Socialists of Rural Andalusia

Socialists of Rural Andalusia

*Unacknowledged Revolutionaries
of the Second Republic*

GEORGE A. COLLIER

STANFORD UNIVERSITY PRESS   1987
STANFORD, CALIFORNIA

Stanford University Press, Stanford, California

© 1987 by the Board of Trustees of the
Leland Stanford Junior University

Printed in the United States of America

CIP data appear at the end of the book

For *Los Chicharreros*

And in memory of
Charles Wood Collier and
Nina Perera Collier

Acknowledgments

In *Long Engagements: Maturity in Modern Japan* (1980), David Plath celebrates the discourse of maturity as it develops among groups of people who shape one another's lives in their mutual experience of history during the life course. This book is a product of such a long engagement—with villagers in the Spanish *pueblo* I call "Los Olivos," with kin and colleagues, and with institutions. The satisfactions of shared understandings have shaped it, as have sad partings and remembrance of those lost to us.

My deepest debt and gratitude is to the villagers themselves, especially those who have opened up their lives to us over the years since 1963 when Jane Collier and I began our study of Los Olivos. This book is about a painful chapter in the history of their pueblo, about events and experiences that many wish to forget. In designating their pueblo "Los Olivos" and changing all personal names in this study, I seek to respect such desires, and I beg my colleagues and others who read this and related studies of Los Olivos to preserve its anonymity.

The kindness and help of certain individuals cannot go unacknowledged. Pepe and Isabel and their children were the first to greet us in Los Olivos and became loved neighbors. Francisco and Modesta made us feel at home in the pueblo in countless ways. We have shared joy and sorrow with Eloina and Magdalena, Loli and Pedro, Cristina and Cándido, Remedios and Miguel, Emilio and Loli, María and Mariano, and their kin. Julia and Gumersindo were among our first neighbors, and we have cherished long friendships with their children, as we have with Esteban and Lorenza and theirs. We relish the times we have spent with Aurelio and Pauli, Félix and Josefa, and Francisco and

Amparo in the pueblo and at their *Finca Rumasa*. Florentina, Fernando, and Angeles, Concepción and José and their Ruth and Noemi hold a special place in our hearts, as do Julia, Pedro, and Juliana. Antonio and Mercedes, and Mariano have helped me in countless ways. To all the *chicharreros*, I express my gratitude.

Several colleagues joined us in research in or near Los Olivos. Richard and Sally Price, Michelle Zimbalist, Sally Simmons, Jean Mullenax, and Richard Maddox all graciously shared field notes and research findings. I am deeply indebted to Richard and Sally Price and to Richard Maddox for countless suggestions regarding this book as it developed in manuscript.

Other colleagues facilitated our study in Spain. Carmelo Lisón Tolosana gave us repeated encouragement and support. Joan Frigolé welcomed us in Catalonia when we began work there and became a steadfast counselor and critic. Juan Díez Nicolás guided me to important work on Spanish demography. We also received helpful advice from Alfredo Jiménez, Isidoro Moreno, and Salvador Rodríguez regarding our work in Sevilla and Huelva.

Of those who helped me by reading and commenting on earlier versions of this book, Benjamin Paul, Renato Rosaldo, Bernard Siegel, G. William Skinner, and Sylvia Yanagisako advised me as only long-standing friends could. Martha Ackelsberg, Herrick Chapman, Lucy Collier, James Fernandez, George Esenwein, John I. Fishburne, David Gilmore, Richard Herr, Catherine LeGrand, Sabine MacCormack, Juan Martínez Alier, Roger Rouse, Adrian Shubert, Peter Stansky, and Temma Kaplan have all contributed in one way or another, some with a careful reading of the manuscript in earlier stages. I am deeply grateful to Nancy Donham and Susan Harding for thoughtful readings that helped me take stock of my undertaking and to formulate revisions. Above all, Jane F. Collier has shared my personal and professional engagement with Los Olivos since its inception, and I cannot adequately acknowledge all the ways she has contributed to this study.

This study would not have been possible without institutional assistance. Jane Collier and I began our research in Spain under the auspices of the Fulbright Commission during 1963–64, and I wish to thank the Comité Conjunto Hispano-Norteamericano para la Cooperación Cultural y Educativa for its support then and through a travel grant in 1980, which helped us return to Spain after many years' work on the highland Maya. The Center for Research in International Studies at Stanford aided us in the summer of 1981. Funds for computation at Stanford's Center for Information Technology were made available by Stanford University. Major assistance for the study came from the National Institute of Child Health and Human Development, grant R01-HD-17351, for research on "Late Marriage, Family Constellation, and Kinship Change" in Los Olivos. Artwork by Charles Collier and a field trip to check some of my conclusions were made possible by support from Stanford's Office of the Vice Provost and Dean of Research.

Finally, I wish to thank William Carver, John Feneron, and John Ziemer for their editorial assistance.

G.A.C.

Contents

Maps, Figures, and Tables

Tables

Illustrations

Socialists of Rural Andalusia

ONE

Introduction

THIS IS A BOOK about the Socialists of an Andalusian sierra
town in the Spanish Second Republic. By examining their organization, their struggle for power, and their accomplishments—
particularly their revolutionizing of labor relations in local agriculture—I try to shed new light on the radicalization of the
Andalusian countryside. The book chronicles the Socialists' virtual extermination at the outset of the Civil War in 1936 and con-
siders their legacy to the pueblo in which they lived and died.
I hope to illuminate the present by reflecting on the past, as well
as to contribute to the Spaniards' recovery of a past that nearly
half a century of dictatorship so effectively obscured.

The study is in some ways an experimental reworking of the
ethnographic subject, delineating its context in time rather than
in space, in history, both large-scale and local. Although depart-
ing from and returning to the familiar anthropological endeavor
of rendering understandable the communities in which we conduct our studies, I center my analysis on a period in the past,
decades ago, whose events decisively shaped the "ethnographic
present" of later research. Although I employ many of the methods that have proved valuable for studying a concrete place and
time ethnographically, I press them into the service of what may
be characterized as serial ethnography, studying through time a
particular subset of villagers and the long-lasting repercussions
of the challenges they posed to the established order.

Before the 1930's, these villagers appeared as a fragmentary lot

---

I am indebted to Susan Harding for perceptive comments and advice that have
helped me formulate this introduction.

of rural laborers, muleteers, and poor landowners who episodically achieved moments of collective identity and efficacy in unrest and protest in tandem with people elsewhere in Andalusia; for a brief time, they achieved a degree of organization under Primo de Rivera. In the Second Republic, they coalesced into Socialist "labor," counterposed to the "proprietors" whom they challenged; the balance of power shifted between them in an ever-widening arc, unweaving the webs of social relations that connected them. Many of the Socialists were killed at the outset of the Civil War, and others fled into exile. An analysis of the succeeding postwar period reveals how those who remained were economically, socially, and culturally stigmatized and stunted, while the village returned to the way things were before the war, but with a vengeance. It is as though the postwar years, extending into the 1950's and even the 1960's, were locked in a negative dialogue with the Republican years, continually affirming values and ideology opposite to those of the Republican era, which no one dared to voice. Years later, under Franco, the ground gradually shifted once more. The poor, now scattered, emerged again with new, largely apolitical identities; those once regarded as rich, the winners of the war and their heirs, though hardly impoverished, faded into the background, bereft of power and prestige.

Theoretical Premises: Political Economy and Cultural Analysis

As a dramatic account, the story of the Socialists of Los Olivos (a pseudonym) may seem to tell itself. But because facts take on significance only within a theoretical frame, the general suppositions that informed the research and analysis on which I base my account are important. They are borrowed from political economy and employed in a manner that reflects some of the concerns of contemporary interpretive anthropology.

Political economy emphasizes production rather than exchange, and it brings relations of production to the foreground in the analysis of a social system. In studying relations of production, political economists are concerned with the mutual determination of political processes and economic activity and affirm the centrality of relations of production in the processes through which political forms are established and maintained. Capitalism is considered as a specific historical system of at least two classes, organizing and reproducing their differential owner-ship of the means of production. Political economy is attentive to the conflict inherent in capitalist class relations and to the goals and objective interests of those involved in such conflict. It thus illuminates the connections between capitalist relations of pro-duction, on the one hand, and consciousness, politics, and cul-ture, on the other hand.

I draw the perspective of political economy into this study in several ways. I place Los Olivos in space and time with reference to the political and economic processes spanning Andalusia more generally. More vitally, I employ political economy as a point of reference and departure for an analysis of conflict and change in Los Olivos. My treatment of the Second Republic in Los Olivos illuminates the basis of conflict there in preindustrial agrarian capitalist relations of class and explores the political ex-pression of conflict as consciousness of class. Political economy further serves me as a vehicle for exploring the linkages between the world of the pueblo and the larger, encompassing systems. Thus, I have attempted to link the background and the fore-ground, using a sequential narrative to relate the conflict and the change experienced in Los Olivos to the experience of other locales similarly situated in the broader dynamics of Spanish na-tional politics. It is from the national context that local events drew inspiration, and it is to that context that they contributed a substantial measure of radicalization in the Second Republic.

As used in one strand of anthropology, political economy has a particular concern for the cultural terms with which people conceptualize their interests, motivate their acts, and experience the consequences of what they and others do. George Marcus and Michael Fischer (1986: 85) point out that interpretive con-cerns of long-standing centrality in anthropology have begun to be wedded to this facet of political economy in analyses such as Pierre Bourdieu's *Outline of a Theory of Practice* (1977) that focus squarely on social action and on the production of cultural meaning and symbols as central to the practices and processes of social action. "Not only is the cultural construction of mean-ing and symbols inherently a matter of political and economic in-

Los Olivos. (Photo from 1963–64 fieldwork season.)

terests, but the reverse also holds—the concerns of political economy are inherently about conflicts over meanings and symbols." This, then, is the point of departure for my own exploration of the cultural expression of conflict in Los Olivos.

In the perspective of such political economic analysis, preindustrial, labor-intensive capitalist agriculture complemented peasant agriculture in Los Olivos during the 1920's. A community of less than a thousand inhabitants, Los Olivos was one of several pueblos oriented to Aracena, the administrative center and principal agrarian market center in the sierra of northern Huelva, the westernmost province of Andalusia. In the nineteenth century, agrarian entrepreneurs had absorbed church property and town commons into agrarian estates and had passed power as a landed oligarchy to their descendants in this century. Los Olivos's *cacique*, or political boss, was part of this oligarchy. His power inhered both in the employment he could offer on lands that constituted one-fourth of the municipality and in being able to deliver the vote to the political machinery of provincial and national government. Lesser agrarian proprietors and merchants from a handful of interrelated families shared power with him. Below them were peasant smallholders and finally a sizable stratum of landless and frequently unemployed poor who labored for wages in the production of olives, hogs, fruit, vegetables, cork, and grains.

The Socialist labor movement would, in the Second Republic, give expression to the conflict inherent in this stratification in terms specific to the ways actors in this setting lived and experienced production relations. In Los Olivos, those terms centered on labor and the relation of proprietor to employee rather than on ownership of land, as the literature on the struggle for agrarian reform would lead one to expect. The Socialists first organized landless laborers to wrest control of local government—and public-works employment—from the cacique and his collaborators. Once they had accomplished this, the Socialists pressed to take the initiative in agrarian employment away from the proprietors.

The Socialists assaulted proprietors in terms of *autonomía*, a cultural construct embodying the proprietors' claim to the right to manage their own affairs in the sphere of production and more broadly in social life. Autonomía was embedded in the property relations and system of honor of agrarian societies of the Mediterranean. Insofar as the property system brought together a couple's productive assets and vested their care in the male head of household, autonomía epitomized the proprietor's prerogative of protecting his family honor and developing his family interests as he wished, free from others' control. Autonomía implied the proprietor's right to hire and fire and to deploy hired labor in production as he wished. But the Socialists of Los Olivos claimed for organized labor the right to determine when and how land should be cultivated, by whom, and under what conditions. In this respect, they attempted to impose on the relations of production a revolution that village proprietors experienced all the more poignantly as a challenge to their personhood. If Los Olivos Socialists were concerned more with revolutionizing labor relations than with landownership, could this have been true of other Andalusian Socialists as well?

Reinterpreting Stratification and Politics

Los Olivos appeared much less stratified when Jane Collier and I first visited it in 1963, shortly to be followed by our friends and colleagues, Richard and Sally Price. It struck us as similar in many respects to the pueblo Julian Pitt-Rivers called Alcalá in *People of the Sierra* (1954). Class divisions, although evident in the choices of marriage partners by which people preserved their standing in the village (Price and Price 1966*a*, *b*), seemed minimal and unmarked by conflict or politics. When we asked, neither we nor the Prices learned much from villagers about politics or about the Civil War. One young man never followed up on his promise to Richard Price to tell him about the Civil War killings in the village, and though Price recorded antiregime banter in one of the mining towns, past politics was not a topic that he pursued. When we asked about the Civil War, we were told that the only event of the Civil War was that "they" had burned the church and that "we" do not talk about politics because that is why people kill one another. In view of the rich new understanding of stratification and politics that we have gained in recent research, why did we learn so little about these topics in 1963?

The theoretical paradigm that informed our view was perhaps most responsible for what we failed to grasp about Los Olivos's past—more responsible than the facts that Los Olivos *was* less stratified in 1963 than before the Civil War and that many villagers were reticent regarding events of that era. Structural functionalism held sway in anthropology in 1963, as it continued to do for some time in the ethnography of Spain. As a theory, it stressed consensus more than conflict and exchange more than exploitation. The best structural-functional approaches to rural Spain accented the boundaries, solidarity, and sociocentrism of the pueblo and the internal coherence and consistency of its values (Caro Baroja 1957, Pitt-Rivers 1954). They emphasized the mutually beneficial relations of Spanish patronage more than its asymmetry and tended to attribute the strains of stratification to relations with authoritative outsiders.

Perhaps because of its focus on problems of community integration and the maintenance of order, structural functionalism diverted our attention from problems that are central in the study of political economy. Thus, we did not appreciate that class struggle had been fundamental in the history of Los Olivos. Although we read Gerald Brenan's account of the social and political background of the Civil War in *The Spanish Labyrinth* (1943) we did not connect it with rural Huelva of the 1960's. We failed to comprehend silence—the refusal of enemies to talk to one another—as the idiom of bitter resentments dating from the 1930's. We were, perhaps, naive concerning the study of politics and conflict within the framework of a repressive dictatorship, but our naiveté stemmed at least in part from the questions not asked, the problems not posed by the theoretical precepts of our discipline in the early 1960's. With the exception of Carmelo Lisón Tolosana's *Belmonte de los Caballeros*, first published in 1966, none of the ethnographies of Spain of that decade dealt with these issues, although later publication of work begun in the 1960's on such topics by Juan Martínez Alier (1971) and Jerome Mintz (1982) suggest that it would have been possible to do so.

By the time that Jane Collier and I returned to study Los Olivos nearly two decades later, political economy had reshaped the issues central to anthropology. In the 1960's and 1970's, it had entered our thinking about problems of kinship, land tenure, ethnicity, politics, history, law, and gender elsewhere than in Spain (e.g., G. Collier 1975, 1978, 1982; J. Collier 1973, 1975, 1979, 1981). By addressing questions of political economy when we returned to research on Los Olivos in 1980, we came to realize that our earlier understanding of the pueblo was an ephemeral product both of Spain's twentieth-century history and of our approach. Our later work made evident how the Civil War and subsequent dictatorship had staved off agrarian change and had enabled preindustrial capitalist agriculture to retrench in the postwar years. It revealed what we had not recognized in 1963, that the capitalist development of the late Franco years had already begun to engulf Los Olivos, marginalizing sierra agriculture and drawing laborers and smallholders into the urban working class. As we learned in brief visits to Los Olivos in 1972 and 1977 and in summer-long visits in 1980 and 1981, these developments had inverted statuses among villagers, drawing the working-class poor into better livelihoods while saddling agrarian proprietors with the drudgery of work in the fields that they could no longer hire others to do.

We embarked on a project to study the transition from agrarian to modern industrial life from the perspective of political economy. We decided to focus on changes in the family system and on the ways lived experience shaped fundamental notions of personhood in such a transition. One central concern was late marriage in Los Olivos, common and understandable as part of a conjugal family system constituted by inherited agrarian property, and the process by which it had given way to earlier marriage after the 1960's. We employed methods of family history and anthropology to study these problems, compiling and combining information from household and vital registries with that from family-history interviews.

When used as we employed them in research concerning an epoch that is still alive in people's memories, such resources provide major advantages and overcome many of the drawbacks that practitioners of family history face when they study the more distant past. The principal advantage of data compiled from systematically accumulated records such as a civil registry is analytical control over a study population, its boundaries, and its internal variation. Such control is essential for the study of social class. Los Olivos's vital registry of births, for example, was kept conscientiously, as far as I have been able to determine from a scrutiny of the corpus and from extensive crosschecking in interviews. The registries establish a basis for systematic inquiry about persons of every social class in successive birth cohorts. They also establish a wealth of other information when used in conjunction with other town records.

This is not to say that these sources have no limitations. Some but not all the vital data one would like to know are to be found in the civil registry and in household registers such as those the Los Olivos authorities compiled in the *Padrón de Habitantes*. Migration both added and removed people from the compass of these records, rendering the data on individuals incomplete for some purposes. The registry of deaths was significantly silent about what we later learned concerning the deaths of many of Los Olivos's Civil War victims. But at a minimum, our compilation of household and vital registry data into a single corpus allowed us to identify and fill gaps in our information and to consider what biases result from irremediably missing information.

On such bases, we reconstructed as complete a genealogical census as possible from civil registries begun in 1871 of births, marriages, and deaths in Los Olivos and from household registries in the *Padrón de Habitantes* of 1950 and subsequent years. Selecting the 1950's as a baseline for our reconstruction of the agrarian family system and its later changes, we embarked on family-history interviews with migrants and nonmigrants of various Los Olivos birth cohorts and class positions. In early 1983, we interviewed some 46 heads of households and their spouses and family members; a few of these had migrated from Los Olivos as early as the 1940's, and many of them lived in Sevilla, Madrid, and the industrial suburbs of Barcelona.

It was in this interviewing that the widows and children of villagers who had been killed at the outset of the Civil War told us of what had happened in 1936. Although we had known some of these people before, it was only now—several years after the demise of Franco and just after the electoral victory of the Partido Socialista Obrero Español in November 1982—that they dared to recount how Falangists had killed their loved ones in the pueblo and how they themselves had experienced the Civil War and postwar years of repression. They told us how their families sank into desperate poverty during the postwar years and how other villagers took advantage of their plight by employing them at starvation wages in domestic service and field work. We discovered that they and other village laborers had begun to emigrate from Los Olivos by the 1950's, leaving behind the more homogeneous village of smallholding families that we had come to know in 1963. Although other villagers whom we interviewed, many of them heirs of the propertied Right, sometimes placed different interpretations on past events, they confirmed much of this history of stratification and conflict. The inequalities of pueblo life, and some of the reasons they had not been apparent to us in 1963, thus began to emerge from these accounts, together with questions about what had taken place in Los Olivos during the Second Republic and Civil War.

As our interviews developed, systematic development of our genealogical data base enabled us not only to fill gaps but to tap the hidden, long-undiscussed, and sometimes forgotten wells of family knowledge that individuals had accumulated and interpreted in the course of their lives. Such data embellished and enlivened the skeletal facts of genealogical relationships and illuminated the analysis of Los Olivos's political history during the

Second Republic by making it possible for me to identify union leaders, Town Council members, plaintiffs and litigants, and Civil War victims within the matrix of their intertwined family histories.

We recompiled such information by computer between seasons of fieldwork and linked them systematically back to the genealogies. For each person, the computer constructed a profile showing his or her parents, siblings, spouses, and children, and for each of these relatives their dates of birth and death, years of residence in Los Olivos, indexes of wealth, public posts held, and Second Republic and migration histories in synopsis. These profiles informed the next season's interviewing. In this way, our corpus of information developed into a Who's Who of Los Olivos in this century, encompassing misfits as well as notables, poor as well as rich, the forgotten as well as the remembered, the Left as well as the Right—and facilitating our reinterpretation of pueblo stratification and politics.

Analyzing Town Council Business During the Second Republic

Interviews of widows and children alone could not reconstruct the circumstances that led to the debacle of 1936 in Los Olivos because they had not been party to the town-hall politics on which Socialist men and youth had centered their struggle. Much of the municipal archive antedating the 1940's had been "recycled," but fortunately the minutes of Town Council meetings during the 1930's and crucial judicial archives survived, as did tax rolls and other records useful for reconstructing people's class position in various years.

The minutes for 1930–36 encompass some 322 folios in three volumes of handwritten summary of business ranging from seemingly inconsequential matters such as the repair of municipal buildings to matters of considerable moment such as the sacking of town authorities by the provincial governor. I extracted meaning from the minutes only after having read them several times to learn their conventions. In doing so, I came to recognize recurrent business, and I developed a scheme to code the minutes and then to select out and copy onto slips all instances of a particular kind of business. I analyzed each such category of municipal action on its own and in relation to other categories, paying particular attention to four questions pertinent to the study of political economy.

1. How did the timing and pace of the activity fit the temporal frame of local politics? I explored this by arranging all references to a category of business—for example, public works—in chronological order, scrutinizing the result for clusters and patterned sequences. Changes in Town Council membership consistently proved to punctuate significant developments in town affairs and to provide the best chronological frame for their analysis. This approach helped me to perceive interrelated shifts and nuances in the conduct of several kinds of municipal business and to understand their local political significance.

2. Who were the protagonists in the activities, and how did municipal business reflect protagonists' objective interests and their relations of kinship, patronage, class, and political affiliation? These are fundamental questions from a political-economy perspective. I found some answers to such questions through internal analysis of the Town Council minutes as a corpus to see where protagonists recurred in them as individuals or in groups. I also situated protagonists in the life-history and genealogical data that we compiled in conjunction with our interviewing. I studied tax rolls for the 1920's and 1930's to help evaluate the relative class position of taxpayers and their family members. It was thus possible to explore just how the town authorities were related to one another and to other village members of similar or different class position.

3. How did municipal business reflect matters of regional and national moment, as distinct from concerns of primarily local significance? To what extent was municipal business initiated by the state? In order to explore these questions, I compared the Los Olivos record to the official chronicle of public business in the *Boletín Oficial, Provincia de Huelva*, and to daily accounts in newspapers such as *El Diario de Huelva*. These resources helped fill the virtual void in published literature on Huelva in the Second Republic and Civil War. They proved to be a vital supplement to synthetic histories of the Second Republic, which generally do not treat matters at the level of regional or municipal affairs.

4. How did municipal business affect and reflect customary usages and practices in the day-to-day conduct of villagers' lives? This question is vital for contemporary anthropology's quest for a political-economy approach that is sensitive to the cultural terms in which people conceptualize their interests, motivate their acts, and experience the consequences of what they and others do. I looked to ethnography, both others' and our own, to explore this question, and I sought answers in the handful of published firsthand accounts of the experience of Andalusian peasants during the Second Republic. Even though almost all of the Los Olivos protagonists in the Second Republic and Civil War were killed or have died, interviewing revealed how bystanders interpreted and experienced municipal politics in relation to the customary conduct of life. As explained in Chapter 5, I found that Andalusian concepts of honor and of the relation of honor to politics were vital in the experience of municipal business.

Contributions to Spanish History

Much has already been written about the Spanish Second Republic and Civil War; thus, it is important at the outset to characterize what I believe to be my contribution to the topic.

This reconstruction of the social and political history of Los Olivos Socialists was an adjunct to research on the contemporary family history of the town's populace. As such, it has benefited from the detailed reconstruction of vital events and genealogical relations that the methods of family history afford. Having built a data base of information on the genealogical relations among townfolk, we found it easy to determine how contestants in the town's political battles were related to one another. By systematically compiling vital registry data with information drawn from periodic *Padrones de Habitantes*, electoral censuses, tax rolls, and such, I ensured that the analysis reflected the town's entire populace, not just its leading figures. The *Padrones de Habitantes* and other records also provided information on the destination of migrants when they first left Los Olivos, data that we supplemented through interviews. In these ways, we learned of many more Socialists active in the events leading up to the killings in 1936 than we would have through oral accounts alone, and we could appreciate how kinship and class conjoined in those events. Furthermore, since the systematic materials of family history facilitated analysis through time as well as cross-sectionally, the corpus of materials from Los Olivos opened up the possibility of studying Socialists as a subset of Los Olivos's population during the Second Republic, to be traced not only longitudinally but beyond the immediate confines of Los Olivos. I hope that my findings will encourage others to use similar methods to study Spanish local history and to improve on them.

This study shares some limitations with our larger project of research. Although ideal for learning about recent family history, Los Olivos was not the best site for reconstructing the political history of the Second Republic because of the loss of much of the pertinent municipal archival material. I have not been able to explore all the alternatives that might compensate for this drawback. I tried but failed to gain access to records of local arrests in the archives of the Court of First Appeal in Aracena, for example. Nor have I been able to learn as much as I would like about Los Olivos's involvement in provincial affairs. This might be possible through police records and provincial governors' official correspondence if they survive and are accessible in Huelva. Instead, I have had to rely on newspaper accounts and the *Boletín Oficial, Provincia de Huelva*, to reconstitute the provincial context for what transpired in Los Olivos. The viewpoint represented in my analysis is thus very much one from within an arena circumscribed by kinship and locality.

As such, Los Olivos affords a perspective that is underrepresented in work on the Second Republic and Civil War. Historians have devoted little attention to places like the pueblo. Studies in labor and social history of the Second Republic and Civil War have burgeoned in recent years, but they have centered on conventional political analysis of the party struggles of the era (Preston 1984a: 10). The view from the pueblo is rare. Ronald Fraser's *Tajos: The Story of a Village on the Costa del Sol* (1973) and his *In Hiding: The Life of Manuel Cortés* (1972; the personal account of that village's Second Republic Socialist mayor) offer an account concerning an analogous place. Other studies are all anthropological. Jerome Mintz's *Anarchists of Casas Viejas* (1982) reconstructs the background and aftermath of the 1933 massacre of anarchists in that pueblo. Susan Friend Harding's *Remaking Ibieca: Rural Life in Aragon Under Franco* (1984) has useful chapters on the experience of anarchism in that town, as does Carmelo Lisón Tolosana for Socialists in another Aragonese town in his *Belmonte de Los Caballeros* (1983). I am not aware of other efforts to ground rural pueblos' experience of that era in a thorough analysis of social organization.

Insofar as my study of Los Olivos Socialists relies on the systematic reconstruction of social organization, it complements what can be learned from oral accounts, however important these may be for interpreting the past. No one can deny the powerful truths orchestrated from hundreds of oral accounts by Ronald Fraser in his masterful *Blood of Spain* (1979). Such oral testimony has been absolutely indispensable for rectifying the Franco regime's obstruction of scholarship and production of tendentious history concerning the Second Republic and Civil War (see Preston 1984*a*). Similarly, Jerome Mintz used oral accounts and reminiscences of the vanquished of Casas Viejas to controvert the official history of newspapers of the time and national historians of a later era. Although I also voice the reminiscences of the vanquished, I consider them in the context of what I have learned from archival research and from the techniques and materials of family history and social analysis. I thus augment and complement the story of the vanquished of Los Olivos, giving it a much firmer grounding than can be derived from the oral narrative of survivors, many of whom were not direct participants in key events. By emending their history, I hope to restore it to them.

The Accomplishments of Rural Socialists in the Second Republic

What I have learned about Los Olivos affords certain important insights into the nature of socialism as it was experienced at the level of the peasant community. I believe that such Socialists accomplished more than historians have given them credit for and that in recognizing what they accomplished, we can learn something about the nature of peasant revolutions.

Rural rank-and-file discontent has come to be regarded as one of the major sources for radicalization of the Socialist party and trade union movement during the Second Republic. At the outset in 1931, leaders of the only working-class party to participate in the Provisional Government (1931) won important reforms for agrarian labor. But conservative landed and church interests rallied to delay and water down their subsequent efforts to legislate land reform. According to the analyses of Edward Malefakis (1970) and Paul Preston (1978, 1984b), disappointment and frustration with the pace of land reform, particularly in the agrarian south, welled up through the Socialist landworkers' federation, the Federación Nacional de Trabajadores de la Tierra (FNTT) and accelerated the radicalization of such Socialist party leaders as Francisco Largo Caballero.

The case of Los Olivos does not controvert the general outline of this current of radicalization, except with regard to its initial source and inspiration. I think that Los Olivos Socialists may have accomplished considerably more than historians generally have credited to agrarian workers in the south, even though they were probably never a focal point for party recruiting and mobilization. It is true that the tactics of an entrenched local landed oligarchy beset Los Olivos Socialists at the outset of the Republic. But by 1933 the Socialists gained control of municipal government in Los Olivos and initiated changes of revolutionary import in employment relations. Their fervor surely arose not from failure and frustration but rather from accomplishment and success.

The measure of the achievements of Los Olivos's Socialists, I argue, must be taken in terms of the goals *they* sought in the concrete experience of their circumstances. Scholars have placed much emphasis on the Second Republic's land reform, but this was apparently not what concerned the Socialists of Los Olivos, nor was it the sole concern of militant agrarian workers elsewhere in Andalusia. In Los Olivos, the relations of proprietor to employee to which ownership of the means of production gave rise were much more immediate than land tenure per se. And it was over employment, not land, that agrarian workers fought with proprietors.

The nature of their struggle only becomes intelligible in terms that are culturally specific. As I have already indicated, property enabled a man to be *autónomo*—to be self-sufficient and independent of any other man's beck and call. Lack of property forced a man to bow his head to others in order to support his family, and it made him suppress his own will in any matter that might anger his employers. Villagers experienced autonomy as masculine honor and family honor, asserted by a household head commanding enough property to be self-sufficient; it was questioned in those whose insufficiency was demonstrated by their need to labor for wages. Although customary usages had developed around wage labor to ameliorate its inherent humiliation, they did not eliminate it.

When the Socialists took power in Los Olivos in 1933, they revolutionized employment by seizing for labor the prerogative of determining what land should be cultivated, by whom, and when. By stripping proprietors of their autonomous power to decide such matters, the Socialists deprived landownership of its cultural meaning and inverted the relation of employer to employee. Although they acted on the basis of the early Republic's agrarian labor reforms, they did so in ways that were revolutionary for the times.

Socialism in Los Olivos thus concerned local affairs first and foremost and continued to do so even after repression radicalized leftists in the region. During the period of reactionary government in 1934 and 1935, local Socialists were repressed, and some of them were jailed together with anarchists and libertarian Communists. Although they voiced a more eclectic rhetoric when they returned to power in 1936, the Socialists continued to press for the same revolutionary transformations of the relations of production that they had sought two years earlier. When peasants make revolutions, they may be inspired from the outside and may use others' rhetoric, but they act in terms that are most meaningful to their experience.

The Vanquished in the Postwar Years

It is crucial that the political history of villages like Los Olivos in the Second Republic be set forth because postwar Nationalist propaganda vilifying leftists—in the media, in sermons, and in

school lessons—cruelly maligned the motives and purported
deeds of the vanquished. Few people survive in Los Olivos who
can reconstruct what transpired in local affairs leading up to the
war. Almost all the Socialist men and youth who had knowledge
of town affairs were killed in 1936; few of their opponents who
are still alive are willing to talk about the era. I believe that my
reconstruction of municipal affairs during the Second Republic
goes much further than reminiscences in setting forth the motives behind events that must have been replicated in countless
rural towns of that era.

The story of the vanquished also deserves telling. The widows
and children of men killed in 1936 were not allowed to mourn,
and they suffered immediate humiliation and more extended exploitation during the postwar years. It was at their expense, in
part, that labor-intensive agriculture revived in the 1940's and
early 1950's; during that time they had little alternative but to
conform to the norms of those who had subjugated them. Not
surprisingly, the vanquished were among the first of the villagers
to emigrate from the town when it became possible to do so in
the postwar years, paving the way for others to follow in an emigration that reached massive proportions after 1965. Yet the impact that they and others like them have had on contemporary
Spain goes largely unacknowledged.

Since the war, the vanquished of Los Olivos have lived in considerable fear, which still is tangible despite the return to democracy and the election of a Socialist government in 1982. Only
those whom we interviewed away from the town felt free to talk
to us openly about what had happened to them and to other formerly Socialist families. With but one exception, those who
spoke about these topics with us in the pueblo did so behind
closed doors, sometimes in whispers. Although many elderly
people still hesitate to profess political views, some of the middle
generation living in urban areas have taken up working-class
politics. But they insist that those in the pueblo are reluctant to
do so because of the continued grip of propertied interests on
the town. They point out that Los Olivos consistently voted for
the conservative Alianza Popular and Unión de Centro Demo-
crático, even in the 1982 elections, and that an "independent"
slate representing vested interests won the municipal elections

of 1983 despite the general trend of landslide Socialist victories elsewhere. Spain will not return fully to democracy until it can overcome such apprehension and mistrust.

For someone like myself born after the 1930's, the Spanish Second Republic and Civil War seem enigmatically distant in direct experience and yet immediate in their felt impact on our world. Spaniards of our generation experience this contradiction even more sharply because of the way the fear and repression of the Franco years have obscured the reality of what transpired. One of the purposes of this book is to illuminate some of that reality, both for the villagers and for other Spaniards.

Outline of the Book

In the chapter that follows I introduce Los Olivos in terms of the fateful changes wrought by history in people's lives. By tracing shifts of personal and family fortune in three representative cases, I illustrate how family and history conjoined class relations and politics in these trajectories.

Thereafter, I develop two principal themes: the nature of the Socialist experience in Los Olivos and the role of the vanquished in the pueblo in the postwar years. In Chapter 3, I examine the antecedents of Socialist organization in the province of Huelva and of agrarian labor activism in the Sierra de Aracena. Andalusia is generally described as a stronghold of Spanish anarchism, but Socialist collaboration with the government of Primo de Rivera in the 1920's gave them the upper hand over their rivals in organizing mining in Huelva. Socialists capitalized on this advantage to organize agrarian labor beginning in 1929, building on long-standing ties between mineworkers and agrarian laborers.

Socialists formed part of the left-Republican coalition that declared for the Second Republic in 1931, and they used their position to bring about a number of significant reforms in agrarian labor. Thereafter, they were beset by increasingly articulate and strident conservative opposition, and their political fortunes slipped. The Socialists of Los Olivos experienced an opposite trajectory during the first years of the Second Republic—intransigent opposition assailed them from the outset, but they eventually overcame it. In Chapter 4, I examine the onset of the battle of Los Olivos Socialists with an entrenched landed oligarchy for control of public-works employment in the town. Appealing to the provincial governor, the Socialists first won recognition as a legal union and staved off illegal disregard of the early Second Republic agrarian labor decrees. But it was not until 1933 that the Socialists came into power in their own right. In Chapter 5, I follow their reforms in education, their successful program of major public works to provide work for the unemployed, and above all their revolutionary reorganization of agrarian employment in 1933 and 1934 even in the face of a national climate of growing conservative reaction.

After the November 1933 elections removed Socialists and left-Republicans from the governing coalition, Spain experienced the *bienio negro*, two years of increasingly reactionary rule. In October 1934, the reaction assumed repressive dimensions with the quelling of the Socialist-led Asturias Revolution and other lesser but related movements. In Los Olivos, as recounted in Chapter 6, the provincial governor sacked the Socialist municipal officers in the name of law and order and installed conservative property holders, who proceeded to prosecute the Socialist leaders on charges of malfeasance in office. They also harassed rank-and-file union members with civil suits and collaborated with the Civil Guard in instigating scores of arrests and fines for purported petty wrongdoings in the countryside.

Not surprisingly, the experience of overt repression further radicalized an already fervent Left, not only in Los Olivos but throughout the country, where thousands of leftist leaders found themselves thrown together in jails. When new elections in February 1936 resulted in a Popular Front victory, Los Olivos Socialists reassumed the municipal posts from which they had been ousted and proceeded to govern the pueblo with newfound militance, pressing further their revolutionary changes in employment relations. In Chapter 7, I follow these developments to the eve of the *Levantamiento* (the military uprising against the Republic) and suggest that the libertarian communist and anarchist overtones of some of the events stemmed from the Socialists' sustained contact with other leftists in the bienio negro.

Insurrectionary forces took Los Olivos within a few weeks of the Levantamiento, but not before militant youth, abetted by outsiders, gutted the church. In Chapter 8, I begin the story of the vanquished by recounting the reprisals taken against Socialists in three massacres and in the terrorizing of their families. Outsiders were responsible for the reign of terror, but not without collaboration from within the village.

Desperate famine beset the early postwar years, but agriculture in Los Olivos revived and actually thrived under Franco's agrarian policies. In Chapter 9, I characterize the revival as an uncontested reign of property in several senses. The propertied class, restored to power by the victors, were able to exploit the vanquished in poorly remunerated agrarian labor. The gap between propertied and poor villagers grew as town authorities favored one group and hindered the other. Moreover, the propertied class articulated village life on its own terms, not only in the public arenas of church, school, and town government, but within people's private lives, as is shown in an analysis of marriage patterns.

Under such circumstances, the vanquished were understandably among the first to depart the village when circumstances allowed, as agrarian change began to affect Los Olivos in the 1950's and 1960's. Such agrarian change grew out of the development of capitalism throughout Spain that marginalized the agriculture of Los Olivos and attracted villagers to urban-industrial employment. In Chapter 10, I sketch the impact of these changes on Los Olivos, pointing out that the vanquished initiated the emigration and set its patterns. Recent years have brought an ironic inversion of status to the village. Vanquished families and other workers of yesteryear have done well in urban Spain, while many propertied families who were once their subjugators have declined and been reduced to penurious drudgery in a countryside they have not wished to abandon.

As I indicated at the outset, this study experiments in reworking the ethnographic subject in a historical context. It explores a past that is elusive yet alive, forged and reforged by those who live and interpret it. One needs to bear in mind, in reading my extended reconstruction of Second Republic pueblo politics and conflict, that they have been distorted or forgotten in postwar memory. One important finding of this study is that Spain's postwar years were locked in a negative dialogue with the past that extended through our first fieldwork in Los Olivos. Official postwar ideology vigorously affirmed and reaffirmed the antithesis of Second Republic ideas, which no one dared to articulate. Postwar political and personal identities formed in negative relation to those that had preceded—much as kinship emerges on a temporal dimension in a process of dialogue between generations (e.g., Yanagisako 1985).

In our 1963 fieldwork, we did not initially recognize the character of this dialogue, which came into focus only through kaleidoscopic changes of perspective, each of which has to be acknowledged. One such change was in our theoretical perspective, the paradigm shift in anthropology away from structural functionalism toward political economy and interpretation. Meanwhile, a sea change in Spain's political economy began under Franco in the 1950's that gradually involved villagers and made them conscious of an irony of history, the inversion of the relative status of the victors and the vanquished. As the Franco regime passed away, as political discourse reawakened in metropolitan Spain, and as the Socialists won landslide electoral victories in 1982, the villagers whom we sought out in interviews, among them the vanquished and their heirs, gave new and different voice to their evolving vision of the past. These changes and their interaction have to be considered in understanding the past. Without doubt, there are pitfalls in such a complex repositioning of analysis with respect to the historical subject. I have attempted to circumvent them by anchoring my interpretation in archival research and in systematic analysis of family history. I seek thus to augment and emend the memory of the Socialist revolutionaries of rural Andalusia and to acknowledge their legacy.

The Traditional Order and the Tides of History

Los olivos is one of the unprepossessing smaller pueblos of the Sierra de Aracena. Thus, we were initially surprised, when we began to investigate family histories there, to find how directly Spain's central twentieth-century drama had entered into the life of the town. In this chapter, I explore how historical developments shaped and then radically shifted agrarian stratification in the experience of individuals and families in Los Olivos. Against a background etched in terms of the commonplace shifts of individual and family fortune are placed in sharp relief the catastrophic losses that the Civil War and its aftermath dealt to the vanquished Socialists.

Los Olivos had three strata early in the century: a handful of moderately well-to-do merchants and landed proprietors; a middle group owning enough land or other productive assets to aspire to independent livelihoods; and a substantial group of poor with limited or no means of livelihood other than laboring for wages in domestic service or farm work.

These strata were by no means impervious to shifts. Within limits, individuals could move up or down by virtue of whom they married. And as conjugal families worked integrally in shared enterprises, fortune or misfortune to one or another member meant that all risked shifts in status even in comparison to close relatives in other families. In the conjugal family systems of southern Europe, daughters inherit as well as sons; in Los Olivos they inherit equally. A couple's relative class position initially reflects how much property each spouse brings to the marriage, although a couple's assets remain separate until there is a child. Once a child is born, both parents' property "belongs" to that child and its future siblings. Parents' obligations thereupon turn away from their own parents, siblings, and more distant kin, and the obligation to maintain and enhance their children's estate takes precedence. Brothers and sisters often come into conflict over inheritance in pursuit of their own children's interests. Thus constituted, a conjugal family's fate and relative class position are unmoored from those of other kin and rise or fall with some independence.* Strata are thus crosscut by countercurrents of kinship. They are also traversed by patronage, through which the weak seek advancement and the powerful reward compliance while sanctioning the loyal or scorning the disloyal.

During the Second Republic, a historic wider-world tide of class concerns and conflict altered the experience of stratification in Los Olivos. For an extended moment, stratification in Los Olivos parted along lines of class, overwhelming those relations of kinship and patronage that ordinarily tended to ameliorate class-based conflicts. In the cataclysm that ensued, individuals and entire families found themselves propelled along unforeseen trajectories of class change. In this chapter, I trace three examples.

1. Librada Moreno's merchant-class father and brothers cast their lot with agrarian Socialists and espoused their Second Republic cause. In doing so, they lost their lives and doomed Librada and her mother to humiliation by the Civil War victors, loss of the family's assets, and working-class existences. Theirs was an unexpected downward trajectory that other leading Socialists shared.

2. By contrast, the war affirmed the class position and power of Celestino López as Los Olivos's wealthiest landed proprietor. The war stymied the Socialists' challenge to the control of labor by López and other proprietors. And the postwar revival of agriculture reversed the slippage of Sierra de Aracena farmers like López relative to merchants.

3. In this context, the war bestowed unexpected good fortune

---

*See Creighton 1980 for a useful discussion of family, property, and relations of production in Western Europe. Campbell (1964) offers the best monographic treatment of a Mediterranean conjugal family system.

on Manuel Santis, a onetime worker, by enabling him to invest in land that war victims were forced to sell. His was an unusual upward trajectory from a humble station in life.

Nineteenth-Century Legacies

The Sierra de Aracena is a westward extension of the Andalusian Sierra Morena, which covers the northern third of the province of Huelva. In contrast to the Extremaduran plains to the north, whose extensively cultivated croplands and vineyards are rain fed, the more rugged Sierra de Aracena has artesian springs that favor a broader range of horticulture. Although much of sierra agriculture has been abandoned today because it cannot be mechanized, manual labor once cultivated irrigated gardens and orchards; park-like stands of chestnut, cork oak, holm oak, and olive under which hogs foraged for acorns or where grains grew; and flatter land devoted to grains (Maddox 1986: 302–16).

These crops and the way people cultivated and marketed them were, in important ways, legacies of nineteenth-century developments that concentrated land and property in the hands of an already established regional gentry, enabling some of them to become truly well-to-do in a national frame of reference for the first time. Simultaneously, developments widened the gap between the gentry and the poor who worked the land of the region, impoverishing the latter group more deeply. In the era before 1750, when Los Olivos was an *aldea* (hamlet) of Aracena, poor peasants of the region subsisted in part through access to commons and to small leased or sharecropped holdings of Aracena's noble families and corporate church institutions. But nineteenth-century disentailments and alienation of corporate church property and municipal commons concentrated property in the hands of the region's gentry, who often abrogated poorer citizens' access to them in the process, exacerbating their impoverishment and their dependence on wage labor (Moreno Alonso 1979: 154–72; Maddox 1986: ch. 6).

The markets for agrarian commodities that developed in the nineteenth century also shaped the region's agriculture. Catalonia's expanding wine industry sharpened the demand for cork in the 1870's, encouraging the gentry to establish stands of cork oak alongside the native holm oak of the region and to expand the husbandry of hogs, which foraged on acorns. Demand for the region's products also grew with the development of mining immediately to the south (see Map 2.1). The state opened exploitation of mineral deposits in the center of the province to French and British firms in the 1860's and 1870's. The Riotinto mines soon grew to be the largest exploited copper deposits in Europe, drawing workers from afar as well as from the province. Los Olivos and other Sierra de Aracena pueblos provisioned the mining zone, where pollution from open-hearth calcination of pyrites ruined farmland (Maddox 1986: ch. 6; Checkland 1967; Harvey 1981).

Political developments in the nineteenth century enhanced the power of the region's gentry. The region's elites had long-standing political ties with Sevilla. The establishment of provinces as political entities added new links to the centralized bureaucratic state through Huelva. It was with the advice of the region's gentry that successive provincial governors, appointed by the Ministry of Interior, designated mayors in municipalities. The gentry were also the beneficiaries of late nineteenth-century electoral politics in that they facilitated the process by which the moderate and progressive parties tacitly agreed to alternate in national government late in the century. This so-called *turno pacífico* operated on the basis of political arrangements at the provincial and local levels to guarantee the election of slates of candidates previously designated by the Ministry of Interior. The gentry of the Sierra de Aracena, with their behind-the-scenes control of municipal politics and their ability to deliver the vote of the landless workers who depended on them, emerged as caciques (political bosses) of particular towns. They manipulated local affairs in consort with provincial counterparts closer to national powerholders. After the turn of the twentieth century, for example, Aracena's leading gentry managed regional politics in close accord with the political boss of Huelva, Manuel Burgos y Mazo of the rich agricultural town of Moguer, one of Andalusia's most powerful caciques (Herr 1971: 87–88; Maddox 1986: 279–90; Tusell 1976: 32–33, 69–71).

An emerging merchant and professional class was also part of

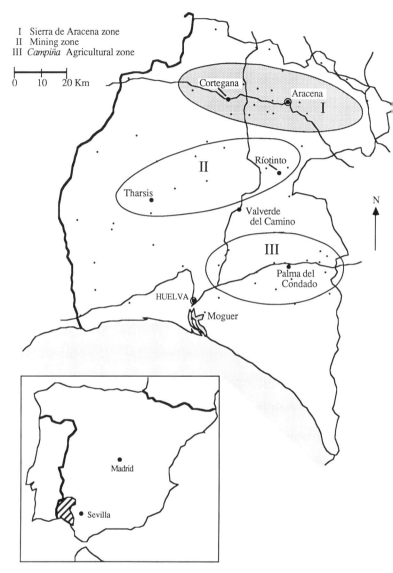

Map 2.1. Key Zones in the Province of Huelva. The subject of this study is Los Olivos (a pseudonym), a pueblo in the Sierra de Aracena, the mountainous agricultural zone in the north of the province of Huelva. Mining of some of the world's richest pyrite and copper ores dominates the zone at the center of the province. Rich agricultural plains of the Andalusian *campiña* stretch between Huelva and Sevilla to the south. (After Forneau 1980: 51, fig. 14.)

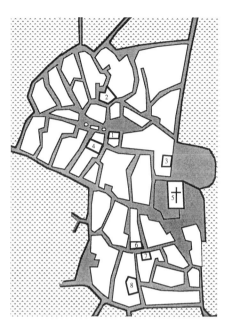

Map 2.2. The Pueblo of Los Olivos. Surrounded by gardens and orchards, the pueblo is compact. (1) The town hall; (2) Celestino López's house; (3) Patricio López's bar; (4) the schoolhouse for girls; (5) the church; (6) the Socialists' Casa del Pueblo; (7) the bar de izquierdas (run by Socialists); (8) the barracks of the Civil Guard.

the nineteenth-century legacy in the Sierra de Aracena. Artisans and shopkeepers made up about 15 percent of the adult male population in Aracena at the turn of the century and about 6 percent in the case of smaller pueblos like Los Olivos (electoral census, 1900). Many of these engaged in livelihoods oriented to the merchandising and industrial processing of cork, hides, and other commodities for provincial and external markets that had formed in response to nineteenth-century developments (Maddox 1986: 297–300).

Los Olivos was one of the smaller pueblos in the rugged sierra (see Maps 2.2 and 2.3). From one side, olive groves sloped steeply down to the pueblo proper, nestled around two ancient spring-fed fountains. Their runoff joined with stream-fed irrigation, jealously divided among rich valley-bottom orchards and gardens by the hours of a week's water vested in each plot. The stream once powered mills along its green course through a dryer, rain-fed landscape that sustained stands of olives and of various oaks—cork, live, and holm—valued for their abundant

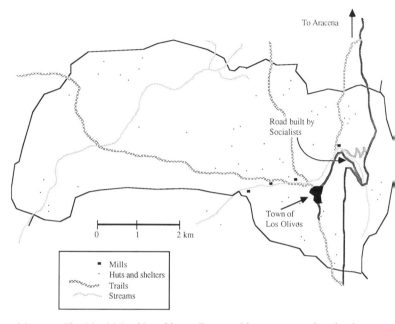

Map 2.3. The *Municipio* of Los Olivos. Traversed by streams and trails, the *municipio* was dotted with shelters and small houses for herders of livestock, caretakers, and some smallholders. Most people lived in town, which was linked to Aracena by roadways, notably that constructed by the Socialists in 1933–34.

acorns (for fattening hogs) and for the charcoal and fuel that their pruning provided.

This landscape afforded poorer villagers only seasonal employment. The yearly cycle of agriculture began in September and gained momentum in late autumn and winter with the harvesting of olives (and chestnuts in neighboring towns). Proprietors hired teams of men to shake or beat the fruit from the branches; teams of women and older children collected the olives, which were then transported to oil presses. Meanwhile, pruning could be undertaken, and the hogs that were to be slaughtered in the winter were fattened on acorns. Sometimes the hogs were left to forage under the oak stands in the care of a swineherd. Sometimes they were penned up and fed acorns gathered by men, women, and children hired for the purpose.

The slaughtering of hogs provided work only through the winter season since cold weather was essential to prevent butchered pork from spoiling as it was prepared for curing. But after winter, employment slackened. Irrigated plots would be tilled, stands of trees might be cleared of scrub growth toward the end of spring, helpers might be hired to harvest cork, grains, and fruit in the

Fetching water at the fountain. (Photo from 1963–64 fieldwork season.)

Washing at the fountain. (Photo from 1963–64 fieldwork season.)

early summer. But summertime provided almost no employment to those who lacked irrigated garden plots of their own. The annual cycle thus ended in hardship for landless workers and for smallholders who needed to supplement a subsistence income by having family members labor for wages.

In the context of this seasonal unemployment and underemployment, proprietors followed the practices of employment that Richard Maddox (1986: 313–15) has described for nearby Aracena shortly after the turn of the century. Proprietors there "recognized that neither more intensive cultivation nor new agricultural techniques would significantly increase crop yields and that holding down the price of labor was the principal way to maintain or increase their profits." Through their control of the town council, proprietors in Aracena kept daily wages at minimal levels, paying day workers barely enough to provide a family of four with bread alone. As the situation of prevailing poverty

drove women and children into the already underemployed labor pool, where they worked for from one-half to two-thirds of a
man's wage, Aracena workers had little recourse. Instead, some
of them accepted agreements, advantageous to landowners, to
prune stands of trees in return for the right to make and sell
charcoal or to sharecrop poorer land in need of clearing. In the
latter instance, Aracena proprietors held lotteries to offer yearlong sharecropping contracts. Day workers and smallholders
who accepted the contracts cleared the land and farmed wheat
or barley for one year, after which time the proprietors profitably
put the land to pasture. Proprietors not only received one-tenth
of the harvested grain; they also avoided having to hire workers
to clear the land for use.

Los Olivos reached its historic peak of some 800–1,000 landless day workers, peasant smallholders, and wealthier farming
proprietors and merchants shortly after the turn of the century.
Most lived in the pueblo proper, although a few absentee landlords lived in Aracena or another nearby town, and some peasant families lived on their smallholdings. Some caretakers and
shepherds inhabited huts and shelters that dotted the countryside. Within the pueblo, stores and the homes of the wealthy
fronted the plaza, the church, and the principal streets. The
poor occupied humbler dwellings at the fringes of town, many of
them rented. This was the populace whose strata—differentiated
by wealth but knit together by kinship and patronage—split
along lines of class conflict in the Second Republic and Civil War,
propelling individuals and families along unexpected trajectories
of class change.

Twentieth-Century Lives

In Los Olivos, Socialists experienced cataclysmic Civil War
losses, both of family fortune and lives. Librada Moreno's testimony of brothers killed and of degradation from merchant to
working class exemplifies the experience of leftists in the village
and their families. We questioned Librada about her family's experiences in an interview arranged by her son Justo, a service
worker in a Catalonian transport firm. In May 1983 on the outskirts of Barcelona, we had been interviewing neighbors from

our 1963 stay in Los Olivos, and they had invited us to join other former villagers in their regular Sunday picnic. There we had met Justo, two years my junior. Justo's sister had cared for our infant son in 1963, and though we had never met him, Justo knew of us and readily consented to an interview. From the standpoint of our research, we thought that Justo could shed light on early emigration to Catalonia from the pueblo (annotations in Los Olivos's 1960 *Padrón de Habitantes* indicated that he had left the pueblo in 1958). We hoped that he could fill gaps in our compilation of vital events in the lives of relatives on his mother's side, gleaned from the pueblo's civil registries and earlier censuses. We were also curious about how his mother's brother Felipe had come to be killed in 1936 under authority of a *bando de guerra* (declaration of state of war), a fact indicated in a posthumous entry in Los Olivos's registry of deaths 45 years after the fact.

It turned out that Justo had learned much from his mother about his uncle Felipe and about another uncle, Pablo, who had been a Socialist town councillor in the Second Republic. Justo thought that his maternal grandfather had been the Socialist mayor of Los Olivos in the 1930's, but this contradicted our own understanding that another man had been the Socialist mayor. Since the discussion had raised questions that he could not answer, Justo arranged for us to meet with his mother, whom he knew to have a keen memory for events of the period.

Librada Moreno had worked for others as a field hand and domestic when we first visited Los Olivos in 1963. She now lives in a small apartment in El Prat de Llobregat and spends much of her time in the company of her grandchildren in the nearby apartment of her daughter, who is married to a metalworker. It was there that we interviewed her, but only after preparing genealogies of the once-influential Moreno family and drawing up a list of all those who I knew or suspected had lost their lives in 1936 or who might otherwise have been involved in Second Republic politics. By exploring her own family's misfortunes, I hoped to learn more about the fates of these others as well.

Fifty years ago, 14-year-old Librada Moreno was of the carefree age at which young women of prosperous and influential Los Olivos merchant and farming families were supposed to have their minds on the next dance rather than on the declining family fortune. Yet she knew that her family was in trouble, that the capital her parents had brought to marriage was in decline. (See Figure 2.1 for a genealogy of Librada's family.)

Her mother, Felisa Mora, one of five children who split the Mora Muñoz inheritance, had brought good farmland to the marriage; and her father, Pedro Moreno, brought his share of the Moreno's commercial capital: a store, a hog-slaughtering business, a truck, and part interest in a store in Sevilla. Felisa and Pedro had taken the appropriate first step for preserving their status by marrying within their class, but they had not had much success in using that capital to advantage. Indeed, their fortunes had slipped.

Pedro had not been raised as a farmer and did not manage Felisa's property well. His involvement in town politics and a term as mayor during the 1920's led him to neglect his affairs. His sons were too young to work, and Pedro farmed the land with hired help, whose wages cut into revenues. In the early 1930's, by the time the children were older, agriculture had slipped into a decline because of drought and the gradually declining world demand for Spanish agricultural commodities during the world depression. Pedro also suffered reversals in his commercial ventures. One year, the herd of hogs he bought for slaughtering took ill and died; another year the hams he was curing spoiled. Pedro opened a bar to try his hand at something different, but he ran up more debts than income. Only his truck, which his sons drove as soon as they were old enough, returned a reliable profit for him, despite his having to share the transport business with a competitor.

Little by little, Pedro sold off Felisa's farmland to cover his debts and to retrench. Matters worsened: "Todo iba pa' atrás y pa' atrás," Librada reminisced as we interviewed her. At the outset of the Civil War in 1936, Pedro died of a heart attack. Felisa was left with just the family house, one large farm property, and the truck.

Then came the war and sharper disaster. Librada's father and elder brother Pablo had been deeply involved in Los Olivos's Second Republic politics. Pablo, twelve years older that Librada, had learned about socialism while working in the Sevilla store

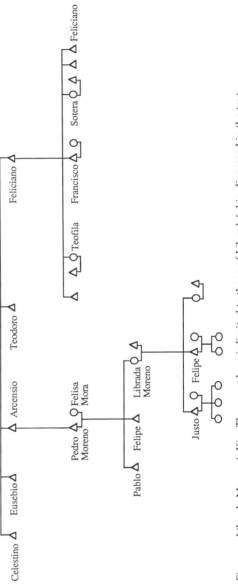

Fig. 2.1. Librada Moreno's Kin. The genealogy is limited to those of Librada's kin discussed in the text.

where his father eventually hoped to place him. He had returned to Los Olivos to take part in the leadership of the Socialist union that twice wrested control of town government away from land-owners and that forced labor reforms on employers. When Falangists took the town in August 1936, Pablo and other Socialist leaders fled.

As he prepared to flee, Pablo advised his younger brother, 21-year-old Felipe, to stay with Librada and their mother. Pablo reassured the family that Felipe need fear nothing since he had not been politically active. Pablo—and many other Socialist protagonists—erred. Felipe and the other younger brothers and sons of activist Socialists were dead within weeks, and the Falangists humiliated their mothers and sisters by shaving their heads and marching them through the streets, all victims of the insurgents' policy of terrorizing civilian populations behind the lines.

The Falangists confiscated the family truck and turned it over to the rival trucker, a rightist whom they installed in town office. With no men in the family, Librada and her mother were reduced to field work and maid service throughout the war, experiencing constant harassment from the Falangists, who wanted to get their hands on Pablo. When Pablo surrendered at the end of the war, the Falangists sentenced him to 40 years in jail. Felisa and Librada went to work for relatives in Sevilla to escape Los Olivos. When Felisa learned that prisoners' sentences could be shortened by bribing the proper officials, she sold off almost all the rest of her property and bought Pablo's release.

Librada married in Sevilla but returned with her mother to the Sierra de Aracena in the 1940's because doctors had sent her husband there in hopes of curing his ill health; he died shortly after, leaving Librada pregnant, with two children and her mother to support. With almost no other place to turn, Librada returned to Los Olivos to labor for a pittance in the fields and homes of anyone who would give her work. Her fortunes irretrievably lost, except for a small house that she managed to fix up, Librada had joined the ranks of the village poor who had to take whatever seasonal jobs they could get. Nonetheless, she managed to send her sons, Justo and Felipe, to church schools in Sevilla, and it was they whom she eventually followed to El Prat de Llobregat in

1965 after her mother died, joining the massive exodus of pueblo poor seeking blue-collar employment and better lives.

Had it not been for the war, the slippage in the fortunes of Librada's family might be interpreted in terms of the dynamics of a conjugal family system, constituted in a particular way by inheritance of property in a stratified agrarian society. These are the terms in which Librada herself interprets why some of her cousins fell on difficult times and others prospered. Her father's family owned most of Los Olivos's commerce before the war and were influential in its public affairs. Librada's great-uncle Teodoro Moreno owned the second largest hog slaughterhouse and managed the town's cloth and dry goods store. He served as the last mayor in the reign of dictator Primo de Rivera. Teodoro's brother Feliciano, a merchant and landlord, was justice of the peace. Two other brothers controlled the church and the school, Celestino serving as parish priest until his death in the mid-1920's, and Eusebio teaching school in quarters rented from Teodoro with municipal tax moneys. But in the next generation, the fates of the Morenos began to diverge. The children of Feliciano, for example, had started out less wealthy than their cousins because their father's property was split among the six of them. But Francisco, who got the *estanco* (the official tobacco and grain store), married a woman with land. With their capitals joined, they began well and prospered. Similarly, Feliciano, the youngest brother, married well. His rich wife brought him capital in Fuenteheridos that he used to continue building their fortune. But Teofila married less well, and her wealth dissipated as her husband lost money in his business. And after her husband abandoned her, Sotera did badly because she had only what she had inherited from her own father.

The war sheds a different light on the experience of Librada's family, however, because the cataclysmic shifts that she and others experienced in its wake call so much attention to the relations of class that underlay the conjugal family system constituted by property. Family fortunes rose and fell on the tides of Spanish history that shaped these relations and propelled their shifts.

The nineteenth century had empowered a landed oligarchy in

the Sierra de Aracena as it did in many areas of rural Spain, and it had established what had become in Librada's day a traditional order in which property owners profited at the expense of poorly paid rural laborers who lacked land altogether or who did not own enough land to live on and thus had to rely on seasonal employment. The established order did not go uncontested. Labor unrest after the turn of the century posed one kind of challenge until Primo de Rivera's "gentle dictatorship" quieted protest in the 1920's. But the dictator opened the countryside to development, advancing those involved in rural commerce who could pose a different sort of challenge to the gentry farmers of the region. In Los Olivos, merchants such as Librada's father and great-uncles were a progressive influence that counterbalanced the established powerholders. Some held office under Primo de Rivera. And in the Second Republic, some of these merchants sided with activists in renascent Socialist agrarian unions to contest the landed gentry's oligarchical power.

The Second Republic reoriented divisions in Los Olivos along the lines of the nationally emerging consciousness of class. Thus, although the leaders of the town's Socialists included two of the town's 20 wealthiest men, most of its active participants came from the village poor (see Figure 2.2), who saw themselves as workers even though some had small holdings. The Socialists increasingly acted in the name of the *clase obrera*, the workers. The other side, the Right, while including a few active collaborators who were poor, was led by 12 men of the wealthiest stratum, the one-third of the men in the village who owned 75 percent of the town's mercantile and farm wealth (see Figure 2.3). These included merchants and a few artisans, as well as farmers, but as conflict between Left and Right unfolded in the Second Republic, the Right increasingly became thought of as *propietarios*, labor-employing property owners whose interests coincided with the landed oligarchy of the sierra.

The war brought this confrontation to a head and resolved it decisively in favor of the landed gentry, Franco's principal allies throughout rural Spain. Thousands of Spanish families suffered losses similar to those of Librada's family. Winners gained much at the expense of losers, and for 20 years afterward property owners enjoyed an uncontested reign in Los Olivos. The traditional order had been given new life.

In Los Olivos, the principal winner was Celestino López, the pueblo's wealthiest landowner, village cacique, and the Socialists' chief opponent during the Second Republic.

We know of Celestino López only through others' accounts and from Los Olivos archival records because López left no heirs or close relatives for us to interview. Not willing to marry beneath themselves in Los Olivos, yet probably below gentry from other, generally more prosperous towns who might have sought their hands, Celestino López and his sisters lived out their lives unmarried in Los Olivos, where the last of them died in 1957.

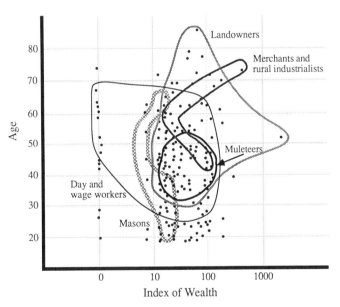

Fig. 2.2. Occupational Status in Los Olivos, 1930. Men in the electoral census of 1930 are plotted by age and by wealth as inferred from tax rolls. Key occupations listed in the census are plotted in terms of their prevailing distributions across these individuals. Although the data are synchronic, they suggest that most men could expect to become landowners later in life through inheritance. There were vast differences in wealth among landowners, however, the richest of them owning more than 100 times that owned by the poorest smallholder.

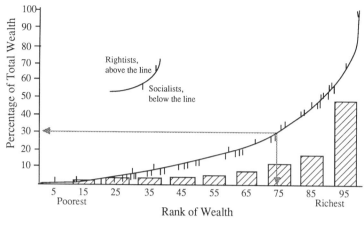

Fig. 2.3. Wealth and Politics in Los Olivos, 1934. The 232 men listed in the electoral census of 1934 are arranged along the horizontal axis from poorest (left) to richest (right). Bars show the aggregate wealth of successively wealthier deciles of these men, as inferred from tax rolls. The curve is the cumulative distribution of wealth owned by an individual and all those poorer than him, expressed along the vertical axis in terms of the proportion of total male-owned wealth. The graph illustrates, for example, that 25 percent of the men owned 70 percent of the wealth. The relative wealth of leaders on the Left and the Right in pueblo politics is also indicated. Socialists and their affiliates are indicated as ticks below the curve. Right-wing activists appear as ticks above the curve, and they are on the whole substantially wealthier than leftists.

Celestino López and his siblings were part of the Sierra de Aracena's landed gentry, which had absorbed church estates and town commons during the nineteenth-century divestitures. The López estates spanned three towns, and the family owned 24 percent of the land in Los Olivos. As the town's wealthiest residents and principal employers, the Lópezes controlled local affairs behind the scenes during the era of "elections" in the first decades of the century when the threat of firing field hands was sufficient to deliver their votes to the governor's candidates. Ousting a rival in 1920 and consolidating his power just before the dictatorship of Primo de Rivera, López became an ally of Aracena's cacique and a henchman of the Huelva provincial oligarchy. As such, he handpicked men for the governor of the province to appoint to the town council. He tried to continue running Los Olivos as a fiefdom during the Second Republic, but a coalition of laborers, tenant farmers, and merchants hotly contested his despotism.*

In many respects, López epitomized the rural *patrón*; he could favor clients not only by offering men and women secure employment in his fields or in his house, but also by loaning money and by using his influence with outsiders to help people deal with state bureaucracies. Conversely, López had the power to disfavor those who crossed him, by blackballing them from his and others' employment. He could do well by doing good, but also by being brutal.

Celestino López managed his estates and the town's political affairs through a distant cousin, Patricio López, to whom he entrusted the hiring and firing of permanent and seasonal employees, the renting out of land to tenants, and the marketing of hogs and crops produced on family estates. Patricio shared with Celestino a stake in controlling the town's tax levies on property and commercial capital since he owned and ran one of Los Olivos's two principal hog slaughterhouses. He also owned the olive press and ran the Casino, the wealthy people's bar and meeting place. Patricio served repeatedly on the Town Council during the dictatorship as councillor and as mayor. During the Second Republic, Patricio continued as Celestino's agent in public affairs.

Second Republic agrarian and labor policies empowered Socialists to contest the Lópezes and the handful of other wealthy landowners by wresting the control of labor away from them. The Socialists' agrarian union—El Sindicato de Agricultores de la Provincia de Huelva, Unión General de Trabajadores, Sección de Los Olivos—implemented labor reforms, enforcing better wages and hours and forcing property owners to hire workers provided by the union. The Socialists took the initiative in agrarian employment away from the property owners and thus undermined their local hegemony.

---

*Data on the López estates are drawn from the *Registro de la Propriedad Expropriable* of the Instituto de Reforma Agraria compiled as a consequence of the 1932 Ley Relativa a la Reforma Agraria. The *Registro* was used by Malefakis (1970) in his study of agrarian reform in Spain, and its use is described in his Appendix A, pp. 407–9. The *Registro* can be consulted at the Biblioteca del Instituto de Colonización in Madrid at Av. de la Castellana 112.

But Franco's forces brutally repressed the Socialists and returned the Lópezes and their allies to uncontested control of the village for at least two decades. For 20 years after 1936, no one challenged the large landowners' control of Los Olivos, not even the wealthier merchants to whose class Librada's family had belonged. Landowners regained total control over employment; wages dropped, and poor villagers, many of them women, found themselves working—as Librada described it—"like negroes, like slaves, just as before the Republic. Workers dared not raise their heads [in protest]." These were the relations of class that enabled a traditional order based on landed property to retrench and then flourish after the war.

Under these circumstances, the farms of Celestino López and other landlords thrived, and with them the fortunes of those who invested newly in property. The renaissance in farming enabled a few families to rise in class position.

Manuel Santis is an example of those few whom the war helped raise from the working class to farming proprietorship. Manuel and his brothers had grown up as workers after the Santis family migrated to Riotinto in search of employment at the mines. Mining slumped after World War I, however, and layoffs provoked massive labor unrest. In the early 1920's, Manuel emigrated to the United States. After some misadventures, in which he and other Spaniards found that they were being hired as scabs, Manuel found decent employment in a paint factory in Harrisburg, Pennsylvania, where he met his wife-to-be, a Spanish coworker.

Manuel Santis returned to his ancestral pueblo with his wife in 1930. Investing some of their $5,000 savings in land, Manuel fulfilled the rural worker's aspiration of becoming an autonomous producer, independent of anyone's control. Because of his working-class background, Manuel at first welcomed the prospect of Second Republic labor reforms. But by investing in land he had cast his lot with property owners, and his sympathy for local workers who sought to reform agrarian employment waned. His allying with property owners probably helped make it possible for him to save a younger brother from sure assassination at the outset of the Civil War when Falangists rounded up youth accused of being leftist.

After the war, Manuel Santis was one of those who bought up land from families in distress, including some from Librada Moreno's mother. The postwar years thus benefited him, together with other proprietors. Manuel gradually rose to prominence in the pueblo and served as mayor during the 1960's.

There were, of course, many families of poor or modest means in Los Olivos whose fates were affected by the sides their men took in the contest for power during the Second Republic. Some small farmers and artisans sided with landowners because they saw the autonomy of their livelihoods threatened by organized labor. Most tenant farmers of modest means joined proletarian laborers against their landlords. Muleteers tended to side with the Socialists because their transporting of produce to the Riotinto mining zone to the south brought them into contact and sympathy with labor activists there. Most landless laborers, but not all of them, sided with the union leaders. But some who had *fijo* (year-around) contracts to work for prominent villagers or whose wives and daughters had served for years as domestics remained loyal to their employers.

Before the Republic, there was much ambiguity regarding many persons' loyalties because kinship and patronage crosscut and complicated class. During the Second Republic, the contest over power in Los Olivos forced individuals to take sides in a class confrontation. The electoral censuses of 1928, 1932, and 1934 give a sense of this forming of sides in local affairs and official discourse. The electoral census of 1928 listed at least 24 different occupations for men eligible to vote. By 1932 and 1934, the era of a "republic of workers," although the classification of occupations was ostensibly similar (except that women had been added), most Los Olivos men were listed either as *obrero* (worker) or *propietario* (proprietor)—that is, in class rather than occupational terms (see Table 2.1). The shift in categories embodied a contradiction that individuals remember: many of them, small farmers and artisans who also worked seasonally for wages, were at once workers and property owners. But the organization of labor—and of census categories—forced them

TABLE 2.1
Occupations Listed on the 1928 and 1934 Electoral Censuses, Los Olivos

Occupation	No.	Occupation	No.
		1928 CENSUS	
Smallholder (*campo*)	52	Schoolteacher	2
Field hand	41	Career soldier	1
Agrarian proprietor	26	Carpenter	1
Muleteer	13	Doctor	1
Day worker	11	Itinerant vendor	1
Farmer (*labrador*)	11	Mail clerk	1
Mason, unskilled	5	Priest	1
Manufacturer (*industrial*)	4	Road repairman	1
Mason, master	4	Sheriff	1
Merchant	4	Store owner	1
Shoemaker	4	Town Council secretary	1
Barber	2	Veterinarian	1
		1934 CENSUS	
Male occupations		Chauffeur	1
Worker	148	Doctor	1
Agrarian proprietor	46	Farmer	1
Mason	9	Field hand	1
Manufacturer (*industrial*)	6	Mail clerk	1
Shoemaker	4	Priest	1
Smallholder (*campo*)	4	Student	1
Schoolteacher	2	Town Council secretary	1
Barber	1	*Female occupations*	
Blacksmith	1	Housewife	244
Butcher	1	Agrarian proprietor	7
Career soldier	1	Schoolteacher	2
Carpenter	1		

for a time to pose either as one or the other rather than as a "farmer" or a "mason." The shift in census categories reflected the emergence of class relations into the foreground of villagers' consciousness of their life and the displacement of traditional conceptions of status in the old order. The point had arrived when even close kin and formerly loyal patrons and clients threatened one another in open class conflict.*

Federico García Lorca spoke of the era as one in which "we (I

*The Second Republic electoral censuses of Los Olivos also help identify villagers present just before the war. The electoral censuses can be consulted in the Archive of the Diputación Provincial de Huelva in Huelva.

mean men of intellectual significance brought up in the atmosphere of what we can call the well-to-do classes) are called upon for sacrifice. Let us accept the call. In the world not human forces but telluric are now at grips" (tr. Herr 1971: 166). Inexorably, the common villagers of Los Olivos were joining their lives to those same forces.

THREE

The Antecedents of Socialist Organization in Rural Huelva

IN ANDALUSIA, most agrarian workers inclined toward anarchism (Díaz del Moral 1967; Kaplan 1977; Mintz 1982; Rosado 1979). Yet workers and peasants in Los Olivos and other villages in the province of Huelva organized under socialism during the transition from the dictatorship of Primo de Rivera to the Republic. In this chapter, I explore how the evolution of the labor movements in Huelva enabled the Socialists to organize agrarian unions in the Sierra de Aracena at a time when anarchists and Communists spearheaded agrarian agitation elsewhere in Andalusia. I have not been able to determine the precise beginning of Socialist organizing in Los Olivos, but it almost certainly took place in conjunction with Socialist organizing in other Sierra de Aracena towns just after the conclusion of the Socialists' campaign to organize miners to the south in 1929.

By addressing the origins of Los Olivos socialism, I am grappling with the historiographical problem of authenticating the Socialists' pedigree. The lines between socialism and anarchism in the Sierra de Aracena seem difficult to draw before the 1920's. Late in the Second Republic, the villagers of Los Olivos whom their fellows remember as Socialists and who affiliated with the Unión General de Trabajadores (UGT) nonetheless voiced some of the rhetoric associated with Spanish anarchism and libertarian communism. These two findings pose a challenge for historical interpretation: Is the identity of the Left in Los Olivos as socialist reliable, particularly since anarchism is known to have had such a prominent role in Andalusia? The problem raises issues concerning the very nature of socialism and anarchism in rural Andalusia: Were they in fact so different?

In this chapter, I endeavor to bring the nature of rural socialism into clearer focus. I argue, with Antonio Calero (1976), that the lines between socialism and anarchism (and even communism) among the rank and file were weakly drawn to begin with, but that in Huelva the Socialists were distinct and clearly predominated over their rivals at the level of formal organization and leadership. There is substantial positive evidence in the Socialist press for the party's extensive campaigning and union organizing in Huelva during the 1920's. During that period, the Primo de Rivera dictatorship forced anarchism and communism underground, making their influence in Huelva difficult to assess. Anarchists in the Huelva mining zone are known to have affiliated with Socialist unions as the only legal alternative open to them for organizing under Primo de Rivera. But in Huelva, Socialists appear to have had a secure grip on organizing, in contrast to Sevilla province, for example, where Communists and anarchists rebounded in rural organization as soon as the dictatorship gave way. Only later in Huelva do we see the lines between socialism, anarchism, and communism breaking down among the Left, probably because of their common experience of repression in the second *bienio*, particularly after October 1934.

Early Socialist and Anarchist Organization in Huelva

Socialists and anarchists in Spain had a long history of rivalry. They differed in goals and tactics. As followers of Bakunin, Spanish anarchists from the nineteenth century onward advocated the general strike to bring down the state as the ultimate arbiter of capitalist property. Anarchists eschewed politics, concentrating on organizing loosely federated syndicates and labor collectives both to implement the revolutionary general strike and to rebuild society from the bottom up. After the turn of the century, the anarchists loosely federated their workers' collectives along French syndicalist lines into the Confederación Nacional del Trabajo (CNT) for these purposes. In the First International, Marxists split with the anarchists and formed the rival Spanish Socialist Workers' Party (PSOE) in 1878. The Socialists believed in a strong state and in the inevitability of a bourgeois revolution to capture it as a step toward socialism. Unlike the anarchists, they took part in politics while building an organized working-class movement from the top down. In 1888, the Socialists joined their unions into an overarching association with centralized leadership, the UGT (Díaz del Moral 1967: 124).

Anarchism and socialism diverged along regional lines as well. Anarchism took hold in Catalonia among industrial workers and in southern Spain among agrarian laborers, for whom the promise of village collectives based on land to be expropriated from the huge Andalusian estates had a tremendous appeal. The Socialists grew through the organizing of craft and trade workers in Madrid and central Spain and among Basque metalworkers. Although competing with the Socialists in other areas, the anarchists retained their initial strength among the industrial and craft workers of Catalonia and among agrarian workers through most of Andalusia. The Socialists spread among peasants in central Spain and Extremadura and among mine- and railworkers in Asturias as well as in the Andalusian Sierra Morena, once an area of greater anarchist strength.

Huelva was located between regions in which the two movements developed their respective strength, but over time it leaned increasingly toward socialism because of the headway Socialists made in organizing mineworkers in the center of the province. The mines had begun to expand after British interests took them over for development in 1873. Anarchists were the first to organize effectively at the Riotinto mines in the 1880's, but the socialist UGT also organized among mineworkers after 1888. After the turn of the century, the Socialists recruited more vigorously in the mining zone, displacing anarchists not only there but in adjacent regions as well.

There were good reasons why labor organization at the mines affected working-class orientations in adjacent regions. As in the recruitment of mine labor in Asturias (Shubert 1984: 27–43), mining in Huelva recruited laborers from afar as well as from the nearby agricultural villages—from Los Olivos, for example (see Figure 3.1), which was barely 20 kilometers to the north and from which migration to the mining settlements roughly paralleled trends in mining output. Even in the barren countryside

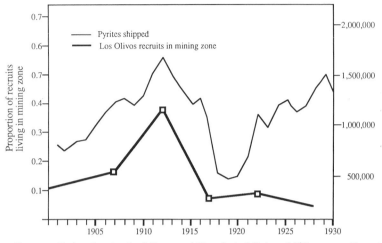

Fig. 3.1. Emigration to the Mines and Trends in Mining. Military recruitment records for Los Olivos indicate that migration from the pueblo flowed to the Riotinto mining zone at rates that correlate with mining output. The heavy line shows the proportion of Los Olivos males of a given five-year birth cohort who recruitment records show to have lived in the mining zone at age 20 and may be inferred to have migrated there for employment by age 15. The lighter line plots production figures for pyrites shipped from the mines.

near the mines, many mining families rented land to farm or worked as farm labor in order to supplement mining wages. Until they reached 14, the minimum age for minework, boys usually would be contracted out by the year to herd pigs and goats in return for food, sandals, a bolt of cloth, and a country shelter.* In periods of slack employment such as after World War I, miners and their families sometimes returned to their native agrarian villages to seek a livelihood. Peasants were thus linked closely enough to miners to share working-class goals and organization. Moreover, for their part, agrarian day workers and smallholders had long-standing grievances against the regional oligarchs who had taken advantage of disentailment laws in the nineteenth century to absorb church-owned land and village commons into their estates (Bernal 1974: 143–47; Maddox 1986:

---

*Suero Sánchez (1982: 25) was himself such a goatherd before joining his father in minework, and his father leased land to farm near Cerro de Andévalo in times of slack minework.

400–410). Periodic calls for revolutionary *reparto* (land redistribution) echoed such grievances. But more frequently, protest in Huelva, whether anarchist or Socialist, united agrarian workers and miners in common concerns over employer-employee relations, work conditions, and wages.

As early as 1888 (the birth year of several of Los Olivos's Second Republic Socialist leaders), anarchist mineworkers joined forces with peasants and farmers in the Riotinto region to demonstrate against the calcinating of pyrites in open-air furnaces at the mines. One market-day Saturday, several thousand workers and farmers gathered in Riotinto to voice their complaints to the mayor. Workers protested the level of wages and working conditions at the furnaces; farmers the despoliation of the surrounding countryside by noxious fumes. Although the authorities disbanded the crowd violently and quelled the protest, the incident led to the growth of mutual-aid associations of peasant, craft, trade, and mine workers outside the immediate mining zone, for example, in Aracena, where such a workers' organization formed in 1894 (Calero 1976: 57–58; Harvey 1981: 132–34; Kaplan 1981: 49; *see also* Instituto de Reformas Sociales 1913).

Such associations were often short-lived, but they reflected a growing consciousness in the Sierra de Aracena of the possibilities of collective action, often through miners attuned to broader currents of working-class dissent. Militancy in Riotinto following the Barcelona Tragic Week of July 1909 inspired dissident smaller shopkeepers and artisans in Aracena to organize day workers to strike for higher wages at the outset of the winter olive harvest. The strike continued until this "socialist" organization was closed by the Civil Guard (Maddox 1986: 320–21). Coinciding as they did with the military service of the cohort of Los Olivos men who later were to be the Socialist leaders of the pueblo, the events of the Tragic Week may have galvanized that generation's political consciousness. There was agrarian unrest throughout the Sierra de Aracena in 1912 and again in 1915. The latter instance was related to the slackening of mining at Riotinto at the outset of World War I and the layoffs of some 20,000 miners, many of whom returned to Sierra towns. Throughout the Sierra, miners and agrarian workers pressured authorities to divide up unemployed workers among landlords to feed (Maddox 1986:

321). In 1915, villagers in Los Olivos rose up against Fermín Moreno, a hated *cacique* who had governed the town at the behest of the regional and provincial oligarchy for over 15 years, killing his wife as she rode into town on a burro and causing him to flee to the nearby town of Jabugo until order was restored. This was probably not an isolated incident since it coincided with a wave of unrest in the Sierra that did not subside until the authorities began road-building projects to hire the unemployed (Maddox 1986: 320–23).

Another outbreak in the sierra in 1919 and 1920 overlapped with the prolonged Socialist-led Riotinto strike of 1920, which became a national cause célèbre. This in turn was a response to the revolutionary agitation that spread through southern Spain during the *trienio bolchevista* (1918–20) in the wake of the news of the Bolshevik Revolution, whether because of rising expectations of revolutionary possibilities or in response to worsening economic conditions following the drop in demand for Spanish exports after World War I (Meaker 1974: 133; Harvey 1981: 178).

These incidents notwithstanding, the landed oligarchy retained tight control of the Sierra de Aracena throughout this period and effectively thwarted any lasting worker organization. Huelva's Conservative party leader, Manuel Burgos y Mazo, had developed a particularly strong grip on the province after the turn of the century, proving powerful enough to dictate the composition of provincial slates for Huelva to the Ministry of the Interior in the arranged elections that characterized Spanish parliamentary politics after the First Republic. Within the framework of his oligarchical control, politics in the Sierra de Aracena were managed through Aracena's *Gran Cacique* and Burgos y Mazo's firm ally, Francisco Javier Sánchez Dalp (the Marqués de Aracena), and through subordinate local-level caciques in the region's villages. These in turn delivered prearranged electoral outcomes by buying votes, using scare tactics, rigging voter rolls, or ensuring that opposition slates were not put up. Electoral outcomes show that this conservative, oligarchical hierarchy managed Aracena district elections unwaveringly up to the dictatorship of Primo de Rivera. By contrast, opposition candidates, including Republicans and Socialists, had some success in the

Valverde del Camino electoral district, encompassing most of the mining zone, particularly after 1914.*

The Sierra de Aracena oligarchy readily resorted to repression in order to blunt working-class organizational or political initiatives. Time and again, the authorities called on the Civil Guard to restore order, both in the mining zone and in adjacent areas. After the 1909 unrest at Riotinto, the mining company there paid for new barracks to house 450 Civil Guard to keep order. Towns such as Aracena beefed up their small garrisons, and barracks were set up in some small villages for the first time. In Los Olivos, for example, landlord Celestino López and his manager, Patricio López, brought in the Civil Guard in 1920 on the pretext of jailing members of the Iglesias family accused of acting as a bandit gang to extort money from local property holders. The Lópezes then rented quarters to the Civil Guard to use as regular barracks. Although the putting down of banditry was a time-honored justification for bringing in the Civil Guard, it seems likely from the timing of this incident and the character of later antagonisms between its protagonists that "banditry" was in this case used as a pretext for preventing incipient worker protest: during the Second Republic, the Lópezes led the Right in Los Olivos, and three members of the Iglesias family were among the Socialists killed in 1936.

Socialists in Huelva under Primo de Rivera: Miners and Farmworkers

The 1923–30 dictatorship of Primo de Rivera quieted worker and peasant dissidence in Spain and in Huelva in a number of ways and channeled permitted labor organization in a manner that ultimately gave an advantage to the Socialists.

Having "pronounced" for order against the threat of revolution from below, Primo's regime categorically put down labor agitation and those advocating it. Organizations of the Spanish

---

*See Tusell (1976) for a discussion of the *encasillado* (government-orchestrated) system of oligarchically arranged elections in Andalusia, for a detailed discussion of the exceptional power held by Burgos y Mazo (1976: 32–33, 69–71), and for electoral data from the Aracena and Valverde del Camino districts (1976: 227–31, 249–51).

Communist Party (PCE), which had splintered off from the Socialists in 1921, and trade unions of the anarcho-syndicalist CNT disbanded or went underground in 1923, not to reemerge until 1930. The dictatorship was not an enemy to labor, but it insisted on the resolution of social issues through state-corporatist institutions, with which the Socialists decided to collaborate. In consequence, the state recognized Socialist trade unions as legal. But even the UGT lost organizations and members, notably in rural areas. In Huelva, where the unsuccessful 1920 strike at the Riotinto mines had already left working-class organization in disarray, the reverses were considerable. Working-class organization did not revive there until the Socialists reorganized mineworkers' unions in a corporatist framework in 1929 (Tusell 1977: 320–22; Preston 1984b: 163).

Primo pursued an interventionist policy of protectionism and public investment in infrastructure that energized the Spanish economy. Even though agriculture benefited from the economic revival less than other sectors, agrarian workers and peasants found that living costs eased relative to wages, in comparison with the post–World War I years. Working-class old-timers from Los Olivos remember the dictatorship nostalgically as an era when food was plentiful and cheap, in contrast to the dire food shortages after the Civil War and the present-day inflation of living costs relative to their pensions. These circumstances softened working-class grievances during the dictatorship.*

Primo's campaign to eradicate *caciquismo*, however ineffectual it proved in Andalusia and other rural areas, probably reduced rural discontent to some degree, at least temporarily. The campaign attacked abuses by municipal functionaries as well as other public officials, removing many old caciques from office and establishing new commissions to serve in place of the old town councils that the caciques had controlled. In Aracena, these reforms temporarily displaced Sánchez Dalp and even led to an investigation of his purported wrongdoing, although Sánchez Dalp returned to favor and to a measure of power within a

*See Ben-Ami (1983: 240–82) on Primo de Rivera's economic policies and achievements and on the stabilizing of wages and the slight decline in prices during the dictatorship.

couple of years. In Los Olivos, the new commissions set up three-year terms for mayors, breaking the old Town Council pattern of perpetuating the same mayor in office for years. To be sure, the mayor and other commission members continued to be drawn from among the leading landholding and merchant families, and Patricio López (Celestino López's manager and henchman) played a strong behind-the-scenes role, but for at least one term the mayorship was held by Pablo Moreno, who later aligned with the Socialists in the town.*

The Catholic mutualism encouraged by the Primo de Rivera regime also mitigated agrarian unrest. Before the dictatorship, the church-affiliated Confederación Nacional Católica Agraria (CNCA) had made headway in organizing the peasants and farmers of Castile and northeastern Spain in a network of rural cooperatives and organizations for insurance, savings, and credit. These entities ostensibly promoted the mutual welfare of proprietors and laborers that they brought together. But their championing of authority and of the rights of property and their paternalistic approach to social problems generally reinforced proprietors' interests—so much so that the CNCA has been characterized as politically subordinating the smallholding peasant (Castillo 1979). Seeking a nonpartisan civilian base for his regime, Primo de Rivera turned to the Asociación Católica Nacional de Propagandistas (ACPN) to help set up a patriotic, apolitical party, the Unión Patriótica, and this in turn linked the dictatorship with social Catholicism and facilitated the spread of such institutions as the CNCA (see Castillo 1984; Payne 1984: 140–48; Ben-Ami 1983: ch. 4).

Catholic agrarian syndicates dominated by proprietors made modest inroads in Huelva (Castillo 1984: 122). Aracena's gentry set up two such syndicates and published a regional newspaper, *El Distrito*, to disseminate Catholic mutualism. There was no Catholic agrarian syndicate in Los Olivos, but church influence was very strong. The village had a native-son priest in the Moreno family and broad membership in two *hermandades* (confraternities). One of these, the Hermandad Sacramental, founded in

---

*For the attack on caciquismo, see Ben-Ami (1983: 90–92); on Sánchez Dalp, see Maddox (1986: 415–19).

1560, was reorganized in 1929 as a funeral association managed by the gentry for needy members.* The spirit of Catholic mutualism thus invigorated old as well as new institutions in Sierra de Aracena villages, reinforcing patronage and undercutting class divisions (Maddox 1986: 355–70).

Working-class unions did not revive in Huelva until 1929, when the Socialists capitalized on their privileged involvement in the dictatorship's corporatist institutions to establish their Sindicato Minero as the sole representative of labor on the new *comités paritarios* (arbitration boards) for mining in the province.

The Socialists considered the comités paritarios as the major achievement of their collaboration with the dictatorship. The Socialists had refrained from agitating against the dictatorship at its inception and had collaborated in implementing corporatist institutions. Asturian mine leader Manuel Llaneza assented to Primo's early overture to participate in the new Labor Council, and in 1924 the UGT designated Francisco Largo Caballero to join Primo's new Council of State. In 1926, the Socialists accepted the corporatist arbitration boards, comités paritarios, that Primo de Rivera's minister of labor, Eduardo Aunós, set up for specific industries and professions. Composed of equal numbers of representatives of employers and unions under government-appointed chairmen, the comités paritarios had the legal power to negotiate agreements and settle disputes between employers and workers in an industry. Only legally constituted unions representing a majority of workers in an industry could represent workers on the boards, an arrangement that advantaged the Socialists over the outlawed anarcho-syndicalists and Communists in attracting union membership in several industries. Although the Socialists withdrew from political collaboration with the weakening dictatorship after 1928, they continued to promote the comités paritarios as the best way for organized labor to win favorable contracts (Ben-Ami 1978: 105–17, 1983: 290–97; Preston 1978: 4–11).

The campaign to organize Huelva mineworkers grew out of a

---

*The Hermandad Sacramental of Los Olivos is active today, and a recent *mayordomo* has been seeking records of its early history in the archive of the diocese of Sevilla. Unfortunately, most of its records were lost in the 1936 burning of church archives, but its 1929 *Libro de cuentas y actas* survived the conflagration.

more generalized promotion of the UGT in western Andalusia and Extremadura in 1928, chronicled in the "News from the Provinces" section of the party newspaper, *El Socialista*. Leading Socialists such as Fernández Quer, Andrés Saborit, and Enrique Santiago toured those regions, explaining Socialist political and social policies to purportedly packed and enthusiastic audiences in local theaters; they outlined how to constitute labor unions legally under the Law of Corporative Organization, and they urged subscriptions to *El Socialista* onto local Socialist groups to help educate prospective party and union members. In the wake of these propaganda tours, local correspondents began to write short articles for *El Socialista* on the abuses of *cacicazgo* (political bossism), on employer breaches of the restrictions on hours of work and work on Sunday, and on issues concerning union and party membership.

When Ramón González Peña and other leaders of the Asturian Miners' Syndicate inaugurated the campaign to organize Huelva mineworkers in 1929, they centered the campaign on defense of the comités paritarios and Socialist involvement in them. On the one hand, they had to challenge the Catholic syndicates that the mining companies had set up as an alternative to the UGT. On the other hand, in organizing the mineworker rank and file, they had to counteract the anarchist charge of having sold out to the dictatorship through collaboration in state corporatism. Answering that charge while on tour in Nerva, González Peña insisted, "We have nothing to apologize for. We were interventionists before [the dictatorship], as we are today and will be tomorrow, because that is our tactic, as it is that of the Unión General and the party, and it is a tactic that we defend with heads held high and a clean conscience" (*El Socialista*, Feb. 6, 1929). The campaign was intense and successful; in the December 1929 elections, the UGT's Sindicato Minero de Huelva overwhelmingly won the right to represent labor on the comités paritarios set up for mineworking in the province (*El Socialista*, Dec. 11, 1929).

Agrarian activism in Huelva, when it revived after 1928, grew out of developments in the mining zone, much as it had done in the past. The Socialists began to reanimate their agrarian undertakings after 1924, publishing extensively on agrarian problems in *El Socialista* and wooing tenant farmers and small landowners as well as day workers. They came within a hair's breadth of having corporative organization of the countryside decreed in 1928, but opposition from landowners and Catholic syndicates defeated them. They initiated propaganda tours in agrarian zones in the same year to revive their rural affiliation (see Map 3.1), making inroads in predominantly anarchist areas of Andalusia and considerable headway in Extremadura (Ben-Ami 1978: 113–16). But these early efforts bypassed Huelva geographically, as Socialist attention there centered on mineworker organization.

Instead, it was the mining campaign itself that revived agrarian activism in Huelva, beginning in settlements near the mines where both miners and agrarian workers lived. Socialist organizer Remigio Cabello visited Cabezas Rubias, near the mines at Cerro de Andévalo, to lecture prospective recruits to the Miners' Syndicate about social security and retirement. Within a week,

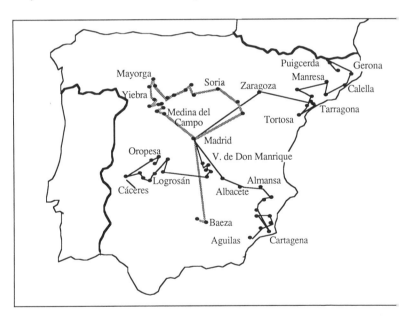

Map 3.1. The Socialist Agrarian Campaign, 1928. The routes in the map are those followed by prominent Socialists campaigning for the unionization of agrarian workers in autumn 1928. (Adapted from *El Socialista*, Dec. 11, 1928, p. 4.)

The Socialist appeal to harvest workers. The Socialists campaigned vigorously among farmworkers and gained support particularly among workers in the wheat-growing areas of central Spain and Extremadura. This constituency was important to the Socialists throughout the Second Republic. (From *El Obrero de La Tierra*, Oct. 22, 1932, p. 1.)

workers there formed a party subsection and took steps to set up an agrarian union affiliated to the UGT (*El Socialista*, Feb. 23 and Mar. 1, 1929). Alosno, near the Tharsis mines, was another such place. Having heard so much about the comités paritarios for mining, agrarian workers there organized themselves and echoed party leaders in appealing to the minister of labor to set up comités paritarios for agrarian employment as well (*El Socialista*, Oct. 23, 1929).

In August 1929, to take another example, mine organizers from Valdelamusa visited Almonaster la Real and Cortegana, agrarian municipalities with some mines in the Sierra de Aracena not far from Los Olivos, to campaign for the Miners' Syndicate. Almonaster's mayor and several citizens wined and dined the organizers before accompanying them to visit nearby settlements. The visit set Socialist agrarian organization into motion in Almonaster. In December 1929, after the mineworker's campaign was completed, Almonaster Socialist Antonio Pérez lamented to *El Socialista* the lack of agrarian organization there and called on his fellows to educate themselves by reading the working-class press daily and to prepare to organize themselves. On February 12, 1930—just a few days after the collapse of the dictatorship—Socialist "militants" in Almonaster announced that they had formed a local party chapter and called on workers to sign up. Not long thereafter, Almonaster's new farmworkers' syndicate sponsored campaign visits, including one by González Peña himself, to promote his candidacy as parliamentary deputy for Huelva in the first elections after the dictatorship (*El Socialista*, Aug. 21 and Dec. 21, 1929; Feb. 12, Oct. 5, and Nov. 6, 1930).

By the end of the 1929 mineworkers' campaign, Socialist organizations in direct touch with *El Socialista* spanned the length and breadth of the mining zone and included several agrarian organizations in adjacent towns to the south and the north (see Map 3.2). Flushed with the successes of their campaigns among miners in Huelva and Asturias, the Socialists launched an even more ambitious drive to organize agrarian laborers throughout Spain. As support for the Primo de Rivera dictatorship crumbled in January 1930, they established the National Federation of Agricultural Workers (FNTT), convening its first national congress

● Socialist organizing
   by 1929

Aracena

1 Almonaster la Real	9 El Cerro de Andévalo	17 Paterna del Campo
2 Alosno	10 Cortegana	18 Peña del Hierro
3 Aracena	11 Cueva de la Mora	19 Puebla de Guzmán
4 Aroche	12 Escacena del Campo	20 Rosal de la Frontera
5 Beas	13 Gibraleón	21 Tharsis
6 Cabezas Rubias	14 Huelva	22 Valdelamusa
7 Calañas	15 Minas de Ríotinto	23 Valverde del Camino
8 El Campillo	16 Nerva	24 Zalamea la Real

Map 3.2. Socialist Organizing in Huelva up to 1929. The Socialists campaigned primarily in the mining zone before 1930. The map is based on news reports in *El Socialista* and indicates places in which Socialists were already active in unions or were attempting to form them.

in April 1930. It was FNTT campaigning from 1930 to 1932 that consolidated agrarian representation throughout the province of Huelva for the Socialists (see Map 3.3). Huelva mineworker leader Ramón González Peña personally led the campaign, which inaugurated agrarian unions in 25 towns in 1930 alone (*El Socialista*, Jan. 2, 1931).

The FNTT began its drive in a year of considerable agrarian agitation in Spain, which was coupled to more generalized disaffection with the monarchy. The stability of prices had eroded in the last years of the dictatorship, and unemployment had risen. Although 1929 had been a peak year in many sectors of the economy, agriculture suffered from overproduction of some crops coupled with declines in exports to troubled world markets. Drought in Andalusia compounded agrarian unemployment in 1930 (Ben-Ami 1983: 335–38; Tuñón de Lara 1978: 138–41). Thus, there was cause for unrest. Meanwhile, following Primo de Rivera's resignation in January 1930, Alfonso XIII appointed a government led by General Dámaso Berenguer. He relaxed dictatorial controls, which permitted anarchists and Communists to resurface to tap that unrest. This the PCE and CNT did. They fomented a wave of agitation and strikes that peaked in a general strike that spread from Sevilla through Sevilla province in the summer of 1930 (Tuñón de Lara 1978: 142–49). For their part, the Socialists were also casting their lot against the monarchy by entering the coalition led by Liberal Republican Niceto Alcalá Zamora and calling for the establishment of a Republic.

Despite the intense agitation to the southeast in Sevilla, developments in the Sierra de Aracena under the aegis of the Socialists were of more moderate tone during 1930. Socialists aired their grievances against the regional oligarchy but cautioned against revolutionary excesses while pressing for broad agrarian organization.

The Socialists sought a broad agrarian base including not just landless workers but smallholders, tenant farmers, and sharecroppers as well. Yet the latter groups had to be wooed from their loyalties to the landed oligarchy with whom they were associated through patronage and Catholic mutualism or from whom some of them leased land. To counteract smallholder

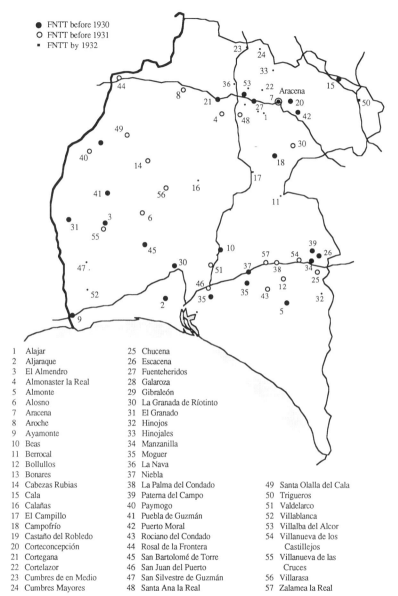

- ● FNTT before 1930
- ○ FNTT before 1931
- ■ FNTT by 1932

1	Alajar	25	Chucena
2	Aljaraque	26	Escacena
3	El Almendro	27	Fuenteheridos
4	Almonaster la Real	28	Galaroza
5	Almonte	29	Gibraleón
6	Alosno	30	La Granada de Ríotinto
7	Aracena	31	El Granado
8	Aroche	32	Hinojos
9	Ayamonte	33	Hinojales
10	Beas	34	Manzanilla
11	Berrocal	35	Moguer
12	Bollullos	36	La Nava
13	Bonares	37	Niebla
14	Cabezas Rubias	38	La Palma del Condado
15	Cala	39	Paterna del Campo
16	Calañas	40	Paymogo
17	El Campillo	41	Puebla de Guzmán
18	Campofrío	42	Puerto Moral
19	Castaño del Robledo	43	Rociano del Condado
20	Corteconcepción	44	Rosal de la Frontera
21	Cortegana	45	San Bartolomé de Torre
22	Cortelazor	46	San Juan del Puerto
23	Cumbres de en Medio	47	San Silvestre de Guzmán
24	Cumbres Mayores	48	Santa Ana la Real

49	Santa Olalla del Cala
50	Trigueros
51	Valdelarco
52	Villablanca
53	Villalba del Alcor
54	Villanueva de los Castillejos
55	Villanueva de las Cruces
56	Villarasa
57	Zalamea la Real

Map 3.3. Socialist Organizing in Huelva, 1930–32. During and after 1930, Socialists campaigned in Huelva almost entirely in agrarian regions surrounding the mining zone. The map differentiates locations in which the FNTT had formed unions by the end of 1930 from locations in which unions formed thereafter. Each successive year saw further Socialist penetration of agrarian Huelva. (Data drawn from *El Socialista* and from Federación Nacional de Trabajadores de la Tierra 1932.)

fears of losing property under socialism, FNTT propaganda stressed that farmers' smallholdings were precapitalist rather than capitalist in nature and thus different from large estates and not a target for redistribution. The propaganda pointed out ways in which wealthy agriculturalists exploited others. It explained how landlords cheated workers hired for piecework at harvest time and tricked sharecroppers and tenant farmers who lacked proper contracts (for examples of these appeals, see *El Socialista*, July 11, 25, and 26, 1929).

The voicing of grievances against local caciques and their sponsors among the regional oligarchy in the Sierra de Aracena responded indirectly to this thrust of the Socialist campaign. Party members from Carbonera, a hamlet of Aracena, complained repeatedly to *El Socialista* about the neglect of their fountain and roads at the hands of Aracena mayors designated by Sánchez Dalp:

[Although] we pay every kind of tax, levy, and surcharge, . . . the city [Aracena] enjoys every kind of convenience, including public entertainment and facilities for recreation, while we of the hamlets are left abandoned. They only think of us when they need us to vote for some cacique, and then just by inviting us to hunt in the game preserve of the marqués [Sánchez Dalp]. . . . In this hamlet our needs are many. Our children, barefoot, have to go to work prematurely in agriculture because of the miserable wages their parents earn, and as a consequence they receive almost no schooling, which might help them defend themselves against the tyrants who amass their capital at the expense of our work (*El Socialista*, Dec. 18, 1930).

Yet in railing against the tyranny of caciques, Socialists also cautioned against revolutionary excesses of the kind being practiced by anarchists and Communists. In an allusion to anarchism, Socialist militants in Almonaster la Real warned workers to reject "the false radicalisms that once were preached to Andalusian workers and that led them to disaster and to the breaking up of workers' organizations. . . . [For that left] the capitalists with a free hand to impose their whim without any check to force them to comply with existing social laws" (*El Socialista*, Feb. 12, 1930).

That the socialist appeal was persuasive in Huelva, and espe-

* Towns with Communists
○ Towns with Anarchists
◉ Towns with both

5
22
4
Aracena
16
14
11
13
10
9
18
8
28
17
25
26
3
23
21
12
6
27
19
15
24
1
Huelva
7
20
2

1   Aljaraque
2   Almonte
3   Alosno
4   Aroche
5   Arroyomolinos
     de León
6   Beas
7   Bollullos par
     del Condado
8   Calañas
9   El Campillo
10 Campofrío
11 Cerro de Andévalo
12 Gibraleón
13 La Granada de
     Ríotinto
14 Higuera de la Sierra

15 Huelva
16 Jabugo
17 Minas de Ríotinto
18 Nerva
19 La Palma del Condado
20 Palos de la Frontera
21 Paterna del Campo
22 Rosal de la Frontera
23 San Bartolomé
     de Torre
24 San Juan del Puerto
25 Tharsis
26 Valverde del Camino
27 Villarasa
28 Zalamea la Real

Map 3.4. Anarchist and Communist Organizing in Huelva, 1932. Anarchist and Communist organizations were active in Huelva, primarily in the mining zone and in the agricultural *campiña* to the south, and apparently did not encompass the Sierra de Aracena. (Map based on parish reports compiled in Ordóñez Márquez 1968.)

cially so in the Sierra de Aracena, is attested by the vigorous spread of FNTT- and UGT-affiliated agrarian organizations compared with the relatively desultory growth of anarchist and Communist organizations. Socialists in Huelva had effectively worked the advantage that the dictatorship had given them over competing parties and ideologies. During the dictatorship, workers who otherwise inclined toward anarchism or communism had no choice, if they did not go underground, but to join with the Socialists to defend their interests. This was particularly true of anarchists in the CNT in the mining zone, many of whom joined the UGT during the ascendance of the comités paritarios (Suero Sánchez 1982: 26).

In contrast to the nonmining regions of Andalusia, in which anarchism and communism resurfaced with vigor on the fall of the dictatorship in 1930, in Huelva the Socialists retained most of the workers whom state-corporatist policies had channeled into Socialist organization. Although anarchism and communism later resurfaced in Huelva (see Map 3.4), their organization remained low and their impact on agrarian zones (particularly the Sierra de Aracena) minor until the Republic's second bienio, when the common repression of leftists brought Socialists, Communists, and anarchists closer together in radicalization (see Chapter 7). Even then, socialism continued to hold sway in the agrarian organizations of the Sierra de Aracena.

FOUR

Control of Labor in Early Second Republic Los Olivos

THE PROSPECTS for Socialists in the national government were bright at the outset of the Republic. Alone among the organized forces of the Left as participants in the Provisional Government, the Socialists basked in the Republic's initial euphoria. As ministers of labor and of finance, Socialist leaders Francisco Largo Caballero and Indalecio Prieto decreed reforms in favor of agrarian labor for which the Socialists long had pressed, without success, under the dictatorship. But the Socialists suffered setbacks during the first two years of the Republic in large measure because of agrarian conflict. These decrees, and the intention of adding land reform legislation to them, inflamed the conflict, particularly in the south, and the conflict welled up into politics at the national level, where it beset Socialists both from the Right and from the Left.

No one has traced this agrarian conflict and the decline it caused Socialist fortunes more clearly than Paul Preston (1978, 1984*a*, *b*). Preston argues that Largo Caballero's decrees, intended only to mitigate the plight of agrarian day workers, seriously challenged the reliance by the inefficient latifundia system on a subservient reserve army of labor. Landowners responded quickly, reviving employers' federations, intransigently resisting reforms, and building a mass party, the Confederación Española de Derechas Autónomas (CEDA) to channel their opposition into national politics. Ultimately their efforts would bring down Manuel Azaña's Republican-Socialist coalition government. Agrarian workers at the local level, meanwhile, initially flocked to the Socialist FNTT and UGT, but they grew increasingly desperate at right-wing obstruction of legal reforms. As anarchist extralegal action increased, rank-and-file Socialists pressured their national leaders toward ever more radical positions. Ultimately the Socialists broke with the Republicans, rendering their party vulnerable to electoral setbacks in 1933.

Although accurate, Preston's analysis of the agrarian conflict does not sufficiently credit the Socialists of agrarian villages for their accomplishments in the early Second Republic. In this chapter and the next, I follow the essentially upward trajectory of Los Olivos Socialists from their embattled beginnings to their taking and proudly managing the reins of municipal governance to benefit laborers in 1933. My account thus complements Preston's analysis by highlighting an irony of the early Second Republic: even though initially frustrated in the quest for more radical agrarian change, village Socialists began to consolidate their modest accomplishments in 1933 just at the time when Socialists at the national level were on the wane. Ultimately, the conservative reaction whose growth Preston traces at the national level overtook Los Olivos and other village Socialists during the bienio negro, the "two black years" of conservative repression that Socialists experienced everywhere in Spain.

The Transition to the Second Republic

The story of Los Olivos Socialists' struggle to control labor begins in the fifteen months of transition from the dictatorship to the Second Republic.

A crescendo of discontent accompanied Primo de Rivera's January 1930 resignation and Alfonso XIII's ineffective attempts to restore a constitutional monarchy. General Berenguer, to whom Alfonso XIII turned to form a government, ostensibly broke with the dictatorship, easing its repression and abrogating some of its legislation. But Berenguer's delays in calling legitimate elections gave time for dissidence to coalesce. Drought in 1930 worsened unemployment, and labor unrest broke out in June in a wave of anarchist- and Communist-led strikes in and around Sevilla. A coalition of opponents to the monarchy, including the Socialists, met at San Sebastián in August to plot for a Republic; in December they unsuccessfully attempted a revolution. Berenguer's dismissal shortly thereafter did not allay deepening antimonarchist sentiment, which ultimately led to a repudiation of the monarchy by plebiscite in the municipal elections finally held on April 12, 1931. Alfonso XIII abdicated within days as the Republic was joyfully proclaimed in city after city. The San Sebastián coalition formed a Provisional Government (Herr 1971: 154–56).

In Los Olivos, those 15 months proved no less eventful, but their outcome was different. At the outset, a new Town Council with socialist leanings attempted to alleviate unemployment by diverting municipal funds into public works, thus challenging the landlords' domination of local labor. But the Town Council leaders found themselves overwhelmed in the April 12, 1931, elections by the reactionary tactics of the town's monarchist cacique, who then acted to reestablish his own and other employers' control of labor.

Los Olivos's new Town Council took office on February 25, 1930, under one of General Berenguer's first decrees. Ostensibly breaking from the pattern of local governance set up by the dictatorship, the decree ordered existing councils to be replaced; half of their new members were to be drawn from a town's leading taxpayers and half from councillors elected from among those with the greatest number of votes in the last three elections before the dictatorship. The decree seemingly looked to an earlier past, to the restoration of the 1876 constitution and of the pre-1923 system of orderly, managed elections (Ben-Ami 1978: 22). But its application in Los Olivos launched municipal governance in uncharted directions under new leadership. Opening a new volume in which to record the minutes of Town Council activities (the record that informs this narrative of municipal affairs), the Los Olivos Town Council secretary convened the councillors designated by decree and oversaw their election of José Antonio Ramos as mayor.

José Antonio joined the Town Council by virtue of the Berenguer decrees as one of those who had won most of the votes for council membership before 1923. He and co-councillor Isidoro Sánchez both had held office during the dissidence-ridden trienio bolchevista years (1918–20) that had led up to the 1920 jailing and deposing by Los Olivos landlords of the Iglesias family gang. Although José Antonio had once been a property holder of modest means, his fortunes had declined after his wife's death in 1924 and the sale of some of his land. Moderately educated and experienced—he had also served briefly as town secretary during the 1920's—José Antonio held a reputation for independence: both his political experience in the trienio bolchevista and his personal history inclined him to oppose the local oligarchy and probably to support the region's nascent agrarian socialism. Whether he was a Socialist at the outset of his mayoralty is not clear, but he was later a militant Socialist.

For a person other than one of Los Olivos's wealthy landlords or leading merchants to serve as mayor was quite a change from practices under the dictatorship, and this may in part account for the unstable council membership during José Antonio's mayoral term. Altogether 20 men rotated through the eight council positions during his 14 months in office. To some degree, the mechanics by which council members were drawn from the tax rolls contributed to the instability. Because the wealthy Lópezes and Morenos had protected their holdings from taxes, aging lesser landlords headed the tax rolls in their stead, and several of these older men refused to come out of retirement to serve on the council. Two other men held judgeships, which disqualified them for service. But class antagonisms also entered into the resignations and refusals to serve. In addition to José Antonio, three who accepted council positions were men who leased land for farming or made a living running pack trains; wealthier men closer to the propertied and merchant elite, and even cacique Celestino López himself, refused to serve with them.

Both politicking and labor organizing in the region were by this time shaping challenges to the Sierra de Aracena oligarchy with whom Celestino López was allied. As indicated in the previous chapter, Socialist agrarian organizing was well under way. Although I have found no documentary record to pinpoint exactly when Socialists began to organize in Los Olivos, the Socialist prevalence in the region, coupled with the coalitional Socialist-Republican electoral campaigning in the winter of 1930–31, almost certainly assures that they began to do so during José Antonio's incumbency. At a minimum, villagers could have attended Ramón González Peña's electoral campaign visit to nearby Almonaster la Real in November 1930 or his campaign for the FNTT there and in other nearby towns such as Santa Ana la Real (*El Socialista*, Nov. 6, 1930, Jan. 2, 1931).

Electioneering at the end of 1930 highlighted alternatives to the old oligarchical order. With elections in prospect, the Sierra de Aracena oligarchy resuscitated old vote-getting tactics, but not without vociferous opposition from the Socialist press. Socialists in Aracena excoriated the monarchist campaigning of the Sánchez Dalp family and urged workers both to organize and to support the Republican-Socialist candidacies announced for the province (*El Socialista*, Nov. 9, 1930). Socialists in Cortegana ridiculed the sons of Sánchez Dalp and their "lackeys" when they visited Cortegana and Aroche in December 1930 to buy drinks for all comers at the local bars (*El Socialista*, Dec. 9, 1930):

What was the motive of this visit? Comrades, it was the following. They used their bankroll, the money given them by the working proletariat, to flood the bars of Aroche with wine so that the townfolk would get drunk and be won over to them. . . . Aroche, town of capable and forceful men, teach them that workers will not be tricked by a glass of alcohol! Refuse the cup whose poison is offered to cloud your consciousness!

Nearby Socialists found imaginative ways to embarrass the powers that opposed them. In El Campillo, a dependency of Zalamea la Real, the oligarchy pressured the authorities to refuse Socialists the use of the bullring for a public campaign meeting. Shortly after, when the town held its fiesta, including the traditional bullfight, the Socialists prevailed on townfolk to boycott the sale of meat from the butchered bulls through which the town authorities financed the event. When the mayor tried to force butchers in the public market to sell the meat, the Socialists spread the boycott to the market. The upshot was that several hundred kilos of meat rotted and had to be buried by the authorities. The report of the El Campillo correspondent to *El Socialista* (Oct. 2 and 3, 1930) compared the mayor to Calderón's despotic protagonist of *El Alcalde de Zalamea*, reminding him that "no olvide quien siembra vientos que cogera tempestades" (he who stirs up a breeze may catch a storm).

José Antonio's council in Los Olivos responded to this new region-wide articulation of working-class concerns. During the last weeks of the Berenguer government and afterward, as towns throughout Spain prepared for the first municipal elections since before the dictatorship, José Antonio pressed forward with plans for municipal public works favoring day laborers in the town. He committed an initial 3,200 pesetas of municipal funds to public-works construction, a sum equal to wages for nearly 1,100 man-days of labor, and solicited approval and support from the provincial government for a road to the main highway to replace the town's existing link, which had been built in 1921 before the advent of trucking and had so many switchbacks that loaded trucks could not make the grade to export the town's produce. The plan was progressive, one that fit the growing national concern about rural unemployment, at this time swelled by the 1930 drought and subsequent abysmal olive harvest. At the same time, it was a controversial plan, multiplying sixfold the moneys ordinarily dedicated to public works. By funding public works in the context of incipient Socialist agrarian union organizing, José Antonio challenged employers' traditional control of labor, which arose from chronic unemployment and the oligarchical management of relief for unemployment crises.

Employers long had held the upper hand over labor because chronic seasonal unemployment made men vulnerable to their power. Such unemployment had always characterized Andalusia, particularly in the vast plains of the Guadalquivir River in which whole towns of virtually landless workers had no employment for months after the winter harvest of olives and the spring and early summer harvests of wheat (Martínez Alier 1976: 33–42). Although unemployment was less severe in mountain areas such as the Sierra de Aracena, where ecological diversity favored more complex cropping throughout the year and where small garden holdings ameliorated the plight of laborers during seasons of want, it was still substantial, particularly among men. The unemployment of men stemmed in part from the accepted practice of paying women less than men for field work; women almost always could find work, but men could not. Such circumstances enabled major employers such as Los Olivos's cacique to sustain a subservient work force by picking and choosing laborers to be favored by yearlong work contracts and by blackballing dissidents. The action of José Antonio's council potentially facilitated Socialist organization of Los Olivos's labor and thus threatened this employer hegemony.

Furthermore, by diverting municipal funds to substantial public works, the council called into question the traditional oligarchical management of unemployment relief. Public works, though recognized as a mechanism for unemployment relief, had been undertaken only on a small scale by earlier town councils, which the local oligarchy had controlled. Instead, employers had utilized the paternalistic *alojamiento* system of dividing unemployed workers among themselves to feed during periods of acute crisis (see Malefakis 1970: 102–3). José Antonio's measures undercut alojamiento paternalism and raised the question of why traditional powerholders had not done more in the way of public-works relief.

Huelva's traditional powerholders, indeed, had begun to react to such challenges by Socialists and would-be Republicans. After the abortive December 12, 1930, revolution at Jaca (Huesca) and Cuatro Vientos (Madrid), the authorities arrested many leading Socialists throughout Spain. In Huelva, the authorities closed down a number of newly formed Socialist agrarian syndicates, some of which were not allowed to reopen until just prior to the April 1931 elections, despite protestations by Socialist leaders that the closures were tantamount to turning towns' elections over to the traditional caciques (*El Socialista*, Feb. 10 and 18, 1930; Mar. 19, 1931).

Celestino López and other Sierra de Aracena caciques did indeed prevail on April 12, 1931, through old-fashioned tactics for rigging elections, returning Los Olivos and other towns to monarchist control—ironically, in the same municipal elections whose outcome in major cities persuaded Alfonso XIII to abdicate and led to proclamation of the Republic. Resorting to the tactics by which rural caciques of an earlier era of electoral politics had perpetuated their control of public office, Celestino López and his manager, Patricio López, somehow prevented the posting of an opposition slate in the municipal elections and took office under the terms of Article 29 of the law governing town councils. This provision held that a slate that had "no opposition" could dispense with an election. Jailing the opposition slate on the eve of an election was a common tactic of Andalusian caciques to control public office under the terms of Article 29, and the Lópezes probably did so.

The electoral deception in Los Olivos accompanied widespread vote fixing throughout the province. The Sánchez Dalp slate in Aracena contrived a similar outcome, and Republicans and Socialists immediately sued to overturn the election. Fraud was in fact so prevalent in rural areas of Spain during the April 12 elections that the Provisional Government ordered new elections a month later in municipalities where fraud had been denounced. In the province of Huelva, 40 of the 79 municipalities were ordered to hold new elections, but Los Olivos was not among them (*Boletín Oficial*, May 14, 1931, no. 93; Ben-Ami 1978: 273–74).

In addition to Patricio López, Celestino López had included other allies in his slate. Among them were Maximiano Nogales (a wealthy farmer), Maximiano Santis (farmer and baker), and Ramón Nogales (who had returned to Los Olivos to buy up farmland with a fortune in wages saved up from five years' work in California). All had been councillors under Primo de Rivera except for Ramón (who had been abroad) and Celestino (who always had worked behind the scenes). At its first meeting, the council elected Celestino López as mayor.

Celestino López's first substantive action after reviewing the municipal coffers and the budget was to annul José Antonio's public-works allocation. Los Olivos thus entered the Second Republic in the grip of traditional powerholders who had repudiated major public-works relief of unemployed day workers. Socialists were to have to struggle fiercely against them for the control of labor over the next two years in order to attain the stature and legitimacy in governance at the local level that their party held nationally at the Second Republic's outset.

The Early Republican Agrarian Decrees

The Socialists accomplished more through agrarian decrees issued in the euphoria and consensus of the first weeks of Provisional Government rule than through any other initiatives, including land reform itself, as it emerged from bitterly contested legislation more than a year later. Even conservatives in the governmental coalition conceded at the outset that the plight of peasants and rural workers demanded redress. Unwilling to undertake land reform before the Constituent Cortes had been elected and could legislate it, the cabinet nonetheless compromised at an early meeting to press ahead with measures to alleviate rural social problems, especially those related to employment. It was to the Socialist ministers of justice, finance, and labor that the formulation of these decrees fell since no other group in the coalition had formulated an agrarian program (Malefakis 1970: 164–66).

Through one group of decrees, the Socialist ministers established the equivalent of comités paritarios for the agrarian sector, structures that they had failed to win under the Primo de Rivera dictatorship. Labor Minister Largo Caballero's decree of May 7, 1931, set up so-called mixed juries (*jurados mixtos*) to negotiate and arbitrate the terms of agrarian employment. Composed of equal numbers of laborers and employers under government-designated heads, mixed juries operated at the subprovincial level to negotiate *bases de trabajo*, detailed specifications of wages and working conditions to prevail in a region. They also arbitrated labor disputes brought to them. The government empowered the *juntas de policía rural*, municipal commissions equally representing workers and employers under two town councillors, to implement mixed jury decisions at a local level. The mixed juries were especially important for organized labor since they gave local agrarian unions (which Socialists were establishing through the FNTT and UGT) a role in designating labor representatives for local juntas de policía rural. Unions had the right to strike in disputes not settled after mixed jury arbitration (Malefakis 1970: 167).

A related edict increased the power of local agrarian unions. The Ministry of Labor decree on *términos municipales* (municipal boundaries) mandated preferential employment of laborers living within the township of a place of work. In implementing this decree, local unions were charged with managing the *bolsa de trabajo* (labor exchange), which listed individuals living in a municipality available for hire. During strikes it was illegal for employers to import strikebreakers. The términos municipales decree was highly controversial because it interfered with the widespread hiring of migrant labor at harvest season, employment on which many agrarian poor relied for survival. The edict's strict application had to be eased for harvest employment but still redounded to agrarian labor's favor (Malefakis 1970: 168–70).

When coupled with an eight-hour day and overtime wages and an edict to increase employment by forcing landowners to cultivate fallow land, these decrees considerably advantaged day laborers and permanent field hands at the expense of employers. As Paul Preston has pointed out (1984b: 166), the measures implied a redistribution of wealth from landlords to employees since the former had to absorb higher labor costs that they could not offset by raising prices for crops in a depressed market.

More significant, I think, was that the measures created the potential for greater worker control over employment. They removed from the employer the power of deciding whether to farm and of determining whom to employ on what terms. In doing so, they threatened the meaning of property. For under agrarian capitalism based on property, ownership of the means of production implied absolute control over it. Owning property had even broader cultural meaning since it accorded the owner not only a measure of practical autonomy but moral autonomy as well, affecting what it meant to be a good person. Spanish farmers, peasants and landlords alike, thus particularly cherished the autonomy with which they, as owners of property, could make decisions regarding its disposition and use. By giving workers and institutions of the state a say in these decisions, the measures changed the meaning of property in a way that was potentially as revolutionary as land reform itself (for further discussion of this point, see Chapter 5).

In addition to these measures, the Provisional Government tried to alleviate unemployment through public works and unemployment subsidies. The Socialist minister of finance, Indalecio Prieto, announced a three-year program of public works for Andalusia and Extremadura, channeling state funds through provincial governments to municipalities for that purpose. Although his conservative fiscal policies limited the Republic's resources for the purpose, the program was of some significance, benefiting Los Olivos, for example. Minister of Labor Francisco Largo Caballero banned the paternalistic *alojamiento* system of having employers handle unemployment relief as charity and established the *décimo para el paro forzoso*. This 10 percent surcharge on rural property taxes was meant to provide each municipality with a fund for the Town Council and local representatives of labor to hire the unemployed (Carr and Fusi 1966: 614; Malefakis 1970: 171).

The Socialist ministers of the Provisional Government did not limit the benefits of their agrarian measures to workers. Other edicts favored sharecroppers and tenant farmers at the expense of landlords by restricting evictions, compensating tenants for improvements on land, and enabling leaseholders to petition for lower rents if crops failed or if rents exceeded a property's assessed taxable income (Malefakis 1970: 166–67). Even peasant smallholders, many of whom supplemented family farming through leasing or wage work, stood to benefit from the decrees. The edicts gave both labor and the state a role in setting the conditions for contracts that employers had theretofore been able to set independently. They appealed to a broad rural constituency, vastly enhancing the popularity of the Socialists who had promulgated them. As Edward Malefakis (1970: 170) has indicated, their potential impact was substantial:

The agrarian decrees of the Provisional Government constituted a revolution without precedent in Spanish rural life. For the first time the balance of legal rights swung away from the landowners to the rural proletariat. The range of decrees and the rapidity with which they were promulgated are breathtaking in retrospect. New conditions had been created in the countryside long before an agrarian reform bill reached the Cortes for discussion. And since the Cortes, after it convened, translated into law all of the decrees except those governing leases, the benefits of this agricultural revolution seemed assured of permanence.

Needless to say, rural landlords intransigently resisted implementation of the decrees (Pascual Cevallos 1983: 49–65). The decrees challenged their autonomy to manage their own affairs and would have hurt landlords economically. The prospect of additional land reform by the Provisional Government swelled their discontent. During the summer months of 1931, as the Constituent Cortes met to draft a constitution, landlords established employers' federations to speak out against these measures. The long-standing association of Catholic mutualism with rural proprietors made natural allies of opponents of the Second Republic's anticlerical measures, particularly the bitterly contested Article 26 of the Constitution drafted in October 1931, which phased out state support of the church and nationalized church property not needed for religious activities. How landlords channeled their intransigence from the local level through the Asociación Católica Nacional de Propagandistas and its electoral organization, Acción Nacional, into opposition to the Azaña government's Republican-Socialist coalition in 1932 and 1933 has been traced masterfully by Paul Preston (1978). Below I examine that intransigence and opposition as the Socialists of Los Olivos experienced them in attempting to secure implementation of the Republic's early agrarian decrees.

The Struggle to Control Labor

The Town Council headed by Celestino López had used reactionary means to come to power in April 1931, and it set about governing the town in a manner intending to ignore, blunt, or reverse the progressive thrust of early Republican agrarian decrees. Socialists, who organized in Los Olivos by the summer of 1931, were to engage this council in a struggle for the control of labor initially centered on hiring for municipal public works.

From the outset of the Republic through its short life, all parties contending for the control of local affairs in Los Olivos accepted as given that there was a *crisis obrera* there, as there was throughout the Andalusian countryside, and that it was the role of the state to alleviate it through the institutions of town government. When José Antonio Ramos's council had budgeted funds for road construction, it did so to provide jobs. Immediately after annulling these plans for construction, Celestino López drew up plans to repair existing roadways and to repave several streets in the town, soliciting and receiving partial funding for these projects from the provincial government. What was at stake in Los Olivos was control of these mechanisms, of the prerogative to determine just who were the "needy" workers and just how they should be employed. Contending for this control were Celestino López and his council and the recently formed Syndicate of Agrarian Workers.

The syndicate, whch was established by the summer of 1931, drew most of its initial membership from 25 families of relatively poorer townsfolk, among them some who were involved in regional transport as muleteers and some who farmed tiny properties as well as working seasonally for wages. It gradually grew to include almost all of the men of Los Olivos who were not employers or self-employed artisans. Many of the members of the syndicate were related to one another as in-laws and as cousins, given the propensity of marriages to be contracted within the narrow ranges of economic class.

But the leadership of the syndicate was in the hands of a few families more closely related to Los Olivos's wealthier stratum. Former mayor José Antonio Ramos was one of the leaders. Ceferino Santis was the president of the syndicate. One of two sons of an upwardly mobile muleteer who had taken up farming after marrying into the propertied class, Ceferino and his brother Francisco had quarreled. Both are remembered as forceful, unpleasant, and somewhat strange individuals who carried their personal fight into local politics, Ceferino taking up the cause of the Socialist syndicate, Francisco allying himself with Celestino López as one of his councillors. Alfredo González, a tenant farmer of fairly substantial means, was vice-president of the syndicate. Pablo Moreno (Librada's brother), whose father had sent him to Sevilla to work in a store, returned to the pueblo radicalized by socialist thought; he served as one of the syndicate's ideologues and was a founder of the local Juventud Socialista, through which youngsters were affiliated to the union. By this time, Pablo and his father had split with the other Morenos, rivaling them for control of merchandising and truck transport in the town.

The syndicate leaders differed from existing powerholders, to whom they were nonetheless related, in their shared experience of the world with one another as members of an age cohort. Members of a Spanish age cohort form particularly strong bonds of solidarity. Males of a cohort consort with one another in

Quinta members from a Sierra de Aracena town. Young men who reach the age of military recruitment in a given year form a quinta. They carouse together before undertaking their military service. Quinta members tend to remain solidary throughout their lives.

youth, especially when they reach the age of military recruitment, whereupon they are celebrated as a *quinta* (draft cohort) by their families and are allowed the license of carousing in enthusiastic camaraderie before going off to military service. Such solidarity is long enduring; men and women keep track of their cohort mates as they do kin.*

Whereas Celestino López's town councillors ranged in age from 35 to 57 in 1931, by contrast, six of the syndicate's eight leaders were between 40 and 43 (see below, Chapter 6, Figure 6.1). Together with other age mates who joined them as Socialists, they constituted four-fifths of the men born from 1888 to 1890. Their social and political consciousness would thus have been shaped and sharpened by joint military service in other provinces at the turbulent time of Barcelona's Tragic Week of 1909

*In interviewing, we found that villagers universally remembered the members of their quinta, often knowing almost as much about them as about kin.

and by coming into early full adulthood together in the euphoria of the Second Republic's formation. They infused the syndicate with all the enthusiasm and camaraderie of age mates of a Spanish quinta.

The basis for conflict between the syndicate and the Town Council over the control of public works inhered not only in the contending claims of two institutional bodies but also in the ambiguity of who were the needy unemployed and to which body they were allied. The syndicate brought some of the town's elite and some of its upwardly mobile tenant farmers and muleteers into an alliance with families that made much of their living through wage labor. Yet Celestino López's faction was also allied with segments of the village laboring class. Families with year-around employment on local estates enjoyed the leading families' patronage. For the most part, masons, ostensibly "laborers" in that they worked for wages, were continually employed in rebuilding the houses of the wealthy; they also supervised most public construction funded through the Town Council. Women and children of poor families were more regularly employed by property owners than were their husbands and older brothers, doing housework and childcare for food and a small wage and field work at two-thirds or less of a man's wages. Moreover, the class position of the substantial number of smallholding farm families was ambiguous; youthful members often worked for wages but aspired to the autonomy of the propertied farmer in a future adulthood.

In this context, conflict developed over employment in public works in Los Olivos during the summer months of 1931 after the wheat harvest had been completed. Celestino López had secured funding from the Diputación Provincial to repave several village streets, and he set about hiring favored workers in the name of the Town Council to undertake the work. The syndicate contested the legitimacy of this employment, claiming the prerogative of determining who were needy laborers and insisting that workers had to join the union in order to be eligible for wages paid from public funds earmarked to relieve the crisis obrera. Celestino López's response was to threaten to put the paving up for bid, a tactic that would probably have given the work to independent masons.

The street that Celestino López paved. The street whose paving Celestino López contracted to masons led to his house.

Masons at work on the paving of a roadway. (Photo from 1963–64 fieldwork season.)

The syndicate responded by violently disrupting the Town Council session of September 23, 1931. The disruption coincided with a change in provincial government and may have been timed strategically by the syndicate to obtain the maximum effect. Just three days earlier, Dionisio Cano López had taken office as governor of Huelva, following his appointment by the Ministry of Interior. A governor held direct responsibility for the proper functioning of town councils. The syndicate's action could have been designed to present the new governor with a crisis that in the flush of new incumbency he could not ignore. When the Los Olivos Civil Guard appealed to Governor Cano to send an official delegate to restore order in the town, he responded promptly.

Public-works construction. Public moneys provided relief for unemployment in work such as this rural bridge construction. (Photo from 1963–64 fieldwork season.)

Enrique Pallores arrived from Huelva the next day, empowered by the governor to settle Los Olivos's conflicts. Town councils, whether constituted by appointment from above, by election of the citizens, or through some other mechanism, served at the pleasure of the governor, who in turn had the responsibility to see that councils effectively served the interests of the state and the duty to investigate charges of misconduct and to prosecute and remedy abuses of office. After hearing the grievances against the Town Council, Pallores took several steps in the name of Governor Cano to bring the local conflict to a halt.

First, he removed Celestino and Patricio López from the council, turning its presidency over to Victoriano Infante, a wealthy hog trader and farmer. He nonetheless left the remaining membership of the council intact, effectively leaving town government in the custody of the López faction. The tactic served as something of a compromise to stem the conflict.

Second, he ordered the council and the syndicate to cooperate in forming a junta de policía rural to draw up bases de trabajo to regulate employer-worker contracts, steps provided for by the decree and legislation of the Ministry of Labor that López's council had never undertaken. By this act, he legitimated a specific role for the syndicate in the local management of labor relations.

Finally, he ordered the council to fill the vacancy in the position of secretary to the council that had gone unfilled after the sudden death of the incumbent at the end of José Antonio Ramos's term of office. In accounting for some of his questionable administrative acts as mayor, Celestino López had attributed them to the absence of a professional to hold this civil service position. Pallores's action led to the appointment of Francisco Javier Núñez from the professional corps of town secretaries to the position.

Several months of uneasy compromise between the council and the syndicate ensued from this intervention of Governor Cano. A freak cyclone in October 1931 that damaged roadways and rural bridges enabled the council to ask for emergency funds for public works. The syndicate collaborated for a time, and the two bodies revived the original plan of José Antonio Ramos to construct a new entrance road to the town, exacting promises of funding from a new governor, Francisco A. Rubio Callejón, shortly after he took office in January 1932. Yet the compromise was an uneasy one that satisfied neither faction. The residual Town Council took the forceful removal of Celestino and Patricio López as an affront, and they registered their unease by petitioning the governor to relieve them of their duties. One of the grounds for having removed Celestino López from the post of mayor had been that the council, "elected" under Article 29 of the law governing town councils, had been constituted illegally. The councillors argued that if their leaders could be removed from office on this ground, then all of the other councillors should also be removed. As the compromise with the syndicate broke down, the councillors repeatedly tendered their resignations, only to have the governor insist that they remain in office until such time as Republican legislation reforming the norms of municipal government should be completed.

The councillors thus served for the remainder of 1931 and throughout 1932 under protest, and it was probably not with enthusiasm that they implemented Republican measures such as the secularization of the cemetery, the 10 percent surcharge on property taxes to fund public-works employment, and the forming of a local bolsa de trabajo, the office in which employers were supposed to list all job openings and workers their availability for hire. Even seemingly trivial symbolic gestures to the Republic such as replacement of the flag came reluctantly or late. (Instead of replacing the old bicolor flag, the council simply had it altered by adding a purple band to create the Republican tricolor.)

For its part, in the early spring of 1932 the syndicate renewed its complaints to the governor that the council was failing to exercise its responsibilities. It is not clear from the record just how the grudging cooperation of the council and syndicate of previous months had broken down, but the animosities probably were exacerbated when councillor Francisco Santis, brother and bitter rival of the syndicate's president, Ceferino Santis, assumed the post of acting mayor in February 1932 after incumbent Victoriano Infante, who fell ill, took extended leave from the post.

By 1932, agrarian conflict had sharpened throughout the Sierra de Aracena, as it had throughout Spain. In Aracena itself, Republicans and Socialists had taken over the Town Council after successfully litigating against the fradulent "election" of the Sánchez Dalp municipal slate. For their part, Aracena landowners joined counterparts throughout the region, including some from Los Olivos, in forming the Unión Agraria Serrana, an employers' organization for landed proprietors and smallholders, linked through the Catholic Church to the conservative opposition to the government building up in parliament. In January 1932, the Aracena Town Council had established higher wages according to new *bases de trabajo*, but some Aracena employers refused to pay these wages, leading to worker violence in March 1932 on some farms and in one of Aracena's hog slaughterhouses. Socialists threatened intransigent Aracena employers with boycotts, and landlords retaliated in May by deciding not to hire workers to harvest cork. Workers then called a general strike, during which a worker was shot by the Civil Guard, which the landlords had called out to protect their property (*Diario de Huelva*, Mar. 19, July 27, and Aug. 13, 1932; Maddox 1986: 423–29). With such animosities so near to hand, it is no wonder that Los Olivos's conflicts sharpened.

The battle in Los Olivos over who should be deemed needy labor continued during 1932 after the breakdown of compromise, even as the ambiguities of class position within the town began to be sorted out between the two factions. The lines between the contending factions were becoming more broadly drawn. For example, some of the smallholders and artisans who had joined the union initially to have access to jobs found themselves deemed *patronos* (employers) when they hired other workers and thus were held ineligible to remain in the union. But the syndicate welcomed smallholding proprietors who sometimes worked for others but did not themselves hire workers.

The truth of the matter was that the syndicate, having been accorded legitimacy by the governor's intervention, wished to monopolize the representation of workers in opposition to the patrón by gaining control of the Town Council itself. Although the Syndicate of Agrarian Workers was first and foremost a trade union and a local affiliate of the UGT, it was natural for union leaders to seek a political role in Los Olivos's municipal governance. In contrast to Spanish anarcho-syndicalists, who sought a social revolution doing away with the state and its institutions of power, Spanish Socialists had established themselves as a party seeking power through parliamentary and municipal action (in 1902, Pablo Iglesias, one of the founders of the UGT in 1879, served as the first Socialist deputy to the Cortes). In the face of the corrupt electoral politics of the 1910's, dominated in rural areas by the rule of caciques, the Socialists had become the champions of honest and decent government (Brenan 1943: 218–20). Largo Caballero, head of the UGT in the 1920's, participated in the government of Primo de Rivera. The Socialists were members of the coalition government of the Second Republic and had won representation on many city and town councils. The Socialists of Los Olivos had every reason to seek a legitimate role in municipal governance.

When yet another governor, Braulio Solsano Ronda, took office in mid-June 1932, the syndicate was quick to appeal to him against the council. The syndicate proposed that the council be ousted and free elections be held to replace it as remedy for a host of charges against the council enumerated in a letter sent to Governor Solsano in early July (Town Council minutes, July 1932):

We, as Socialists of the Agrarian Syndicate protest the comportment of the council, constituted under Article 29, for the most part made up of men who held office under the dictatorship, all of them monarchists in opposition to this Republic of Workers.*

While 30 fathers lacked even bread to feed their children, this dignified council spent municipal funds to pay for music and religious sermons during the fiesta of San José. They obliged the priest to parade the patron saint through the town under armed guard, attempting thereby to provoke public violence. But we workers recognized this act as a provocation, as an attempt to get us to shed our blood in the streets and thus to break up our union, something that will not happen even if the streets should be washed in our blood.

This council is wholly in the service of the great cacique, who threatens workers who seek employment from him and has them jailed. The council spent all of the tax surcharges for public works in paving a street that only goes to the cacique's front door.

Meanwhile, the councillors cut down trees along the public ways, make them into charcoal, and pocket the proceeds from its sale. Moreover, in the fiesta of San José, they illegally authorized a bullfight without seeking proper permission.

Because we could add innumerable charges to this list, we petition you to remove from office the councillors and above all the town secretary and to order the election of a council by popular vote. We trust that Your Excellency will see justice done. May Your Excellency live many years in favor of the Republic.

*Article 1 of the Republican Constitution declared Spain to be "a democratic republic of workers of all classes."

Governor Solsano sent the protest to the council and asked it to respond to the charges point by point but seems to have taken no explicit formal action to oust the councillors. Nonetheless, the complaints may have forced the councillors to greater circumspection in their exercise of office. For example, in December 1932, when the syndicate accused Celestino López and his sister of violating the bases de trabajo governing agrarian employment, the council investigated the charges, fined the Lópezes 25 pesetas each, exactly the amount prescribed by law for first-time offenders, and notified Governor Solsano of their actions.

The first two years of the Republic were thus experienced in Los Olivos as a period of continuing rightist domination of municipal institutions in the context of a newly legitimated workers' union that sought control in the name of honest municipal government. In this context, villagers experienced some of the innovations of the Republic—the secularization of the cemetery, the opening of public schools. They witnessed the renaming of streets in honor of historical figures such as Juan Bravo, a hero of the sixteenth-century Comunero revolt, and nineteenth-century Spanish intellectuals and Republican statesmen such as Santiago Ramón y Cajal, Isaac Peral, and Nicolás Salmerón. But they also experienced the local continuity of the old order of powerholders, threatened, however, by the newly legitimated representatives of the worker.

FIVE

The Challenge to Proprietors' Autonomy, 1933-1934

THE SOCIALISTS came to power in Los Olivos early in 1933 at an inauspicious moment for the Socialists in the coalitional government of Azaña, which had held power since 1931. Conservative opposition to the government had grown considerably during 1932 after Alejandro Lerroux's conservative Radical party split with left-Republicans and as Gil Robles consolidated organizations representing monarchists, the agrarian oligarchy, the wheat growers of central Spain, and the Catholic church into his Acción Popular party. Combining political ideals and extralegal tactics inspired by Italian and German fascism with parliamentary obstruction of such legislation as land reform, Gil Robles had begun to transform the Acción Popular into a mass party. In February 1933, he founded the Confederación Española de Derechas Autónomas (CEDA), which he was to lead to electoral victory over Socialists and left-Republicans in November (see Preston 1978).

Anarcho-syndicalists and Communists, moreover, threatened the government from the left and blamed the Socialists for their share in the state repression of strikers and revolutionaries. Beginning as early as 1930 and continuing through 1931 and 1932, militants had led strikes to press for revolution, especially in and around Sevilla, where revolutionary strikes reached their climax in 1932. Public authorities, notably the Civil Guard and the Republic's new Assault Guard, had put down the resulting disorder, and the Azaña government had passed laws to control and punish violence in political, social, and religious confrontations. The Left was not alone in resorting to confrontational tactics, but it received more than its fair share of the resultant repression. The Socialists, as the only labor party in the Azaña coalition, were particularly prone to criticism for backing the government's handling of disorder. And in January 1933, when Civil and Assault Guards massacred anarchist prisoners at Casas Viejas (Cádiz) after an abortive uprising, Azaña and the Socialists were deeply shaken by the resultant outcry from both the Left and the Right and by the subsequent investigation (Jackson 1965: 52; Tuñón de Lara 1978; Mintz 1982).

The Socialists became increasingly divided over the appropriateness of their participation in the governing coalition. Doubts about collaboration in a bourgeois republic were by no means new among party leaders, although they had been set aside in 1930 in the forming of the San Sebastián coalition and after the drafting of the Republic's constitution (Preston 1978: 1–25). But the rank and file had begun to question Socialist leaders on the issue. The concessions to the Right in land reform as it finally was legislated in September 1932 and the slow and relatively ineffective measures of the resulting Institute of Agrarian Reform are said to have frustrated the rank and file of the FNTT. Mineworkers in the Sindicato Minero Asturiano (SMA) pressed their leaders to match the militancy of rival anarchists and Communists, and dissident railworkers in the Sindicato Nacional Ferroviario threatened strikes that their leaders had to oppose. As the crisis of Casas Viejas swelled criticisms within the party during 1933, it was rank-and-file pressure, according to writers such as Paul Preston (1978: 69–91), that pushed Socialist leaders toward radicalization and ultimately to withdrawal from collaboration with left-Republicans in October 1933.

But while the Socialists were on the defensive and in decline at the national level, Los Olivos Socialists attained coveted control of the Town Council in 1933, governing it with considerable effectiveness. Unlike their counterparts in Extremadura and the Andalusian plains, I have found no evidence that smallholders and day workers in Los Olivos had been inflamed by the desire for land reform. Instead, they sought reforms in the relations of employment. The Socialists of Los Olivos challenged the autonomy of agrarian proprietors to manage their own affairs. Invok-

ing the 1931 reforms in agrarian employment, they forced proprietors to hire workers and to work their land under new bases
de trabajo. Seizing the initiative for employment away from proprietors was in itself revolutionary. But the cultural terms in
which Andalusians relate autonomy to masculine honor made
loss of this initiative all the more galling for proprietors, humili-
ating them and undercutting the patronage basis of their political power. The Socialists thus altered the relation of honor to
power in local politics, shifting autonomy from proprietors and
their loyal coteries to workers as a class. The Los Olivos Socialists thus found reason to exult in gains made possible by Republican legislation—in education, in honest government, and
above all in the control of local labor and employment.

This is not to deny that pressures from the rank and file radicalized the Socialist debate on collaboration at the national level,
but rather to point out that not all rank and file were equally
frustrated and radicalized. Pressure on the national leadership
may equally well have arisen from the fervor of accomplishments
won at the local level. Los Olivos Socialists became frustrated
only long after the November 1933 electoral setback of Socialists
and left-Republicans nationally and after being beset and eventually repressed by the conservative reaction.

Transition to a Socialist Town Council

Town councils arbitrarily constituted under Article 29 of the
code governing municipal government at the outset of the Republic posed a widespread problem that the Republic finally ad-
dressed in January 1933. As in the case of Los Olivos, many of
these councils were composed of monarchists who had taken
power under circumstances of questionable legality.

The remedy under a new municipal code was to replace such
councils with smaller administrative bodies representing labor,
property, and the state while preparing for municipal elections
under a reformed code that would ensure popularly elected
councils. In late January 1933, Governor Braulio Solsano Ronda
inaugurated a new era of town government in Los Olivos and six
other Huelva municipalities with councils that had taken power
under the provisions of Article 29. He installed moderate coun-

cils that paved the way for elections in April in which the syndicate of Los Olivos would win control of the Town Council (*Diario
de Huelva*, Jan. 11, 1933). In all seven towns, the governor appointed interim councils consisting of a local schoolteacher, a
representative of labor, and a representative of property.

The interim council appointed by the governor took office in
Los Olivos on January 24, 1933. It was headed by Niceto Ortega,
the schoolteacher, in his capacity as a public employee. Teodoro
González, brother of the vice-president of the syndicate and a
tenant farmer, took a council position as a representative of labor. Claudio Teodoro Santis, son of a shoemaker and himself a
farmer, served as a representative of property. It was a youthful
council—Niceto was barely 24, and his co-councillors were in
their early thirties. And in contrast to the council it replaced, it
exhibited progressive leanings inherent in the linkages between
Republican educational reform and the favoring of labor.

This was indeed an optimistic moment in Republican educational policy. Liberal thinkers, who had deep faith in the power
of education to shape the country's future, had dedicated themselves to new educational initiatives. In Madrid, the Faculty of
Philosophy and Letters of the new Ciudad Universitaria campus
had just opened. Leading intellectuals, playwrights, and poets—
Federico García Lorca and Luís Buñuel among them—had organized students in pedagogical missions to carry their ideas to
rural towns. A campaign for rural literacy was under way, and
the Ministry of Public Education and Fine Arts had drawn up
programs to build and staff thousands of rural schools (Herr
1971: 164–66).

It was through Niceto Ortega that youngsters in Los Olivos
began to experience the new Republican policy on education.
Previously, schooling in Los Olivos had been a privilege of the
wealthy, controlled by the pueblo's elites and affiliated with the
Catholic church (to which the Concordat of 1851 had granted
the authority to ensure that public education conformed to Catholic dogma). In the 1920's, boys had attended class in the school
owned by Teodoro Moreno, patriarch of the Morenos and father
of the village priest, and were taught first by his son Celestino
and later by a private teacher. Girls had attended a school run by
Tomasa Valero, wife of a wealthy property owner who served as

councillor and judge under Primo de Rivera; this was another devout family whose son was a clergyman. But the school-teachers had charged students 15 centimos per day, an amount poor families could not afford. Only the rich had attended.

Nor had schooling changed much in the first years of the Second Republic when Niceto Ortega was hired to teach the boys' school. The disassociation of public schools from the church under the Republic simply meant that the Town Council now paid rent for what had previously been private school quarters and paid the salaries of teachers who had previously charged fees. Tomasa Valero continued to teach. And Niceto himself, brought to Los Olivos by his brother-in-law Feliciano Moreno (one of the younger generation of Morenos who had married into wealth in Fuenteheridos), initially represented the continuing power and patronage of the old order. For the most part, poor children had continued not to attend school since their families counted on the income they could earn tending pigs and goats in the countryside. Lack of schooling and of access to schooling on the part of the working class was one of the ills that the Socialist press repeatedly lamented. Differences in education thus played an important part in the experience of class in Los Olivos and continue to this day to be part of the way class is talked about.

As mayor, however, Niceto Ortega set out to improve and broaden education substantially, in accordance with current Republican policy and ideology. He began to spend municipal moneys on refurbishing school buildings and facilities. He obtained funding from the governor to install lighting in the school buildings, and he began to teach evening classes as part of a national adult literacy campaign. It was in these evening classes that many poorer adolescents and young adults who could not attend school by day acquired basic literacy. Juan José Santis, one of the surviving sons of the syndicate's president, claims that he received a much better education than his older brothers because he happened to be of school age at the time of the Second Republic. He remembers that the Ministry of Public Education and Fine Arts sent an inspector to Los Olivos and other towns every week to keep the schoolteachers on their toes.

At the same time, Niceto Ortega collaborated with the Socialist syndicate, accompanying its leaders in a visit to the governor to persuade him to concede the funds promised for the road project. He also allowed them to rent a building owned by the town to use as the Casa del Pueblo. This was the public salon for UGT members and affiliates that Spanish Socialists had adopted from the Belgians as an institution earlier in the century (Brenan 1943: 219). In Madrid, the Socialists set up a Casa del Pueblo in a ducal palace. As in every town in which they organized, the Socialists equipped the Los Olivos salon with facilities for party assemblies and a reading room with newspapers and leftist literature. The Casa del Pueblo was where the syndicate did its business, drawing up the censuses of agrarian workers resident in the municipality and thus eligible for local employment.

Finally, in the special elections on April 23 to replace councils originally set up under Article 29, Niceto supervised the first open municipal elections of Los Olivos of the decade. These were important elections nationally, even though held in only the small proportion of municipalities whose councils had taken power under Article 29, since their outcome would reflect the popularity of the Azaña government. In the weeks before the election, the Socialist press warned local party leaders against the tricks and illegal tactics that the caciques could be expected to employ in these pueblos. On April 15, 1933, on the eve of the election, *El Obrero de la Tierra* emblazoned the headline: "PEASANTS! THE ELECTIONS OF APRIL 1931 OVERTHREW THE MONARCHY. THOSE OF THE 23RD MUST SERVE TO DESTROY THE CACIQUISMO OF THE COUNTRYSIDE IN MANY PUEBLOS. LET US TRIUMPH AT THE VOTING URNS!" In Los Olivos, the Socialist slate dominated the election, delivering control of the Town Council to the union that had coveted it for so long. Ironically, the Socialists came to power in elections that nationally tended to favor conservative candidates of the Radical and Agrarian parties, reflecting the cooling of early Republican support for Azaña's government and for progressive reforms (see Jackson 1965: 104).

Land, Autonomy, and Labor Relations

During their 17-month incumbency in the town hall, the Socialists advanced and consolidated their organization and control of employment on the basis of the initial agrarian decrees and related legislation. In doing so, they laid the groundwork for what I believe were inherently revolutionary challenges to the relations of production in Los Olivos. Yet these challenges apparently did not involve *reparto*, the redistribution of property sought elsewhere in Spain by agrarian revolutionaries and enabled in moderation through land reform legislation in September 1932.

I cannot be absolutely sure that Socialists did not press for land redistribution in Los Olivos, yet I am convinced that it was not an important goal. There is not one mention of land reform in the hundreds of pages of Town Council minutes, litigation, and other documentation I have examined; nor is Los Olivos mentioned in the *Boletín Oficial, Provincia de Huelva* in regard to official land reform initiatives. Although this is negative evidence, villagers' recollections support it. They remember reparto not as land reform but as the 1936 forced distribution of workers to employers (see Chapter 7). When pressed whether there were Second Republic initiatives to redistribute land, villagers cannot recall any. One surviving Socialist told me that land redistribution was not sought because Socialists did not think they had the power to redistribute property.

One possible reason that redistribution was not sought is that land was more equitably distributed in Los Olivos than elsewhere. In a survey of landownership in or just after 1932, the Institute of Agrarian Reform found only one landowner, Celestino López, with property expropriable on the basis of excessive size and six owners of smaller rented or uncultivated properties that could be affected by land reform in Los Olivos, proportionally far fewer than elsewhere (Carrión 1932: 238–46; Maddox 1986: 297–300). Although López's estates comprised one-fourth of the municipality and 70 percent of the land was controlled by the wealthiest 25 percent of household heads, this distribution was more equitable than in other Sierra de Aracena municipalities, some of which matched the Andalusian plains in their concentration of land in large estates. Similarly, the totally landless were not as numerous in proportion to the populace of Los Olivos as elsewhere. Many day workers had smallholdings.

More important, to avoid alienating smallholders from their cause, Los Olivos Socialists probably would have avoided advocating land reform. For their part, ultra-right and Catholic conservatives were wooing smallholders by depicting Second Republic agrarian measures introduced by the Socialists as an attack on all private property. Some Socialist ideologues had earlier countered similar charges by arguing that smallholdings were precapitalist in nature and that only large capitalist holdings were the target of agrarian reform (*El Socialista*, July 11, 1930). Even *El Obrero de la Tierra* (Nov. 11, 1933), which voiced strident appeals for land reform, observed that the line between the proletariat and the bourgeoisie was hard to define in the case of smallholders or renters whose circumstances rendered them particularly prone to the political propaganda of propertied interests in the countryside. The arguments of the Right did indeed persuade peasants in many regions, notably in Castile, where peasants opposed the Left.

Smallholders in Los Olivos were more amenable to the Socialist cause than were their counterparts in such areas in Castile. Unlike peasants in Castile whose experience with day workers was with laborers brought in at harvest time from other towns and cities (Pérez Díaz 1976: 125), smallholders in Los Olivos were closely tied to day workers, who lived in the town rather than coming in from elsewhere to find work. Many were related to one another, and members of smallholding families often worked side by side with day laborers to supplement subsistence farming.

Hence a worker-peasant alliance was quite justifiable in Los Olivos, and when the Socialists offered employment in public works during their incumbency in the Town Council in 1933–34, many smallholders did in fact join the syndicate to avail themselves of jobs. The Socialists thus united laborers and peasants in work, setting aside land reform if it was in fact ever an issue. Indeed, relations of work, of employer to employee, prove to have been central to alliances and cleavages in Los Olivos, much more so than differences in ownership of property per se.

Autonomía, the self-sufficiency to which proprietors laid claim and to which smallholders and workers aspired, explains the significance of employment relations. Villagers in Los Olivos held to the ideal of masculine autonomy characteristic of property relations and the system of honor in the agrarian societies of the Mediterranean. The property system brought together a couple's productive assets and vested their care in the male head of household. In principle, a family estate of sufficient size enabled a man to protect and develop his family interests with autonomy. Such a man could do what he wished, free from others' control; he could thus stand up to others to protect his family's honor.

In practice, however, the property system was always contestable, inscribing an arena of conflict in which a man had to stand ready to defend his family's interests. Conflicts inevitably arose over boundaries, rights of way, the disposition of walls and other structures common to adjacent residences, and the division of family patrimony. As in many Mediterranean agrarian communities (see, e.g., Schneider 1969), the head of household had not only to fend off such encroachment but to forestall it by presenting himself to the world as prepotent and unassailable.

In this regard, Los Oliveños, like other Andalusians and Mediterranean countrymen, gave expression to their individual autonomy and challenged that of others in the familiar idiom of honor and shame (see Peristiany 1966; Pitt-Rivers 1966). The prepotent male discouraged challenges by continually reasserting this masculinity and potential for physical aggression while he guarded against assaults on the virtue of his women and stood up to others to protect his family's honor (see Brandes 1980; Driessen 1983; Gilmore 1983).

Inequalities of wealth nonetheless made it impossible for all men to live up to the ideal of the autonomous male in equal manner or degree. Men who controlled insufficient property had to bow their heads in subservience to employers. Such men sacrificed autonomy perforce and, in doing so, called into question their ability to defend family interests and honor. Conversely, the man wealthy enough to hire labor held in addition to autonomy the power to subordinate others, arbitrarily if so desired, and even in ways that might compromise the subordinate's family honor.

The ideal of masculine autonomy thus charged employer-employee relations with special tension. In having to accept someone else's orders, the employee implicitly acknowledged his lack of full autonomy and his vulnerability to potential dishonor. In giving orders, either directly or through a representative, the employer implicitly asserted his own invulnerability and power.

To a certain degree, the protection that a powerful employer could bestow on faithful employees ameliorated their loss of autonomy. Insofar as political mechanisms defended and enhanced economic interests, men of means built up action sets or coalitions of supporters to help them stand off contenders politically.* Employers included loyal employees in their action sets, serving in turn as their patrons. As such, they could compensate employees for loss of autonomy with political protection, favors, and steady (as opposed to seasonal or uncertain) employment, thus affording them a modicum of economic security. Such patronage tended to set the favored worker apart from other workers, however, and this class disloyalty might provoke insinuations about his inability to stand up to the world as an honorable man.

Many of the usages and attitudes that Juan Martínez Alier (1971) describes as characteristic of Andalusian employment also ameliorated the direct threats to masculine autonomy that employment entailed, but in ways that united workers rather than dividing them. The use of foremen shielded employers and employees from direct confrontation. Through *unión*—workers' solidarity and the strict equality with which what applied to one applied to all—workers not only protected their class interests but also defended against any questioning of their individual autonomy. By having well-defined standards of what amount and quality of work enabled a worker to *cumplir*, to fulfill his obligation to his employer, workers not only resisted exploitation but also subtly protected themselves from appearing to have to take orders.

Seen in the light of peasant and agrarian working-class prac-

*Schneider, in his discussion of "conflicting claims on human resources" (1969: 140–43), links politics to honor through the action sets or groups of supporters that individuals recruit to help them defend and enhance their interests.

Unión

Winter weather; a week of rain; a whole week without a nickel's wage, without bread in my home,

And listening to my little ones cry, asking for food, without my being able to earn it, because the fields are sopping wet.

Now the sun has broken through the clouds, at last; the fields are lush from the rain; the rich smile, because the rain was like drops of silver for their purses.

Joy for them, sorrow for us; abundance for them, hunger in the houses of us who with sweat on our brows work the lands that give them such abundance.

Hunger for us, the unprotected; hunger for us because of our ignorance; because though our limbs produce all the bread, they give us only a few crumbs.

And worst of all is that those who suck our sap are not alone responsible; so too are we, because we do not unite. It makes one mad that they should fill their bellies with our sweat and exploit us because we are not all united as one.

Ah, *unión*, come soon, for we need you!

Working-class ideology in the press. This poetic appeal for *unión*, working-class unity, was published by *El Obrero de la Tierra* (Oct. 7, 1933). Written by a farmworker from Rociano (Huelva), the appeal had political significance in the context of the upcoming November 19 elections in that the anarchists planned to abstain, withholding support for the left-Republican parties, and the Socialists sought anarchist support in the elections.

tices and values, the bases de trabajo of the Second Republic implicitly challenged the automony of the proprietor to manage his own affairs (e.g., as described by Rosado 1979: 69–71). They did so by altering customary usages of employment and by giving labor the upper hand over employers in determining employment relations. They undercut the politics of patronage by asserting the politics of class. The extent to which they did so can be seen in the bases de trabajo drawn up for the Sierra de Aracena region by the Mixed Jury for Rural Labor of Aracena in June 1933, just after Socialists assumed power in Los Olivos (for texts, see *Boletín Oficial*, June 14, 1933; Aug. 4 and 6, 1934).

In general, the bases set minimally acceptable terms for hiring workers. These terms included minimum wages, extra pay for the transporting of equipment, a place to tie up and graze a mule or horse, hygienic lodging if a worker was to live on site, and so forth. Only employment at least as favorable to the laborer as specified in the bases was permissible.

The bases formalized a worker's maximum responsibility to an employer, in many instances reducing what a laborer had to do in order to *cumplir*. Instead of the customary work *de sol a sol* (from dawn to dusk), the bases set the workday at six hours in winter, seven hours in summer, with extra hours paid as overtime. They specified a reduction in the workday to compensate for any travel to work over two kilometers from a worker's home.

"UNIÓN IS POWER!" Socialist appeals for working-class unity resonated with the customary usages through which farmworkers experienced *unión*. (From *El Obrero de la Tierra*, Nov. 11, 1933.)

Agrarios: Cómo emplean el tiempo los que lo son y los que, sin serlo, se lo llaman

The true agrarians. The Agrarian party, representing rural landlords opposed to land reform, sought support from smallholders as well. The working-class press, in articles, editorials, and cartoons such as this one, drew attention to the class line separating landlords from those who actually worked the land. In this instance, the appeal was to peasants not to vote for the Agrarian party in the elections of November 19, 1933. The caption reads: "Agrarians: How they pass the time—those who are real agrarians and those who claim to be agrarians but are not." (From *El Obrero de la Tierra*, Nov. 11, 1933.)

They codified the degrees of respect that employers and workers were to show to one another, to foremen, and to these parties' families.

Worker solidarity and *unión* were institutionalized by the bases in the functioning of municipal employment offices, in which organized labor had a voice and often control. Laborers were to be hired on a weekly or semimonthly basis in rotation and in the strict order that they had signed up for employment in the municipal office of employment or labor exchange. Employers could not hire workers for jobs that had not been listed

¡Y los hay que viven sin hacer nada!

"AND THERE ARE THOSE WHO LIVE WITHOUT DOING A THING!" In their recollections of class contrasts before the Civil War, particularly in nearby Aracena, villagers evoke images similar to this 1932 cartoon. (From *El Obrero de la Tierra*, Mar. 12, 1932.)

Hunger and power. Class was frequently experienced in relation to food. Poor villagers remember class differences in terms of how well their employers ate and how poorly they provisioned their workers. Working-class parties sometimes appealed to the electorate in this idiom, as in this cartoon, which appeared in *El Obrero de la Tierra* on November 18, 1933, on the eve of national elections. The caption reads: "You can and must free yourself, farmworker. You are the perpetual victim of nonsensical capitalism. You suffer at home when your companion and little ones ask you for bread, which they lack, because your young and vigorous limbs cannot provision them, because the bourgeoisie deny you work, either because you fight for your labor organization or merely belong to it and demand a better salary or work conditions. While this happens, he goes on eating from a plate brimming with delicious food at a table set with cloth. In those seasons when you worked for him, along with other workers like you, you left him with enough not to have to worry about your sustenance or that of your family, enough even to divert himself with entertainment. While you and yours starve, because they hound you, or because they don't want to offer work at a salary they are unwilling to pay, they are not concerned with your situation. Either they give you no work, or they offer it on their own terms. When they need your help, they promise and offer you everything, work, a good salary, everything. But as soon as they've gotten what they want from you, they take everything back. Only when there is power to oblige them to keep their word do they do so. Your power is in Socialist control of the authority of the state. Your own power, that of organized workers. Vote for the Socialists if you do not want the cacique to make play of your hunger and suffering."

in these offices. These provisions prevented employers from favoring some laborers and blackballing others. They also affirmed the dignity of work by preventing laborers from having to kowtow to employers in order to get jobs.

The bases considerably restricted employers' autonomy in managing their agricultural property. They prohibited the use of reaping or threshing machinery and of plows in vineyards. They mandated yearlong contracts for a specific number of laborers depending on the acreage a farmer owned and how it was cultivated. They restricted the grounds on which employers could dismiss employees.

Other provisions of the bases tailored wages to specific groups of municipalities to reflect variations in the profitability of local agriculture. They restricted the hiring of nonresidents except on estates spanning territory in more than one municipality and required proportional hiring in these cases. They restricted the employment of women (excepting widows and orphans) to the harvesting of olives, chestnuts, and acorns; women were to earn two-thirds of the minimum wage for men. The bases prohibited the employment of children, except as herders. They exempted tenant farmers and renters from having to hire workers on yearlong contracts unless the land they rented exceeded a certain acreage. It is difficult to say if the bases de trabajo were economically feasible. Since they were established by a joint commission of workers and proprietors for the region, they cannot have been totally unimplementable. But by adjusting the parameters of agrarian production to favor workers, they may well have implied alterations in the region's production.

The bases de trabajo for the Aracena region were by no means unique in tipping the balance of employment relations in favor of workers. Bases issued in other areas of Andalusia during 1933 were equally far-reaching. In the Andalusian province of Jaén, for example, the bases codified the customary harvest practice of *rebusca* in ways that were highly advantageous to the proletariat. This practice permitted foragers to follow harvest teams into the olive groves to scavenge the fruit that had been left behind. Usually the rebusca began after harvesting was completed. The 1933 bases in Jaén authorized the rebusca to begin after one-fourth of the harvest was in, leading proprietors to charge angrily that they were being robbed of their harvest (Aparicio Albiñana 1936: 40–43).

The outcry of proprietors against the bases de trabajo for Aracena was equally angry. "The propertied class of Aracena has its hands up while the *Boletín Oficial* of June 14 takes aim at them with the rifle of the bases contained therein," railed the *Diario de Huelva* (July 4, 1933) as it lambasted the provisions mandating the hiring of workers on yearlong contracts for properties of a specified size. Indeed, the bases were far-reaching. In the hands of representatives of labor who also controlled municipal governance, they posed the potentially revolutionary threat of completely undermining proprietors' autonomy to put property to whatever use they wished in capitalist production. They also changed the rules of the game of local politics by undercutting patronage and affirming the politics of class.

The Socialist Town Council: Labor Relations and Public Works

In office in the Los Olivos Town Council from May 10, 1933, to October 22, 1934, the Socialists initially triumphed in their exercise of legitimate local governance and above all in their organization and control of employment. But during the last year of their reign, they began to experience the strains and ultimately the reversals brought about by the conservative reaction to two years of left-Republican–Socialist government under Azaña.

In the early months of their incumbency in the Town Council, the Socialists engaged in a spate of undertakings. For the first time, the Socialists held a majority in the bodies managing local labor relations, and they immediately used their position to wrest advantages for labor from the town's employers.

Emboldened by having won office, the syndicate leaders pressed their newly won advantage over employers even more than called for in the bases de trabajo. Town Council minutes record that on taking office as mayor, Syndicate President Ceferino Santis's first step was to call Los Olivos property owners to a public meeting to demand that they hire more workers and that they pay an advance on their property taxes for the council to use in public-works employment. There is no record of what transpired in the meeting, but property owners may have re-

sisted, since a few days later Ceferino petitioned Governor Braulio Solsano Ronda to send a representative to intervene with employers on behalf of laborers.

The next step was to raise workers' wages. Under the existing
local bases de trabajo, men were to be paid 4.00 pesetas per day.
A retired mason whom we interviewed near Barcelona recalls
that Ceferino Santis called a workers' meeting in the town square.
"Would you like to be paid better? How about 4.50 pesetas? Yes!"
Ceferino proposed to the crowd. "But don't be afraid to demand
4.50 pesetas. The reign of fear is over." Workers realized how
provocative raising wages would be. As one worker put it, "Now
the burro's gotten out of the corral!"

The Socialists' proudest achievement was the public-works
construction of a new entrance road for Los Olivos. In July 1933,
the Provincial Delegation finally authorized a contract for the
long-awaited project. The contract gave Los Olivos a year in
which to build the road, and the syndicate immediately dedicated most of its energies to organizing the work. Workers not
enrolled in the syndicate were not permitted to labor on the
project, a stricture drawing numerous new members into the
union. To provide the greatest number of jobs, no machinery was
used. Instead, workers used pickaxes, shovels, and dynamite to
carve and grade a roadbed out of a granite hillside. Eusebio Santis, whose father was one of the council members in charge of
the construction, remembers the project as deliberately labor intensive so as to "give the means of living to many poor, illiterate
men who had previously had to beg for employment."

As the work went on, the town councillors grappled with a
troublesome problem of cash flow to pay the workers' wages.
The Provincial Delegation's contract required a performance
bond for the project and paid for work only in installments. The
councillors borrowed municipal reserves for the performance
bond. They assessed property owners a special levy to pay road-
workers, promising to return the levy when the state paid. At
first this provided the needed cash. But after the collapse of the
Azaña government in September 1933, Los Olivos experienced
delays in the Provincial Delegation's payments. The difficulties
began as Lerroux, leader of the Radical Republicans, struggled
but failed to govern. The Constituent Cortes was dissolved,

preparations began for elections on November 19, and the conservative CEDA electoral coalition emerged. During this brief period, Lerroux appointed a new governor for Huelva, Enrique Malboyssón Ponce, a Radical Republican and editor-in-chief of Valencia's *El Pueblo*. Malboyssón represented a swing to the right, and he continued as governor after the CEDA electoral victory and installation of the right-leaning government headed by Lerroux's Radical Republicans (see *El Liberal*, Sept. 20, 1933, for Malboyssón's background). Whether the delays in payments to Los Olivos were a deliberate tactic of conservatives newly in power in Huelva to hamstring Socialist labor initiatives begun under the Azaña government is not clear. The Los Olivos council coped with the dilemma that the late payments posed through a series of transfers within the municipal budget to borrow funds for wages from moneys and reserves already earmarked for other expenditures.

Looking to the future, and probably responding to Niceto Ortega's role in paving their way, the Socialists began to draw up a request for state moneys to construct a complex of school buildings in Los Olivos. Under recent legislation by the Cortes, the state could provide a nearly total subsidy for such construction in a town of Los Olivos's small size.

Above all, the Socialists infused municipal governance with an unaccustomed austere morality and aura of scrupulous honesty. One day Ceferino Santis, the mayor, surprised his son Juan José practicing typing on the secretary's typewriter. Juan José remembers that his father threw him out of the town hall and gave him a stern lecture about the evils of nepotism. "Let no one say I've been preparing my sons to give them municipal jobs!"

Los Olivos Socialists were not alone in their successes. By mid-1933, Socialists held incumbencies in town councils throughout the province. In the September 4–5 elections for the Tribunal de Garantías Constitucionales (the body responsible for determining the constitutionality of laws), which set Socialists back through most of Spain and toppled the Azaña government, Socialists triumphed in 21 of Huelva's 78 municipalities and tied with Radicals in many others. The Socialists campaigned actively in the Sierra de Aracena as they did throughout Huelva for the November 1933 elections, even while candidacies such as

Pablo Iglesias, Socialist party founder and hero. The Casa del Pueblo featured a portrait of Iglesias, perhaps similar to this photograph, later published in *El Obrero de la Tierra* (Dec. 9, 1933, p. 1).

Aracena's Manuel Sánchez-Dalp Marañon for Acción Popular and the center-right coalition of Maurists (followers of Miguel Maura) and Radicals gained ground. The Socialists won a plurality of the November 19, 1933, vote in Huelva for deputies for the Cortes, though not quite enough to prevent a runoff election in December, in which Huelva Socialists won four seats in the Cortes and the center-right CEDA coalition only three. And Socialists continued as incumbents in pueblo governments even as reaction set in (for election results, see *El Liberal*, Sept. 6, Nov. 1, 3, and 20, and Dec. 7, 1933).

The Socialists thus seized the opportunities provided by incumbency with considerable boldness. Their 17-month reign in Los Olivos must have been a relatively proud one. In the town, they used their one peseta per month dues to refurbish the Casa del Pueblo, setting up a salon with magazines and leftist newspapers for townfolk to read and a large portrait of Pablo Iglesias, the "grandfather" and leading figure of the UGT and of the Socialist party. Two Socialists who returned to Los Olivos from years of work in the troubled Riotinto Mines set up a *bar de izquierdas*, a leftist bar that counterposed itself to the Casino of Patricio López that the well-to-do frequented, in a manner characteristic of the role of bars in Andalusian political culture (Gilmore 1985). To make the town more attractive, the Town Council ordered property owners to whitewash all the buildings facing the streets. But the roadway itself was the most tangible symbol of the syndicate's accomplishments. Propertied men even now grudgingly credit it to the Socialists as a major achievement, as did the smallholders who joined the union to get jobs on the project. Exactly a year after the construction was begun, the Socialists recorded in the minutes of the Town Council that new signs marking the completed entrance road had been set up.

Resistance and Reaction from the Right

Despite their accomplishments, or perhaps because of them, the Socialists of Los Olivos experienced growing opposition from the Right during their incumbency, orchestrated with increasing acquiescence and even encouragement from the provincial government.

In spring 1933, the Right still had a handhold on the management of town affairs in the person of the secretary to the council, Francisco Javier Núñez. Francisco Javier had been given his position by the governor's representative, Enrique Pallores, in September 1931 when the Lópezes had been removed from the council. Serving the town with councillors of the Right through 1932, he had won the enmity of the syndicate by helping the councillors resist the syndicate's pro-labor activism. The syndicate's antipathy to him was such that union leaders had appealed to the governor to remove Francisco Javier from office along with the councillors of the Right (see Chapter 4). But legally a council secretary could not be removed from his position without cause, and Francisco Javier continued in his position into the incumbencies of Mayors Niceto Ortega and Ceferino Santis. As secretary, Francisco Javier was responsible for most of the council's bureaucratic paperwork and for its compliance with existing administrative codes; he thus wielded much power over public affairs. Such holdovers of civil servants from more conservative administrations were hampering town councils elsewhere in Huelva, a large number of which were in Socialist control by 1933, and some mayors were retaliating by withholding the secretaries' salaries. After Lerroux's Radical Republican appointee, Enrique Malboyssón Ponce, took office as governor of Huelva, some secretaries complained to him that they were being threatened with bodily harm, and the governor met with representatives of the Comarcal de Obreros y Empleados de Huelva, an organization of municipal civil servants, to hear their grievances (*Diario de Huelva*, Oct. 3, 1933). Just what harassment Francisco Javier suffered in Los Olivos, if any, is not clear. But his resignation on November 22, 1933, must have removed a thorn of resistance in the side of the Socialists.

Failing to control matters through the secretary, the Socialists' local opposition resorted to the courts, primarily in civil suits harassing Socialist leaders. A Ministry of Justice decree of May 25, 1931, had replaced justices of the peace from the era of the dictatorship in towns of less than 12,000 inhabitants and provided for elected judges in their place. This reform installed a judge in Los Olivos, José Antonio Roncero, who proved sympathetic to the Socialists. But the Court of First Appeal in Aracena was still in the hands of the old judiciary, giving Los Olivos rightists hope for support from the courts, particularly in suits against Socialists to collect debts and in suits for eviction.

The resulting litigation is at least partially documented in Los Olivos's judicial archive. The archive preserves records from 258 judicial proceedings initiated in Los Olivos between 1931 and 1942. Although I cannot be sure that all cases from that period are represented, I see no evidence of gaps in the record, and I have analyzed the corpus on the assumption that it is essentially complete.

Whereas suits to collect debts accounted for a relatively unvarying 30 percent of all civil cases litigated in Los Olivos during the Second Republic, eviction suits were a new consequence of Republican decrees and legislation. The Provisional Government issued initial decrees regulating evictions in 1931; the Azaña government followed with legislation in 1933 that was repealed in 1935 and reinstated in 1936. The measures gave renters considerable new rights to extend leases and to forestall evictions. For the most part, this controversial legislation affected rural communities by enabling tenant farmers to continue indefinitely on advantageous terms in long-term leases of farmland. Property owners, for their part, perceived the new legislation as a threat to their power and prerogatives as landlords. They felt sure that leased land would be vulnerable to expropriation if Republican land reform ever got under way; many thus sought to evict their tenants. To break a lease, the owner had to prove that the tenant had defaulted on rent and to indemnify the tenant for any "improvements" to the property. In Los Olivos, as elsewhere, many older property owners leased land to tenant farmers to procure income during retirement. Many of them brought suits of eviction against their tenants under one or another pretext to rid themselves of the threat of indefinite leases on unfavorable terms.

Eviction suits and suits for payment of debt against leading Socialists became prominent in and particularly after 1933. These suits reflected and heightened the growing class conflict in Los Olivos. One landlord, who had been a town secretary of Los Olivos under the monarchists, brought suit against the widowed mother of the man who ran the leftist bar to force her and her sons out of the tenant-farming contract they had held for six years. Another property owner brought an eviction suit against José Antonio Ramos, the mayor during the transition to the Republic. Patricio López took Alfredo González, vice-president of the syndicate, to court to collect the balance due on his charge account in the local store. Meanwhile, Maximiano Nogales, a former co-councillor with Patricio López, sued Alfredo for debt, as did an absentee landlord. José Antonio Roncero, the justice of the peace and himself a Socialist, was sued to be evicted from a farm that he leased.

Celestino López and proprietors from a neighboring town who owned land within Los Olivos municipality also began litigation against property tax assessments drawn up under the Socialists. López claimed that the town authorities had prevented property owners from inspecting the levies when they were initially drawn up and posted, as required by law. The Socialists responded that the landowners questioned the levies only after they had been posted and duly approved. The suit was carried up to the Tribunal Económico Administrativo in Huelva and eventually decided in López's favor—but only after rightists resumed power at every level of government following the Asturias Revolution of October 1934.

Reaction on the right, meanwhile, grew at the provincial and national levels during 1933 and 1934, leading to increasing use of public force against the Left in the name of law and order and culminating in the overt repression of a broad spectrum of leftists in the autumn of 1934.

The resort to force dated back to the early Second Republic and had its roots in the inability of the Republican government to contain extremism at both ends of the political spectrum, but particularly on the left. After a wave of church burnings in May 1931, the Provisional Government had begun to take a hard line against leftist agitation, forming the Assault Guard as a new corps loyal to the Republic to complement the rural Civil Guard. In October 1931, the Cortes passed the Law for the Defense of the Republic empowering the state to use police powers to fend off reactionaries and revolutionaries. As agitation grew, particularly violence provoked by ultra-church and agrarian proprietors' organizations on the right and by anarcho-syndicalists and Communists on the left, the state increasingly resorted to these forces to put down disorder (Jackson 1965: 52; Herr 1971: 161).

The attempts by anarchists to organize general strikes elicited more comprehensive measures to thwart agitation. One of these attempts, the abortive call for a general strike in Catalonia and Andalusia of early January 1933, led to the infamous Casas Viejas massacre in Cádiz (Mintz 1982). Shortly afterward the Cortes began to debate legislation to restrict the use of arms. In Huelva, the governor urged possessors of weapons to turn them in to the police or the Civil Guard. In May 1933, the anarchist Confederación Nacional de Trabajadores (CNT) tried to call another general strike. Shortly after, the Cortes passed a new Ley de Orden Público enabling the government to declare emergency states of prevention, of alarm, or of war, which would suspend a variety of civil rights and give public forces and the military a freer hand to maintain order. Another law, the Ley de Vagos, allowed the state to arrest miscreants and vagabonds. On December 9, 1933, the state managed to contain yet another extremist nationwide general strike, organized around railroad strikes by the CNT and radical Federación Anarquista Ibérica (FAI). Shortly afterward, the state declared the unlicensed possession of firearms a crime and instituted tight controls over the distribution of explosives.

Fortified with such measures, the Ministry of Interior stepped up measures to maintain public order, particularly at junctures at which disorder was expected. Whenever a general strike was anticipated, the Ministry would declare a state of alarm under the Ley de Orden Público, authorizing governors to deploy the Assault Guard and Civil Guard and to put suspects under preventive arrest. Such action began under the Azaña government but became more prominent after Azaña's fall. On October 7, 1933, for example, Governor Malboyssón sent a contingent of the Assault Guard from Málaga to Huelva, using them and Civil Guard to keep order during the weeks leading up to the general elections that gave the rightist coalition of the Radical party and CEDA control of the state in November 1933.

The fall of the Azaña government and the electoral victory of the Right in November 1933 changed the political context in ways

ESTA ES LA VISION
DE TU PORVENIR
SI VOTAS A LAS
DERECHAS

BARBARANO

The specter of fascism in 1933. Campaigning to forestall CEDA electoral victories, the working-class press harped on the dangerous alliance of former monarchists with fascist enemies of the Republic, particularly as epitomized by Gil
Robles and his followers. (From *El Obrero de la Tierra*, Nov. 18, 1933.)

that led to increasingly repressive measures against the Left. Gil Robles's CEDA coalition had won the election, but President Alcalá Zamora, distrusting Gil Robles's loyalty to the Republic, turned to Lerroux and his center-right Radical Republicans to form a government, which Lerroux realized he could do only by appeasing Gil Robles (Herr 1971: 144). The Lerroux government began to use whatever legal means it could to undo or reverse the progressive initiatives of the Republic's first bienio. At the provincial level, this meant efforts on the part of governors to facilitate the undoing of the *tinglado Socialista*, the apparatus of Socialist governance. Pressured by the rightist agrarian press, some provincial governors sent representatives to investigate pueblo affairs to find a pretext for removing Socialist and other left-leaning town councillors from office or for instigating criminal proceedings against them. Although some governors, such as Jaén's governor Aparicio Albiñana, resisted such pressure, Socialists at the local level found themselves pressed by tactics they had not experienced in the first bienio (Aparicio Albiñana 1936: 42–44).

Governors reacted to labor unrest with increased vigor. In the Azaña era, the governors of Huelva had contented themselves with fairly direct intervention in ongoing labor conflicts to negotiate compromises based on already negotiated bases de trabajo. The governors could and in many instances did declare strikes illegal when they found them not to be grounded in legitimate grievances; they could and did fine employers for violating bases de trabajo. Generally, the governors' interventions had been conciliatory. For example, when militant laborers in Aracena refused to conform to the bases de trabajo in December 1932, Governor Braulio Solsano Ronda had allowed the Civil Guard to disperse the laborers, but he also oversaw the installing of a new mayor who negotiated a compromise with them (*Diario de Huelva*, Dec. 8–10 and 15, 1932).

By contrast, the Lerroux government began to take concerted action to prevent or put down labor activism. It encouraged the ignoring or undoing of earlier pro-labor agrarian legislation. In Huelva, for example, landlords of the Aracena region appealed to the minister of agriculture to gut the 1933 bases de trabajo of its antiproprietor provisions and had many of them reversed.

Such setbacks angered working-class militants. After the abortive railroad and general strike organized by the FAI and the CNT in December 1933, the government stepped up efforts against activists. For the first time in the Second Republic, the state began to censor newspapers such as Sevilla's *El Liberal*, hammering reports of labor unrest and strikes in other parts of the country (particularly Catalonia) out of the galleys as papers went to press.

Such vigilance was not without a response; working-class militants began to take a more radical stance. Frustrated by Socialist electoral losses, by setbacks for land reform, and by efforts to reverse the gains won by labor in the first bienio, the leader of the Socialist farmworkers' federation, the FNTT, declared openly for revolution in bold headlines and an editorial on the front page of the February 3, 1934, edition of *El Obrero de la Tierra*. "The government of Lerroux, the reactionary bourgeoisie, rural caciques, and the clergy today form a vast united front whose goals appear to be the destruction of the lay, left, and social evolutionary spirits that were the essence of the Republic and the popular movement of April 12, 1931; the suppression of each small victory achieved by the working class in the first phase of the Republic, to the point of unconditional surrender; and the total undoing of agrarian reform." The editorial accused the reaction of anticonstitutional maneuvers, of subversion of the Republic, of organizing "yellow" syndicates to discredit the labor movement, of illegally boycotting legitimate labor organizations, and of arming fascist squadrons. It concluded that the FNTT "declares without reservation for revolution and calls its affiliates to prepare to undertake and defend it under the red banner of the UGT and the Socialist party." Subsequent issues called for militant action to socialize landholdings along the lines of Soviet models (e.g., the issue of Feb. 10), published hundreds of testimonials about the abuses and repression syndicates were experiencing throughout the nation (Mar. 24 and 31), and appealed to peasants and farmworkers of all parties to join in a united front (Apr. 21) to militate for land and labor reform. The final step (May 1) was to call for a nationwide harvest strike on June 5, 1934.

In Huelva, Governor Malboyssón began to watch and repress

those thought to be subversive, particularly labor leaders and leftists in local government. The vigilance involved not only direct intervention in strikes and labor disputes, but also widespread use of the Civil Guard to conduct house searches for subversive literature and to seek and confiscate firearms and knives. Additionally, Malboyssón began to suspend town councillors suspected of sedition or of encouraging the forming of armed local militias or "illegal" strikes. During this period, the newspaper *Diario de Huelva* published interviews with Malboyssón reporting, after the fact, on many of these actions. For example, on April 6 and April 29, 1934, the paper reported the arrests of councillors and mayors in Cabezas Rubias, Santa Olalla de Cala, and Almonte.

The escalation of repression in the name of order in 1934 reflected the ascendancy of the interests of agrarian property as a concern of state. This became readily apparent in the 1934 wheat harvests. On May Day, the Socialists and the FNTT called for harvest workers throughout Spain to strike on June 5 as part of an effort to form a *frente campesino* with anarcho-syndicalists in a common effort to secure land reform and protect agrarian workers' rights. The FNTT published preprinted forms in *El Obrero de la Tierra* for agrarian unions to fill in and file so as to make the strike legal. Although rhetorically adhering to a corporatist framework, which heralded agrarian workers as part of the *gran familia campesina* whose cooperation in agrarian production was vital for the economy, state agrarian policy clearly aimed at completing the June harvests without disruption or destruction. The minister of interior was given a free hand to prevent the strike. He instigated the wholesale arrest of local Socialist leaders and closed the FNTT's *El Obrero de la Tierra*. Strikes and work stoppages affecting harvests were declared illegal, and the authorities began to arrest those who advocated striking. The wave of arrests extended even to Socialist deputies in the Cortes, despite their constitutional immunities, evoking comparisons to the fascist repressions of German Social Democrats in 1933 and Socialists in Vienna in February 1934 (Aparicio Albiñana 1936: 75–78; Jackson 1965: 134–37; Malefakis 1970: 336–37).

In Huelva, Governor Malboyssón declared his firm determination to maintain order in the harvest and insisted that he had sufficient forces to put down any effort to disrupt it:

For Spain is at a moment of anticipation, its people determined to reconstruct it and make it blossom by peaceful means; and it would be senseless, even criminal, for those of us charged with securing public tranquility, Spain's well-being, and the strengthening of the state not to intervene forcefully to break up the stupid attempts of those who would prevent the country from recovering its glory and the Fatherland from prospering. Citizens! *Viva España! Viva La República!* (*Bando* of Apr. 26, 1934, declaring a state of alarm; *Boletín Oficial*, Apr. 26, 1934)

But such rhetoric may not have been deemed forceful enough; on May 27, 1934, the Council of Ministers transfered Malboyssón to Tenerife, appointing as his replacement Jerónimo Fernaud Martín of Tenerife, a hardliner who would collaborate in putting down the escalating agrarian conflict. When Fernaud took office on June 8, a wave of arrests in rural Huelva had already begun under Enrique Valdés, interim governor.

It was in this context that Los Olivos's Socialists began to experience state repression. "Preventive" arrest became a commonplace experience for the town's leading Socialists, who suspected that police forces were trying to provoke them. Juan José Santis remembers that his father, Ceferino, was arrested at least a dozen times and held without charges. "Whenever he saw the Civil Guard awaiting him, he would put up his hands to be shackled so that there could be no excuse for shooting him down under the Ley de Fugas." (The Ley de Fugas was the common name for a provision that permitted arresting officers to open fire, not an uncommon practice, on anyone who "fled" or "resisted" arrest.)

As the threat of harvest strikes swept the country in May 1934, the arrests quickened. On May 2, the day after the Socialists had proclaimed a common cause with rural anarchists in the Frente Campesino and called for a June 5 harvest strike, Governor Malboyssón suspended Ceferino Santis from his position as mayor and had him jailed. When workers ignored the governor's warnings and went on strike in June in many towns throughout the province, Interim Governor Valdés arrested strike leaders. On June 6, he reported to the press on steps he had taken to break up the strikes, insisting that "tranquility reigns" through-out the province (*Diario de Huelva*, June 6, 1934). It is not clear whether workers struck in Los Olivos, but shortly after Jerónimo Fernaud Martín took office, Alfredo González, who was acting mayor, was also arrested and jailed. To protest the entry of three CEDA deputies into the Cabinet on October 1, 1934, the So-cialists led a series of revolutionary uprisings, of which the most significant was in Asturias (Shubert 1984). As these movements were put down, Governor Fernaud declared that he had orders from Madrid to remove from office every individual whose in-clinations might oppose those of the state. On October 22, a large number of Huelva towns received a form letter from the governor removing known and suspected leftists from their councils and replacing them with rightists. In Los Olivos, the entire council was suspended under the terms of Article 55 of the Ley de Orden Público and replaced with a slate headed by Celestino López.

SIX

Law and Order: The Bienio Negro in Los Olivos

THE SOCIALISTS of Los Olivos had overcome the adversity of local opposition in the Republic's first two years, taking power in 1933 and effectively challenging and reforming labor relations. Yet as their fortunes had waxed locally, their party's lot had waned nationally. Socialist party leaders had become disillusioned of collaboration with left-Republicans because the governing coalition proved incapable of fending off a vociferous and ever more effective reactionary opposition. Electoral setbacks had ensued, and Lerroux's Radical Republicans formed a government sympathetic to the Right. Nearly a year later, Gil Robles and other CEDA reactionaries joined a new cabinet, and the Socialists led the October 1934 revolutions in protest and were crushed. Up to that time, the Socialists had held on to local government in Los Olivos even though their party had fallen from power nationally, but thereafter national developments engulfed them. This chapter concerns the repression that the Socialists of Los Olivos shared with their counterparts throughout the country following the revolutionary movements of October 1934—a repression that contributed to the growing polarization of local affairs by regional and national politics.

Spaniards refer to the period of reactionary Republican government that followed the electoral victory of CEDA, the rightist front, as the *bienio negro*, the two black years of repression and of legislative repeal of many earlier Republican reforms. In the wake of the Asturias Revolution, the state of alarm suspending civil rights was extended through 1935. On the orders of the

Ministry of Interior, hundreds of leftist town officials were suspended, and up to 40,000 union leaders and former officials held
prisoner (Jackson 1965: 161). Socialist casas del pueblo were
closed, as was the party newspaper, *El Socialista*.

Los Olivos Socialists had weathered the first eleven months of
the provincial government's reactionary vigilance and preventive
arrests and had remained in control of town government. Now
they underwent more explicit repression of the sort that had begun earlier in other provinces; in Jaén, for example, pressure to
sack and prosecute Socialist town councils had mounted immediately after the November 1933 elections, according to Governor
Aparicio Albiñana (1936: 42–44). Within a month, Los Olivos
Socialists were overwhelmed by a clean sweep of all public posts
in favor of rightists of the old order; criminal prosecution of former councillors for malfeasance in office; and the reinforcement
of the Civil Guard, who began to arrest and fine dozens of poor
and working-class townfolk in the name of law and order. The
bienio negro was thus a period that Los Olivos experienced as an
escalating polar confrontation, with the state using its repressive
apparatus on behalf of local propertied interests against workers
and the Left.

Governor Jerónimo Fernaud Martín of Huelva removed the Socialist councillors from office in a climate of hysterical vigilance
by the Right. A few months earlier, leaders of the Juventud Socialista (the Socialist youth organization) in Cueva de la Mora, a
Huelva mining town, had been arrested on charges of organizing and arming an illegal militia after the Civil Guard seized militant pamphlets in the home of the fiancée of one of the leaders (*Diario de Huelva*, Mar. 22, 1934). A month later, anarchists
bombed the convent of the Hermanas de la Caridad in Nerva
and desecrated religious images in several other towns, acts that
the governor claimed were part of a national conspiracy that he
vowed to thwart (*Diario de Huelva*, Apr. 26, 1934). During the Asturias Revolution, anarcho-syndicalists burned the church in Paterna del Campo, a rich agrarian town in Huelva's fertile plain,
and set off bombs in the mining town of Nerva. A pitched battle
broke out between workers and employers in the town of Santa
Olalla de Cala, and miners disrupted operations at El Cerro de

Andévalo. The Civil Guard made more and more arrests in these and other places (*Diario de Huelva*, Oct. 9, 1934). In the wake of the Asturias Revolution of October 6–8, 1934, the governor suspended councillors belonging to the Socialist and other leftist parties, first in Huelva itself and then in town after town throughout the province (see *El Liberal*, Oct. 10 and 11, 1934). Rightists in Los Olivos, including one whom I interviewed, collaborated with the Civil Guard, the priest, and Celestino López in mounting a night watch to protect the church from a suspected attack.

With the exception of López, the town councillors designated by Governor Fernaud on October 22, 1934, to replace the Socialists were all new to public office, but their ties with Celestino López's old affiliates were nonetheless strong (see Figure 6.2). The councillors elected Tomás Nogales mayor, Celestino López evidently preferring a lower profile as councillor. Tomás was a property owner and the older brother of Ramón Nogales, who had served with Celestino López in the council of 1931. Isidoro Moreno served as vice-president of the council. Isidoro, who was married to the niece of another of the 1931 councillors, was the trucker who competed for the town's transport business against Pablo Moreno, the Socialist ideologue and young councillor just ousted, and Pablo's father. Lorenzo Infante, a property owner and muleteer and a son of Ramón, a former councillor and a compatriot of Celestino López, held another council position. Francisco Moreno, son of the monarchist judge Feliciano Moreno and owner of the *estanco* (official tobacco and grain store), represented the Moreno family as a councillor. His brother-in-law, Celestino Nogales, a wealthy farmer, also served as a councillor. Marcelino Gómez, a staunch rightist property owner, was the oldest councillor, at age 61 six years older than Celestino López. Agustín Nogales, son of 1931 councillor Maximiano Gonzales, was youngest at age 28. The council thus consisted of middle-aged and somewhat more youthful property owners and merchants close in age to the Socialists they replaced (although *not* solidary as an age cohort), many of them nephews and children of the councillors who had served with Celestino López in 1931. Coming into pueblo politics, they represented the up-and-coming generation of prominent propertied family heads.

The change of councils subtly altered the dynamics of local politics by increasingly polarizing them along lines of national politics rather than of local factionalism. Factionalism had always found expression in Town Council politics. Villagers associated town hall politics with *interés*—self-interested action of a kind that emerges in middle age in peasant life as formerly solidary youthful relatives and age mates mature to compete with their own and their spouse's siblings for inheritance, and perhaps for influence and followings among the village poor. As cohorts came of age, their conflicts were expressed in town politics, and villagers might thus interpret town hall politics as self-interested expression of *rencillos* (personal quarrels). Yet rivalries and potential alliances based on kinship tended to be ephemeral and not to rend the community; such divisions and ties differed from one person to the next, as they characteristically do in cognatic kinship. The politics of the Socialists who came to power in 1933, for example, might well have been passed off as that of a group of young adults competitively related to the councillors of Celestino López's faction whom they had sought to oust. Socialist Mayor Ceferino Santis and his rival and predecessor, Francisco Santis, were brothers, after all. Several of the rightist councillors of 1934 were similarly age mates and potentially rivalrous siblings or in-laws of the Socialists they had ousted (see Figures 6.1 and 6.2).

But the leading Socialists of Los Olivos had introduced a new and potentially more profound fissure into local politics. All men of the age cohort that had experienced Spain's Tragic Week of 1909 as the *quinta* just recruited to military service and that had grown up together in the subsequent two decades of Spanish political life, the Socialists had shouldered the working-class cause with exceptional solidarity and fervor. The struggle to establish the syndicate had bonded them further, drawing sharper than customary lines between them and their opposition. And the councillors of 1934 exacerbated the resulting polarization of town politics, representing the national reaction and becoming the instrument of the state's repression of the local Left. Seemingly irreconcilable differences, articulated first and foremost in the burning national issues of the day, had thus given substance—and increasingly bipolar shape and experience—to lo-

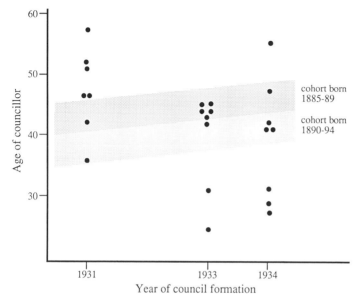

Fig. 6.1. Age Distributions of Town Councillors. The broad-ranging distribution of ages among councils dominated by the Right (1931 and 1934) contrasts with the age-group solidarity of Socialist councillors (1933), all but two of whom were from the 1885–89 birth cohort.

cal factionalism, eclipsing the personalistic bases from which it may originally have risen. In people's memories, the politics of the Town Council divided the pueblo as never before, rending the fabric of kinship and crosscutting patronage. The village was becoming split into two camps.

Upon taking office, the rightist councillors made a clean sweep of all personnel involved in town government. In the case of civil servants who supposedly could be fired only for cause, the councillors simply invoked the governor's mandate to remove leftists from office. The acting secretary to the council was fired, and Francisco Javier Núñez, who had resigned from the position under the Socialists, took his place. Francisco Sánchez, the town sheriff, was also dismissed and replaced by Eusebio Ramos, a cousin of José Antonio Ramos's who recognized on which side his bread would be buttered. But the councillors did not stop with these key civil servants. Other minor functionaries were

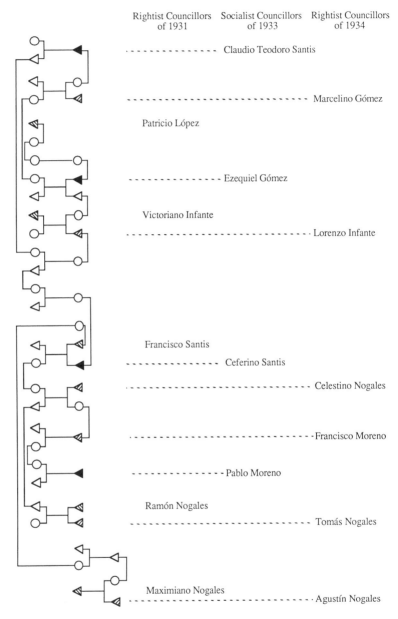

Rightist Councillors of 1931   Socialist Councillors of 1933   Rightist Councillors of 1934

Claudio Teodoro Santis

Marcelino Gómez

Patricio López

Ezequiel Gómez

Victoriano Infante

Lorenzo Infante

Francisco Santis

Ceferino Santis

Celestino Nogales

Francisco Moreno

Pablo Moreno

Ramón Nogales

Tomás Nogales

Maximiano Nogales

Agustín Nogales

Fig. 6.2. Relations of Kinship Among Los Olivos Second Republic Protagonists. Town leaders, whether of the Left or the Right, were closely related to one another as siblings, cousins, or affines. Countervailing bonds and conflicts of kinship ordinarily mitigated against sustained or clear-cut factionalism in the pueblo, but Second Republic politics split leaders into two camps and polarized town life. (The diagram shows only close kin relationships among the town councillors.)

booted out. For example, the council summarily dismissed Federico Santis, the guardo de consumos responsible for registering wheat harvests and the consumption of flour, on the dubious charge of illiteracy. The Socialists had hired Federico temporarily to collect minor taxes for the town, and the council refused to pay the back wages due him on the pretext that his post had never been formally approved as a budget item.

The syndicate itself, meanwhile, had been dissolved by order of the governor. The council closed down the Casa del Pueblo, the Socialists' meeting place, one night just as its proprietor, Teodoro Santis, was about to go to bed. Villagers were treated to the spectacle of the Civil Guard shackling the old man and hauling him in his pyjamas and socks through the streets to jail. The next day, the council instituted formal eviction proceedings to revoke Socialist claims on the building rented from the town for the Casa del Pueblo. In other actions, they packed the commissions supervising agrarian employment and managing public works with allies, firing Socialists and leftists from jobs and allowing private employers to do the same. To add insult to injury, the council declared the new entrance road to the town "impassable" and erected barriers to prevent its use!

Additionally, the council began to hound Socialist ex-councillors with charges of malfeasance, leading ultimately to criminal suits, another tactic that the Right had refined elsewhere in previous months. It was a routine matter for an incoming council to inspect the books and accounts of the outgoing council. The villagers' general assumption about all officeholders was that they acted out of self-interest to benefit themselves while in office, but scrutiny of the books usually turned up only minor amounts for which previous incumbents could be held accountable. For example, Celestino López had held José Antonio Ramos responsible in 1931 for subscriptions to official publications that had not been kept up in Ramos's incumbency, and the Socialists had inspected their predecessors' bookkeeping when they took office. The steps taken in 1934 went much further than these, however.

The council hired an accountant to examine all the fiscal records of their predecessors. The Socialists had transferred items in the budget in a most irregular way in order to pay workers under the road construction contract. Francisco Javier Núñez, the secretary who had resisted the Socialists before resigning under duress, probably knew about these irregularities and called them to the accountant's attention. The accountant claimed to have discovered further irregularities. Because of the Socialists' sloppy bookkeeping, there was no firm evidence that the property tax surcharge destined for public works had actually been spent for that purpose. He found evidence that Ceferino Santis, the Socialist ex-mayor, and two other socialist ex-councillors had accepted wages as workers on the road project for days during which they had actually been in jail under preventive arrest at the governor's orders. This particular charge grew out of the Socialists' practice of working overtime on the road project on behalf of their leaders so that the leaders could be free to attend to union business. Ceferino Santis and other leaders had not been paid a salary in their capacity as union leaders or town councillors. So the union men had worked an extra fifteen minutes per day in these leaders' names.

Having amassed this evidence, the council denounced the Socialist ex-councillors to Governor Fernaud, who sent a representative to investigate the charges. The representative confirmed the evidence, and the governor instigated criminal proceedings against the ex-councillors.

The rightist council also deepened its collaboration with the repressive Civil Guard. Up to 1933, the Civil Guard seems not to have intervened explicitly in the political life of the town. Since the early 1920's, when a unit of the Civil Guard had been brought in to help rid the town of the purported tyranny of the men of the Iglesias family, whom the Lópezes had denounced as a band of thugs, four guards and their captain had been stationed in the *cuartel*, a garrison rented by the council from Celestino López on their behalf. Pairs of guards (*La Pareja*), who were always outsiders assigned to a given pueblo, made daily tours of surveillance in the countryside, occasionally citing villagers found to be grazing pigs or goats on someone else's property. The guards also investigated thefts and quarrels involving insults or assault. Up to 1933, they functioned in Los Olivos as a relatively benign local police force, favorable to propertied interests but not overtly interfering with Socialists' undertakings, which were, after all, entirely legal.

Their function changed at the outset of the bienio negro by becoming overtly oppositional to working-class interests. In many parts of Andalusia, property owners prevailed on governors to use the Civil Guard to crack down on purported thefts of produce. In Jaén, for example, where famine was particularly acute, the bases de trabajo included a provision advancing the date at which poor people could begin the *rebusca*, a customary practice in which proprietors allowed poor people to glean the harvested fields. Proprietors complained that the poor were stealing crops before they could be harvested and called on the Civil Guard to put a halt to the theft (Aparicio Albiñana 1936: 40–43).

There was at the same time a growing general concern on the part of governors to beef up the forces at their disposal for maintaining public order. As governor of Albacete (after being transferred there from Jaén), Aparicio Albiñana (1936: 83–86) complained that he had only 44 investigative and security officers and 365 Civil Guard officers at his disposal throughout the province, and he began a campaign to build a new Assault Guard corps. Huelva's Governor Malboyssón, who had assumed office at the same time as Aparicio Albiñana as a Radical Republican under Lerroux, had begun an identical campaign, bringing in a corps of Assault Guard from Málaga to station in Huelva. He also repeatedly deployed Civil Guard units to maintain order around the province in the face of threatened general strikes. While the state was cracking down on leftists' possession of weapons in the spring of 1934, the Civil Guard helped ten prominent Los Olivos rightists obtain licenses for rifles and shotguns (*Boletín Oficial*, May 19, 1934). During the Asturias Revolution in October, Governor Fernaud authorized local authorities to accept the services of volunteers in maintaining law and order, and Captain Sánchez, who headed the Los Olivos garrison, helped organize the vigilante groups that stood night guard at the church for a month.

Immediately on taking office, the rightist councillors responded to the state's efforts to beef up the Civil Guard. They authorized a contribution of town funds to the "forces that restored peace in Spain." Reinforcements had been sent to the local garrison, and the council paid for their room and board.

Then in December the council took steps to enlarge and refurbish the local garrison to accommodate the augmented forces of the Civil Guard. The garrison belonged to Celestino López, who happily agreed to sell the building to the town for 9,000 pesetas. The council persuaded the heirs of a recently deceased widow to sell the house next door to the garrison for 4,000 pesetas so that it could be expanded to accommodate seven officers and their families instead of five. Although these purchases completely exhausted the town's reserves, the council committed funds from the operating budget to reconstruct and modernize the garrison, putting masons to work on it through the summer of 1935.

For their part, the Civil Guard made their presence felt with a vengeance. Judicial records show that citations by the Civil Guard increased an astonishing thirtyfold in 1935. Almost all of the citations went to townsfolk allegedly caught trespassing or improperly herding in the countryside, primarily on properties of the largest landowners. Poorer townfolk, regardless of their political affiliation, were the target of the Civil Guard vigilance, and villagers remember with anger doing everything they could to avoid encountering La Pareja on their tours of the countryside, as most of the charges were arbitrary and groundless. Patricio López, who was then justice of the peace, upheld most of the charges, and defendants were forced to pay fines of 25 pesetas or more—nearly a week's wages—in tax stamps sold by the state. The Civil Guard vigilance in favor of the wealthiest farmers penalized all of the poorer classes, among whom workers of leftist leaning predominated, probably extracting enough revenue in fines to repay the state for deploying these repressive rural forces.

Repression and vindictive hounding of leftists and their families also characterized the spate of civil suits litigated in Los Olivos during the last year of the bienio negro. State legislation abetted the litigation. In July 1934, the Ministry of Justice annulled the reforms made in the procedures for appointing justices of the peace and reinstated the procedures that had prevailed during the monarchy. Socialist sympathizer José Antonio Roncero had been ousted from the local court under these provisions, and Patricio López had taken his place. Patricio's incumbency obviously promised judgments in favor of the Right. The Cortes also repealed various other Republican legislation, the most significant for Los Olivos being the legislation in favor of tenants, which was repealed in March 1935. This change enabled property owners to sue leftist tenant farmers for eviction with far greater success (Jackson 1965: 109).

In this context, local civil suits trebled in number in 1935 over the average of previous years and were directed disproportionately at Socialists and their relatives, making local litigation overtly political to an unprecedented degree. Criminal suits for malfeasance in office were already in process against the Socialist councillors, and many of them were direct or indirect victims of citations issued by the Civil Guard.

For example, in one case the Civil Guard charged Alfredo González, the vice-president of the disbanded syndicate, with improper herding. The Civil Guard brought another suit against Alfredo's son Hipólito. And his brother, Teodoro, was sued for eviction from a farm that he rented.

Pablo Moreno, the youngest Socialist ex-councillor and ideologue, was accused by Teodoro Moreno, an equally fanatical rightist whom the council had made responsible for banking municipal moneys, of fraudulently delivering to a mechanic in a neighboring town truck parts that Teodoro claimed he owned.

Claudio Teodoro Santis, another Socialist ex-councillor, was charged with abusive herding on Celestino López's property by the Civil Guard, and a wealthy widow sued him for debt. The council brought an eviction suit against his father, in whose name the Socialists had rented public quarters for the Casa del Pueblo.

Domingo Santis, another ex-councillor, was forced to pay a fine and court costs on behalf of his son, Eusebio, who allegedly insulted Eusebio Ramos, the rightist town sheriff. The child was subjected to a lecture by Patricio López, the justice of the peace.

A different Eusebio Santis, also an ex-councillor, learned that his elderly mother had been charged with trespassing by the Civil Guard, and that Celestino López had brought an eviction suit against his father on the pretext that he had neglected beehives on farmland that he leased.

Federico Santis, whom the rightists had evicted from the post of guardo de consumos and had refused back pay as temporary tax collector, was charged twice by the Civil Guard with trespassing on two estates while herding.

Francisco Sánchez, the ousted sheriff, was arrested and jailed for not having licensed the pistol he was supplied with when in office.

Thus, an overtly repressive invocation of law and order characterized Los Olivos's experience of the bienio negro. This is not to say that the rightist councillors were bent solely on vengeance. The council continued to recognize the need and potential benefits of public works that the state might fund, responding to state inquiries about public works with requests for subsidization of projects similar to those planned by the Socialists—road and school construction. What had become clear, however, was that the reactionaries in control of the state had backed the conservative propertied class against agrarian workers in the countryside of Huelva with coercive and judicial power in a manner that polarized life in towns to an unprecedented degree. More than ever before, partisan national politics began to sunder pueblo affairs in ways that bonds of kinship and patronage could no longer contain.

SEVEN

The Vindication of the Left

SPAIN'S WORKING-CLASS radicalization was, if anything, heightened by the two years of repression. We have seen how reprisals from the Right in Los Olivos exacerbated the divisions that had opened in the first bienio and linked them to increasingly polarized national causes. Much the same happened elsewhere. Furthermore, repression made common bedfellows—or cellmates—of Socialists with anarcho-syndicalists and Communists, who had suffered more systematic persecution than the Socialists before 1934. The Socialists moved further to the left, joining Communists and left-Republicans in a Popular Front that gained an electoral victory on February 16, 1936. In this chapter, I explore how Los Olivos Socialists, who returned to power in the wake of the election, invested local affairs with newfound militancy colored by sentiments of anarchism and libertarian communism garnered from other Huelva leftists in the bienio negro.

One old Socialist, explaining to me why the state had invited or imposed so many changes of government in Los Olivos, contrasted the Second Republic with the dictatorship of Primo de Rivera in the 1920's. "Then, public affairs were forever in the hands of eight or ten powerful men of the town to manage to their own advantage. Under the Republic, at least the state allowed different groups to try their hand at managing things better." This is perhaps a not inappropriate interpretation of local events driven at a national level by lapses in the ability to govern and by the need to reassert the popular legitimacy of government through elections.

When the Azaña government failed to resolve the deep social

and economic problems of the early 1930's, the calling of general elections in November 1933 enabled those of the rightist coalition of the Radical party and CEDA to try their hand at governing. But Lerroux, the Radicals' head of government, was hardly any more successful at bringing about the flourishing of the *patria* in whose name Huelva's governor had deployed the forces of law and order. Bringing Gil Robles and other CEDA deputies into the cabinet had precipitated revolution, repression, and the suspension of civil rights for more than a year. Finally, a scandal over Lerroux's complicity in attempts to introduce *straperlo* (a variant of roulette) discredited his government in autumn 1935.

Not daring to turn the government over to Gil Robles, Alcalá Zamora, the president of the Republic, set up a caretaker government and called for new general elections to be held on February 16, 1936. The president noted that free and open expression of public opinion had been made impossible by the growing violence, on the one hand, and by state controls, on the other hand. He voiced the hope that elections, by giving expression to public sentiment, would legitimate a modern majority to counterbalance the extremisms of Left and Right. In Huelva, the unions that had been closed down in October 1934 were allowed to reopen (*Boletín Oficial*, Jan. 9, 1936; Jackson 1965: 176–77, 184).

In the feverish electioneering during the last months of the bienio negro, parties of every political shade began to canvass the country. The people of Los Olivos remember these months as a time of public meetings when orators would proclaim their doctrine from the porch of the town hall to anyone who cared to listen. Right-wing parties, the Acción Popular, the Partido Radical, and the Partido Agrario, lobbied in the Huelva countryside. But the Socialists stirred greater excitement as the rumor spread that Largo Caballero would visit the province on behalf of the new Popular Front electoral coalition, formed to sweep the election, much as CEDA had done in 1933. For the first time, the Socialists had proclaimed common cause with the Communists, as well as with the left-Republicans. On January 16, 1936, newspapers published the text of the "Manifiesto Electoral de la Alianza de Izquierdas," the platform of the leftist Popular Front coalition. Socialist party leaders and the federation of local Socialist party organizations campaigned in virtually every Huelva town on behalf of the Popular Front in the month that followed. In Los Olivos, Socialist ex-mayor Ceferino Santis shared the platform with Juan Gutiérrez Prieto, candidate for deputy to the Cortes from Huelva, on the evening of January 22, 1936.*

Despite Alcalá Zamora's desire to consult public opinion through free and open elections, tactics in Huelva were hardly aboveboard. The city of Huelva itself experienced high-handed political maneuvers with a succession of three governors in barely five weeks. On December 27, 1935, Benjamín Caro Sánchez of the Partido Agrario took office for five days, during which time he deposed Huelva town councillors affiliated with CEDA and replaced them with Partido Agrario members. Fernando Olaguer Feliú, an old ally of Huelva's *gran cacique* during the era of Primo de Rivera, succeeded Caro Sánchez on January 5, 1936, and collaborated with conservative leader Manuel Burgos y Mazo in putting together a "counterrevolutionary" candidacy of the Right for forthcoming elections. But on January 28, Vicente Marín Casanova was appointed governor, and three days later Marín Casanova deposed the Partido Agrario councillors and reinstated the CEDA councillors (see *El Liberal*, Dec. 27, 1935; Jan. 2, 18, and 28 and Feb. 1, 1936). Thus, the political maneuvers were both high-handed and confusing.

Local authorities would not tolerate open campaigning in some rural areas; in the town of Cala, for example, they arrested a visiting politician on charges that his speeches attacked Gil Robles and Lerroux and defamed the Civil Guard. Officials in Los Olivos hastily removed the names of certain Socialists from the electoral rolls to prevent them from voting. Meanwhile, torrential rains inundated Andalusia, flooding many areas. Such measures and the weather did not, however, dispel the popular euphoria, the *exaltación*, that characterized the electoral campaign nationally. For many leftists, the election was a plebiscite to demand the release of the many hundreds of political prisoners still in jails around the countryside (*Boletín Oficial*, Jan. 29, 1936; *El Liberal*, Feb. 7, 1936; Suero Sánchez 1982: 74).

By February 17, 1936, after the votes of the previous day had

---

*As Jackson (1965: 185) points out, similar coalitions formed in opposition to fascism throughout Western Europe after the Communist International "reversed its policy of constant struggle against . . . Social Democrats."

been tallied, the scope of the leftist electoral victory was apparent. The mandate to return the affairs of state to the Left was clear. In Los Olivos, where a delegate of Governor Marín Casanova supervised the election of deputies to national government, the vote favored rightist candidates 235 to 80, similar to the split in other Sierra de Aracena towns where the Right held so much power. But province-wide the vote had been substantially in favor of the Left; of Huelva's seven seats in the Cortes, the Socialists garnered three, electing Juan Gutiérrez Prieto (who had campaigned in Los Olivos), Crescenciano Bilbao, and Ramón González Peña, even though the last two were as yet in prison in Huelva and Asturias. Public clamor for the freeing of political prisoners and the return of leftist rule at the local level grew, and on February 21 a huge crowd paraded through the city of Huelva, prevailing on the government to release Bilbao from jail, where he had been held since 1934. Bilbao and other leftist leaders such as Luís Esquiliche, who had been imprisoned with him, were given a hero's welcome and paraded on shoulders through the city by a multitude of flag-waving men and women (*El Liberal*, Feb. 21, 1936).

Released by order of the authorities in Madrid, some of Los Olivos's Socialists were greeted by their compatriots at the Almonaster railway station and driven home in triumph. They returned to demand control of local affairs, vindicated by the elections, but clashed with the rightist mayor, who had jailed 15 Los Olivos Socialists two days after the elections. In the face of growing confrontation of this sort, the provincial government risked losing control over the countryside. Governor Marín Casanova declared a state of alarm and called on mayors and local Socialist organizations to keep order. Socialist Deputies Juan Gutiérrez Prieto and Crescenciano Bilbao echoed the governor's appeal, warning local Socialist functionaries that they would dismiss them from their posts if they did not cooperate (*Diario de Huelva*, Feb. 18, 1936; *El Liberal*, Feb. 22, 1936).

Within a week after the general elections, Governor Marín Casanova began to restore leftists to local office, including the Socialists of Los Olivos. Town Council minutes show that the same persons who had held office in 1933 resumed the posts they had held before their arrest and removal from office during the bienio negro.

Sources of Ideological Commitment

Restored to power, Los Olivos Socialists governed the pueblo with newfound vigor and a willingness to forge ahead on their own without explicit sanction from the state. They drew their self-confidence in part from the skills of experienced outsiders whom they brought in to help govern. But their newfound fervor also manifested a broader range of leftist thinking than had been apparent earlier. Some discussion of the sources of their ideological commitments will illuminate the course of events in the pueblo in 1936.

The Left in Los Olivos was almost exclusively Socialist and had drawn primarily on various strands of Socialist thought for some time. Mayor Ceferino Santis is reported to have preferred the center of the spectrum of Socialist party ideology, as compared to the militancy represented by Largo Caballero in 1933 and 1934. Young militant Pablo Moreno, who had worked in a store in Sevilla just before the Second Republic, kept in touch with the more radical Socialists there while doing business transporting produce (just as his cousin Inocencio Moreno, educated and working in a Sevilla store, was taking up with the Falangists he had come to know as a student).

Yet exposure to a broader range of leftist thought had not been absent in the town. Many villagers whose families had worked in the Riotinto mines sustained contacts with anarchists and Communists there. Nationally, leftists prided themselves as being intellectuals, as "people with ideas." Similar notions were current in Los Olivos. Ceferino Santis is remembered as a man who had studied a lot and had read widely even though he had had little formal schooling. The emphasis on literacy was strong among the pueblo's leftists. A range of newspapers, including some anarchist literature, circulated in the town. Other facets of anarchism were in evidence: more than one Socialist family forswore smoking and drinking, emulating the reforms in personal life of anarchists elsewhere.

At the other end of the spectrum, anticlericalism had been

halfhearted among Los Olivos Socialists before the bienio negro. Most villagers were practicing Catholics. Ceferino Santis, the Socialist mayor, had had his daughter baptized at birth and confirmed shortly afterward by the bishop in 1930. During the 1920's, there had been two *hermandades* in Los Olivos, and almost everyone belonged to one or the other of these religious confraternities. Villagers enjoyed the Easter Sunday raffle of olives, hams, and candied pastry that one of the hermandades had organized each year from time immemorial. The village's most festive occasion had always been the fiesta of San José, its patron saint, which the Town Council was responsible for organizing. When the Socialists took power in 1933, the council debated whether to sponsor the fiesta and decided to do so. This does not mean that those Socialists who were practicing Catholics were fully at one with the church. As we have seen, the clergy and the town's powerful interests were closely allied, giving anticlericalism a tangible point of departure. But anticlericalism did not have to entail the abandonment of the very individualistic kind of faith that need not rely on the intermediation of the clergy. As one Socialist survivor told me, in explaining his faith, "Many say that Christ was the first anarchist."

Before the bienio negro, in short, socialism in Los Olivos exemplified what Antonio M. Calero (1976: 78) says about the ideological content of the base, as opposed to the leadership, of social movements in Andalusia: "I believe one has to acknowledge a certain relativism to the anarchism, socialism, republicanism, and even the Catholicism of members at the base of worker and peasant organizations. . . . In conversations with old members (those at the base, to be sure; leaders were a different matter altogether), I believe I have verified that for them there was no great difference between belonging to the CNT or to the UGT." After the bienio negro, however, Los Olivos Socialists began to act with newfound militancy. I believe their shift stemmed from the experience of repression that leftists of every persuasion shared in the bienio negro.

In the Huelva prison, for example, hundreds of anarchist, Communist, and Socialist political prisoners shared quarters. Luciano Suero Sánchez, an anarchist organizer from the mining town of El Cerro de Andévalo, was imprisoned there during the bienio negro. According to his description of prison life in his autobiography (1982: 68):

We met with many friends we had come to know in the fray of earlier social and political battles, principally militants of the CNT and UGT, who were the most numerous in that enormous roundup of the province. There were men of every type, and of all ages and professions. Many of them were Socialist mayors and town councillors of towns from all over the province, mostly working class and self-educated, holding a tremendous faith in the future of society, which seemed to them alive and within their tangible grasp.

The prison was new, and it was run by an enlightened warden who allowed the prisoners to run a school in the courtyard. The school was sponsored by a Socialist schoolteacher, Luís Es-quiliche, who organized the prisoners into groups to teach one another. The prisoners also passed their spare time arguing about politics:

They argued about the two philosophies, anarchist and Marxist, about the capacity or incapacity of workers to defend themselves, about the supposed drawbacks of workers' running society for themselves, without hierarchy and without a government based on force.

The Socialists clung to the timeworn thesis that once capitalism was destroyed, a socialist state would be indispensable for mobilizing the mass of workers to reform the community. They held on to the notion that the state ought to be the owner and master of everything and to give workers liberty and education as a stepping-stone to a socialist state.

We anarchists argued that, no, authority was not needed, neither that of the state nor that of the bureaucracy, given that the people would be in a free state only without restrictions other than those agreed on by themselves and for themselves. . . . The anarchists would go straight to the goal of a free community, that of libertarian socialism (Suero Sánchez 1982: 68–69).

Prison, in short, was a caldron of radical ideology, argued forcefully but amicably by proponents of every leftist persuasion. Los Olivos's Socialist leaders, some of whom were imprisoned along with Suero Sánchez, surely extended and deepened both the radical scope of their ideological commitments and the range of their acquaintances with leftists, much as this anarchist organizer did. Juan José Santis, for example, remembers that his father, Ceferino Santis, adulated Crescenciano Bilbao, a Socialist organizer whom he probably met in the Huelva prison, as Suero Sánchez did.

Toward the end of the bienio negro, the union of left-wing parties in the Popular Front must have reinforced the radical turn of pueblo Socialists. Spanish Socialists had looked to the Russian Revolution before, but rapprochement with the Communists in the Popular Front animated the Socialists' drawing of an analogy between Spain in 1936 and Russia in 1917 (Jackson 1965: 207). Suppressed in the bienio negro, the FNTT newspaper *El Obrero de la Tierra* (Mar. 7, 1936), in its second edition after the Popular Front victory, extolled Soviet agrarian collectives as a model for Spaniards to emulate. Shortly afterward, the Los Olivos council even voted funds to a provincial subscription to subsidize the travel of three schoolteachers to Russia at the invitation of the Union of Intellectuals of the USSR; one of the teachers was Luís Esquiliche. This was just one of the ways in which Los Olivos Socialists voiced the more general call for proletarian unity.

The Juventud Socialista, the local youth organization, also adopted a more radical voice at this time, reflecting the union of national Socialist and Communist youth organizations in the Juventud Socialista Unificada in April 1936 (Jackson 1965: 207). The local Juventud Socialista probably borrowed some of its militancy and ideas from youth in the Riotinto area, where anticlericalism was much more current and where youth groups of the militant Federación Anarquista Ibérica were active. One young member, Celestino Ramos, had been an acolyte in the church until he joined the Juventud Socialista in 1936, probably under the influence of his slightly older first cousins who had worked in the mines. Most of the active members were young men, but there was one young woman, whom the Socialists had earlier commissioned to embroider the Socialist party flag, whom villagers remember shouting "¡Viva el comunismo libertario!" in the streets.

Professionals living temporarily in the town also reinforced the local Socialists' zeal. When the Socialists resumed office, they hired Celestino Munís, a former first officer of the Town Council of Huelva and an experienced Socialist, together with another outsider to "help" and then replace Francisco Javier Núñez, the rightist secretary. Since the governor of Huelva had jailed all Socialists in the provincial capital's government on October 11, 1934, it seems likely that Munís had come to know Los Olivos Socialists in prison during the repression. Villagers remember Munís as a distinguished man, a grand figure who carried an embossed staff given him in honor of previous diplomatic service; this image certainly fits the eloquent prose that Munís injected into the council's records and official correspondence.

Then there was the press, which villagers read avidly. The Socialists subscribed to *El Obrero de la Tierra* (the official organ of the FNTT); *La Tierra* (a sensational paper with anarcho-syndicalist leanings); *La Vanguardia* (a short-lived Socialist paper published in Huelva in 1936); and *El Socialista* (the official Socialist organ), among others. They thus were abreast of the redirection of Socialist party policy that encouraged workers and peasant organizers to take the initiative in the Spanish countryside rather than to wait for the Popular Front government to act.

El Obrero de la Tierra's stridency exemplified the new Socialist militancy. The March 7, 1936, edition called on Socialists to voice their demands in meetings to be staged all over the country the day before the opening of the new parliament on March 15:

Immediate turnover of land and credits to peasant collectives. Rescue of pueblo commons. Work for all the unemployed. Return farms to evicted renters. Strict compliance with the bases [de trabajo]. Strict job rotation. Not one social prisoner in jail. No reprisals in the street. Bring the executioners and thieves of the pueblos to justice. Republican government. Left town councils. Kick out public employees who are enemies of the workers. Disarm the rightists. Popular militias.

Fifteen hundred Socialists and sympathizers voiced these demands in a rally in Alajar (according to the paper's March 28 edition), just one of the Sierra de Aracena towns to stage such rallies. The March 28 edition also urged peasant land invasions in Badajoz: AVOID CLASHES WITH PUBLIC FORCES. BUT NOT ONE STEP BACKWARD. HERE I AM AND HERE I SHALL STAY! THE ONLY

GOAL: TO PLOW! The same issue exhorted every town, every hamlet, to form peoples' militias (see Malefakis 1970: 365–66 or these tactics).

Militancy in Action

Immediately after taking office on February 20, 1936, the So cialists made a clean sweep of the town hall, much as the right ists had done before them. They fired Eusebio Ramos and re stored Francisco Sánchez as sheriff. They named Pablo Moreno, one of the councillors, to bank town funds. They formed a new commission to reassess property taxes, which property owners of the previous council had rigged in their own favor. As noted above, they hired two outsiders to "help" the incumbent secre tary, Francisco Javier Núñez, and a few weeks later they formally fired Francisco Javier on charges of poor conduct, malfeasance, and unwillingness to cooperate with the council. They ordered an inspection of the books and records of the previous coun cil, and they requested the governor to send a delegate to inves tigate and bring criminal charges against it. In other words, they acted as vengefully toward the rightists as the rightists had to ward them at the end of 1934.

The Socialists did not control the local court (Patricio López still served as the justice of the peace) or the Civil Guard, which remained in state control; so they could not suppress the Right as effectively as the Right had repressed them during the bienio negro. Instead, the Socialists deployed their own power—the control of labor—as effectively as they could against Los Olivos's large property owners. The syndicate had reopened in Los Olivos just before the February elections. Organized labor's le gitimacy had been reaffirmed by the Ministry of Labor's March 1 decree ordering reinstatement of all workers fired during the bienio negro for union membership or political motivation, as it would be again by later legislation restoring tenants' rights and reestablishing local juntas de policía rural to regulate rural em ployment (*Boletín Oficial*, Mar. 4, June 15, and July 14, 1936). But the Socialists organized labor much more militantly than before. They harassed independent artisans who did not join the union, forcing them to do menial tasks for the council usually done by women, such as mopping the floors of the town hall after council meetings. They also enforced Sunday as a secular day of rest and purportedly beat up at least one rightist carpenter who continued to work on Sunday.

The Socialists' most militant deployment of labor was the practice of *repartimiento*. The syndicate divided union workers into groups and assigned them to employment on larger estates whether the owners accepted them or not. If not given work, workers were to sit with their tools at the landowner's doorstep and demand their wages on Saturday anyway.

The repartimiento was a new practice, not explicitly sanctioned by law, although it was widely used, for example, in Ronald Fraser's Mijas (1972: 106, 122). Not to be confused with earlier *alojamiento*, in which proprietors took on workers as an act of charity in times of famine, it had a precedent, instead, in the legally sanctioned stipulations of the bases de trabajo that forced employers to hire workers. Employers had abrogated the bases during the bienio negro. In the city of Huelva, the municipal government distributed unemployed labor to employers in this way on March 13, 1936, but the next day Governor Miguel Luelmo Asencio (of the Unión Republicana party, who had taken office just two weeks earlier) suspended the practice (see *El Liberal*, Mar. 13 and 14, 1936). But under current circumstances, this meant little in Los Olivos. With the Socialists back in power, labor once again held the upper hand. Leftists in Los Olivos still believed that they did not have the power to dispossess landowners of their property; to do so would have required the backing of the state. But they could enforce employment through the repartimiento.

This militant deployment of labor is what villagers remember most about the spring of 1936 since it struck deeply at the autonomy of property owners. Rightist property owners experienced the repartimiento as a threat to their ability to manage their property and thus as a step toward its dispossession. "You were no longer the owner of what you possessed," one proprietor reminisced to me. "If you wanted someone to prune your trees, the syndicate would force you to hire someone who couldn't even dig a ditch." The forceful repartimiento of labor thus threatened proprietors' autonomy in the same way that the Socialists' bases de trabajo had threatened their autonomy in 1933—by questioning the prerogative of a proprietor to be free from any other man's beck and call. But the repartimiento differed from the bases in that local authorities enforced the repartimiento on their own authority.

Thus, when Enrique López, Celestino's cousin from a neighboring town who owned land in Los Olivos, fired some Los Olivos workers, the syndicate sent a team of these and other workers onto his land to prune the olive trees, disregarding Enrique's objections to the courts. And one week, when Celestino López tried through a court officer to pay the wages he claimed to owe the laborers assigned to him, rather than the wages they demanded, they and their leaders refused to receive the pay. On its own authority, the syndicate was pressing the revolution it had begun three years earlier in the relation of employee to employer, if not in the ownership of capital.

Theoretically, the state still exercised legitimate dominion over the region, but in fact the Socialists seem to have shifted the balance of initiative to the local level more than ever before. Throughout Spain, the Left and the Right increasingly took matters into their own hands in these months that Preston (1978) refers to as the abandonment of legalism. As happened in many other towns, it is likely that the Socialists formed a *guardia cívica*, a local vigilante group, to back themselves up. The provincial governor, Miguel Luelmo Asencio, clearly saw these groups as a threat to the state, arguing that "the state is the absolute owner of the sources of legitimate rule"; he reserved the prerogative of appointing local authorities and ordered such groups to disband. Although the Socialists carried out the decrees and legislation restoring fired workers to their jobs, reinstating juntas de policía rural, and reestablishing local commissions to administer public works, in fact, as we have seen, they assumed more direct and militant control of labor relations. As the summer harvest of wheat and cork began, the governor appealed to mayors not to interfere in the harvests, as property owners complained to Madrid they were doing. In Los Olivos, the Socialists refused to take action against youths who threw rocks at Patricio López's Casino, which the Socialists were trying to boycott, leading

Patricio to charge that they were contributing to the disruption of public order and engendering disrespect of the authorities.

Thus, the Socialists were taking the law into their own hands in a manner much more consistent with the anarchist ideas of legitimate authority. Anarchism held that legitimate governance should spring from consent and be exercised on the level of the municipality, rather than being imposed from above by the state.

The Socialists engendered a sense of utopian expectations similar to those that prevailed elsewhere in Andalusia (Jackson 1965: 222). Many people of the village believed that a time was coming in which all property would be shared. There were no land invasions in Los Olivos, as there were in nearby Aracena. But the more militant leftists went into the countryside to bring back cows and goats to slaughter and distributed the meat free, even to rightist families. Poor people remember these as days of feasting, but wealthier villagers claim that a lot of meat was wasted, that there was a glut of fresh meat, more than could be eaten.

Finally, Los Olivos Socialists were for the first time exhibiting overt anticlericalism. Before 1936, the Socialists' anticlericalism had been halfhearted. When the Socialists had first come to power in Los Olivos in 1933, they did not take a militantly anti-clerical line but emphasized, instead, the separation of church and state embodied in Article 3 of the Republican constitution. The Republic had secularized cemeteries some time before, and the preceding council, under representatives of property, had already assumed the cemetery's management. Republican legislation had restricted public religious functions, but this seems to have meant little in Los Olivos. The councillors hotly denied an accusation by the archbishop of Sevilla that the clergy in several Huelva towns, including Los Olivos, were being taxed for ringing the church bells. It is true that the Socialists charged their predecessors with provocatively parading the image of San José during his fiesta through the village streets under the guard of public forces and with using public moneys to pay priests for sermons during the fiesta, but during their first incumbency, after some debate, the Socialist councillors decided to continue the council's sponsorship of the fiesta of San José.

Matters had changed by 1936, however. Practicing Catholics found themselves harassed if they attended mass or tried to have their children baptized. For the first time in history, the council decided not to sponsor the public festivities of San José (which they allowed the priest to celebrate only in the church); rather they decided to sponsor a school festival to begin several weeks later on the fateful 18th of July.

EIGHT

The Levantamiento and the War Years

ON JULY 18, 1936, rural Spaniards learned by radio of the *Levantamiento*, the military uprising against the Republic that many had realized was in the making after the Popular Front electoral victory. As popular forces rose to defend the Republic in Madrid, Barcelona, and other major cities, most people thought that the uprising would be put down in short order, just as the abortive coup led by General José Sanjurjo had been put down in 1932. But within days, it became obvious that the uprising was more serious and that the insurgents were making headway in Castile, Galicia, Navarre, and Aragón, as well as in Andalusia.*

Dramatic developments gripped western Andalusia. General Gonzalo Queipo de Llano flew in crack troops from Spanish Morocco to consolidate his seizure of Sevilla on July 27 and of Huelva on July 29. The involvement of the Moroccan troops particularly chilled Spaniards because of the ruthlessness the *Moros* had shown under Franco in the taking of Oviedo on October 12, 1934, during the Asturias Revolution. Queipo de Llano immediately imposed martial law and took harsh measures against the Left (Herr 1971: 177).

The insurgents then swept close to the Portuguese border into Extremadura to join up with a column from the north, seizing Badajoz on August 14 and slaughtering hundreds of prisoners in the bullring. French, English, and Portuguese reporters wit-

---

*José María Gironella's novel *Los cipreses creen en Dios* (1953) evokes a sense of the widespread Spanish anticipation of the coup attempt.

nessed the taking of Badajoz and publicized the atrocities in the international press (Jackson 1965: 268–69).

In the province of Huelva, meanwhile, having secured the capital, the insurgents moved toward the interior. As a tactic for overcoming organized resistance in the Riotinto mining zone, they first outflanked it to the north by taking Aracena on August 18 and sweeping through the towns of the Sierra. Then they closed in on resisting miners at Riotinto, Nerva, El Cerro de Andévalo, and other towns, consolidating control of the province by late September.*

The Levantamiento had unfettered revolutionary and anticlerical fervor in Los Olivos, threatening landlords' property and resulting in the burning of the church. But when the Nationalists arrived, they took over the town without resistance; not a shot was fired. Harsh reprisals against the Socialists ensued nonetheless, directed by Falangist occupiers and their collaborators within the town. Although Los Olivos passed the Civil War years far from the Republican-Nationalist front and was never involved in armed conflict, it suffered the insurgents' systematic terrorism and repression of the civilian population in conquered territory behind the lines. Thirty-eight Socialist men—12 percent of the town's adult males—were killed within the first year of the war, and their family members were terrorized and humiliated.

In this chapter, I chronicle the events of the Levantamiento and Civil War in Los Olivos and the manner in which villagers experienced and remember them. Town Council and judicial records understandably did not document events of the period that could be considered atrocities or crimes. Consequently, my chronicle draws much more heavily than the previous chapters on oral accounts and on a systematic reconstruction of the fates of townfolk known to have lived in Los Olivos just before the war from the evidence of census and civil registry records. Many details came to light in interviews we conducted with villagers to learn about their family history and to fill gaps in our knowledge of what had happened to relatives documented in earlier records but missing in later ones. This approach and other clues made it possible to compile a list of the men who lost their lives and

---

*See Suero Sánchez (1982) for a gripping account from an anarchist viewpoint of what transpired at El Cerro de Andévalo.

EL OBRERO DE LA TIERRA

Órgano semanal de la Federación Española de Trabajadores de la Tierra • Redacción y Administración: Santa Engracia, núm. 7. • Teléfono 32 437

2.º Batallón de Trabajadores de la Tierra

En una semana transcurrida, 800 campesinos acuden a nuestro llamamiento

Nuestra previsión y nuestros deseos se han visto cumplidamente satisfechos. A nuestro primer llamamiento, los campesinos han acudido sin vacilar. No dudábamos nosotros de que así fuera. Conocemos de sobra el espíritu de heroísmo que los anima. Tan grande como su espíritu de sacrificio. Y a éste nadie podrá igualar. Pues bien: si algo es preciso buscar para contrarrestarlo, ese algo es su heroísmo. No es que nos ciegue el cariño. Pregúntese a los responsables de los batallones de campesinos que están luchando en el frente desde que la sublevación fascista dió comienzo. Mejor aún: pregúntese a los milicianos de profesión. Y que ellos confiesen quiénes, de cuantos milicianos vayan a sus órdenes, ponen a mayor altura el precio de una vida.

Por eso nosotros confiamos en que, a la hora de llamar a los que aún no estaban enrolados, la respuesta no se tardaría. Y ahí están. Ha sido tal la prontitud con que han acudido, y tal el número de camaradas, que nos hemos decidido a abrir el alistamiento en un segundo batallón.

Otra vez, como hace unas semanas, nuestras oficinas se han visto invadidas de camaradas que venían a pedir. Pero, esta vez, también a ofrendar. Y la petición y la ofrenda encaminadas a un mismo fin: ganar la guerra. Pedían un fusil. Ofrecían su vida.

Así son los campesinos españoles. Arrojados de sus hogares, no quieren una vida que les ponga en el trance de mendigar eternamente, buscan la liberación completa. Y, por eso, se lanzan, apenas se les da la voz de llamada, a la reconquista de su hogar perdido.

¡Bien, camaradas! Estamos satisfechos de vosotros. Igual que pensamos estarlo, dentro de breves días, de todos cuantos, de momento, no hagan falta en la retaguardia.

¡A vencer, campesinos!
¡La victoria tiene que ser nuestra!
¡Acudid sin vacilar!

BARDAJANO

¡CAMPESINO! LAS MILICIAS TE LLAMAN

El 2.º Batallón de Trabajadores de la Tierra os espera

The call to the defense of the Republic. After the insurgents swept northward from Huelva and southward from Salamanca to join forces in Extremadura for an assault on Madrid, the Socialist press appealed to peasants to join in the defense of the Republic. For the Socialists of Los Olivos, the appeal was too late. (From *El Obrero de la Tierra*, Oct. 31, 1936, p. 1.)

to confirm and amplify details concerning them in interviews about the war given me by respondents both on the Left and on the Right.

Needless to say, some interviewees were reluctant to talk about events that implicated specific villagers, whereas others had self-serving or vindictive motives for doing so. Some were still afraid to talk about the past; others refused to do so because their memories were too painful or bitter to discuss. I have deliberately rendered a less detailed account than I might have in order to avoid attributing individual responsibility for events that I believe were beyond individuals' power to control, and I have taken pains to honor the desire of some not to have their story told.

The Levantamiento

It was during the Socialists' secular school festival of July 18 that the villagers of Los Olivos learned, by radio, of the Levantamiento. The town's official records are absolutely silent on the eventful month that preceded the arrival of the Falangists on August 22, giving one the impression that the ordinary rule of law had been abandoned. Throughout Spain, both sides were taking matters into their own hands, as did the Communists and anarcho-syndicalists whom George Orwell described in his *Homage to Catalonia*. The most revolutionary undertakings of the Second Republic were under way (Bolloten 1979).

Villagers vividly remember certain key incidents of this period and the euphoria that surrounded them. For the first time, "spirits were heating up and no one knew to what extremes they might go." In the very first days of mid-July following the Levantamiento, leftists began to distribute the goods of nonresident property owners to villagers. Elites from a neighboring town owned large tracts alongside the López family holdings in the southern part of the municipality, and villagers assigned by the Socialists to work on these lands appropriated cattle there to bring to Los Olivos. The local butcher helped them slaughter the cattle and distribute the meat to happy villagers both of the Left and of the Right.

As the seriousness of the Levantamiento became apparent,

militants of the Riotinto area (like their counterparts nationally) began attacks against the church and the Civil Guard. Local militias formed and armed themselves to resist the expected onslaught from the south. Anarchist miners besieged the Civil Guard garrison in Higuera de la Sierra and finally assaulted it with an armored truck, killing the officers. Militant youth of the Federación Anarquista Ibérica (FAI) and the Juventud Socialista initiated a wave of church burnings in the mining area and then in surrounding towns. Militants mined key bridges to prepare to blow them up in the path of the Falangist troops.

Los Olivos's ties to the Riotinto area embroiled the town in these activities as they spread out from the mining zone. Ceferino Santis formed a local militia, although everyone knew its rusty shotguns would be of little use against army forces. Some villagers were later accused of participating in the siege of the Civil Guard in Higuera de la Sierra, a plausible charge, for Captain Sánchez, who had built up the garrison in Los Olivos and directed the wave of repression there in 1935, had been transferred to Higuera de la Sierra to head the garrison there. Teodoro López, a former miner and one of those thought to have helped lay siege to the Higuera de la Sierra garrison, supposedly hid dynamite and bombs left over from the siege to blow up a bridge near the entrance to Los Olivos when troops arrived.

The burning of the church and the statues of saints are what villagers remember most vividly about this month; they interpret the severe measures taken by Falangists a month later in part as reprisals against those participating in it. The Socialists did not burn the church until militants from the mining area insisted that they do so. Some of the older Socialists were reluctant to have the town's treasures destroyed, and they ordered villagers to take the saints' images to their homes for safekeeping before allowing militant youth of the Juventud Socialista to burn the church altars and furnishings. After the fire, they forced some of the rightists to begin cleaning up the blackened, gutted church interior.

The militants held out for destroying the saints' images as well, however, and a few days later the Socialists ordered women and children to carry the images down to the millstream. The more militant leftists harangued fellow villagers to the effect that

"50,000 Peasants Battle in the Front." (From *El Obrero de la Tierra,* Sept. 26, 1936, p. 1.)

the images were nothing but carved limbs of orange trees (*palos de naranjo*). Federico Gómez, whose son was president of the Juventud Socialista, snatched the Virgin's veil to use as a toreador's cape while other militants carrying saints charged at him in a mock bullfight, throwing the vanquished images into a bonfire, as villagers looked on.

In contrast to some parts of southern Spain where priests, property owners, or members of the Civil Guard were shot, however, the militants killed no one in Los Olivos (cf. Suero Sánchez 1982: 76–78; Fraser 1972: 143). It was the burning of the church and saints' images that is remembered on both sides as the most provocative act, one that certainly did not merit the harsh retribution that followed.

And yet, who knew what the militants might do next? In Barcelona and Madrid, people were being taken at night from their homes to the outskirts to be shot. Militants in Aracena had jailed a number of prominent landowners and clergy and threatened worse. A rumor spread among the propertied families in Los Olivos that the militants had drawn up a list of rightists to eliminate. Meanwhile, insurgent General Queipo de Llano, in a July 25 radio broadcast from Sevilla, threatened dire reprisals for any action against rightists:

In various villages of which I have heard, right-wing people are being held prisoner and threatened with barbarous fates. I want to make known my system with regard to this. For every person killed I shall kill ten and perhaps even exceed this proportion. . . . The leaders of these village movements may believe that they can flee; they are wrong. Even if they hide beneath the earth, I shall dig them out; even if they're already dead, I shall kill them again. (Quoted in Fraser 1979: 128)

Within four short weeks, it had become obvious that the Falangist forces would soon arrive. Although the mining towns had not fallen, they were on the defensive. Los Olivos's militia would be of no use in protecting the town. By August 18, the insurgents had reached Aracena, freeing the property holders and clergy that leftists had jailed there. Reprisals had begun, and Los Olivos inadvertently suffered its first victim—a slightly retarded young man on an errand in Aracena whom the occupying forces shot when he failed to heed their orders. Leaders of the syndicate and the Juventud Socialista prepared to flee. They knew that town rightists held them responsible for the militant managing of labor, acts against property, and the burning of the church. They assumed that only they would be singled out for reprisals by the occupying forces, and so they left their families behind with reassurances that nothing would happen to them. In this they were wrong.

The troops encountered no resistance when they entered Los Olivos on August 22. The Socialist Town Council and most of the village had decamped to the countryside because of the reports of how ruthlessly *Los Moros*, the Moroccan regulars, had seized other towns. From a promontory, they watched the Falangists arrive. Ceferino Santis had left the Socialist flag flying on the church steeple, insisting that "this town will remain socialist to the last minute!" In the village, prominent rightists—Patricio López (justice of the peace), rightist ex-councillor Isidoro Moreno, former mayor Tomás Nogales, and Teodoro Ramos (a rich barber)—and only a handful of sympathizers awaited the troops. The troop commander invested Tomás, Isidoro, and Teodoro with the authority of the Town Council and appointed Francisco Javier Núñez and Eusebio Ramos to their old posts as secretary and sheriff, and he ordered the Socialist flag hauled down.

Meanwhile, the Falangist squadron, guided by Sevilla-educated Inocencio Moreno (who came dressed in full Falangist regalia—blue shirt and pants, leather boots, and a whip), raced around in search of leftists. Under the threat of death, they seized Maximiano Infante, a young mason who worked for Celestino López, and ordered him to point out, house by house, where the leftists lived. Patricio López rescued young Maximiano from this predicament by sending sheriff Eusebio Ramos to do the job. Finding the town almost empty, the Falangists began to break into leftists' houses to requisition beds, taking linens and valuables. They took over the girls' schoolhouse for their quarters. Troops quartered themselves in the *cuartel*, the garrison of the Civil Guard, which became the headquarters of Los Olivos's military occupation.

Within a day or two, the bulk of the occupying troops moved on, and villagers began to return to the town because empty houses were being looted. Everyone was required to report to military headquarters at the cuartel, where the authorities questioned them about the whereabouts and doings of Socialists and other leftists.

It became apparent that the occupying forces intended to remain. Martial law prevailed, directed by Falangists from elsewhere and the Civil Guard, which had been reinforced by a consignment of troops. These, in turn, used local rightists, who collaborated by running the Town Council and local court at their behest. The authorities also began to co-opt other villagers by forming local Falangist squadrons, giving men who cooperated *un mono, un fusil, y un duro*—a uniform, a rifle, and five pesetas per day.

The authorities began to oppress those whom they could hold accountable for the deeds of the Left. In going over the town's accounts, the new councillors claimed to have found that the Socialists had absconded with all the cash reserves. Celestino Munís, the secretary to the Socialist Town Council, who had not fled, was called to account for the missing funds and was beaten. Francisco Sánchez, who had served the Socialist council as sheriff, was horribly battered and died from his injuries.

The Falangists were convinced that Socialist councillors and leading leftist militants were being harbored in people's houses or in the countryside. They began to terrorize Socialists' families to learn their whereabouts. Some men and boys were beaten and whipped in the cuartel or in the church. There were no rapes in Los Olivos, but one day the troops rounded up the leftists' wives and adolescent daughters (among them Librada Moreno and her mother) and marched them to the church, where two barbers were waiting to shave their heads. Those who cried or resisted were given ample doses of castor oil. The women were then put to work cleaning the charred ruins of the church. To humiliate them further, the troops forced them to parade through town as the castor oil took effect, while Falangists jeered at them. These were becoming standard Falangist humiliations for leftists' wives and daughters (see Suero Sánchez 1982: 83).

The terror quickly escalated. Teodoro López, the former miner from Riotinto whom Falangists suspected of having hidden explosives left over from the siege of the Civil Guard garrison at Higuera de la Sierra, was called to military headquarters. According to a secondhand account, the authorities beat Teodoro and forced him to consume a bucket of oil and bread. Then they took him to the roadway to force him to reveal where he had hidden the explosives. Finally, they released him, only to shoot and kill him as he fled downhill toward the village, as though he were a fugitive.

A day or two later, the Falangists organized villagers in the first of many manhunts to track down fugitives in the countryside. These *batidas* employed the Andalusian hunting tactic of stringing men out in a line that advanced through the woods, forcing game out in front. One of the villagers sighted Juan José Gonzales, a Socialist councillor, in hiding but kept his mouth shut. Another villager also noticed Juan José, however, and shouted, "A rabbit is getting away from us." Juan José was dragged into headquarters, beaten, and shot.

On the ordinarily joyful morning following the annual pilgrimage to the shrine of the Virgen de los Angeles, patroness of the Sierra, in Alajar, barely half a month after the Falangist occupation, the authorities sent villagers out with a list of ten men and boys, all brothers and fathers of militant Socialists and youth of the Juventud Socialista, to bring to the cuartel. Family members were told that the men were being hired to prune olive suckers on one of the larger estates. This was a veiled taunt, in that such pruning was one of the jobs for which Socialists had forced workers on proprietors. When the men arrived at the cuartel, the Falangists trucked them off, not to work but to a nearby town to kill them, but the authorities there refused to grant them permission to execute the group in territory under their jurisdiction. The Falangists trucked the group back to the edge of Los Olivos, tortured and shot them, and then hauled their bodies to be buried clandestinely in an unmarked grave in the cemetery.

This was the first mass killing; two others followed, one of a group of men first imprisoned in Aracena and then killed at the end of September 1936, and one of seven men from Los Olivos and many others rounded up by truck from nearby towns and killed en masse in reprisal for the ambushing of a Falangist in a nearby town. Once again, those killed were primarily brothers and fathers of principal leftists rather than the principals themselves.

Other leftists met death individually. Falangists sent Felipe Moreno with the family truck ostensibly to run an errand for them in Riotinto; there he was seized and shot. Various victims were hunted down in the countryside and killed. Domingo Santis, a Socialist councillor, was caught in one of the batidas and shot by an officer of the Civil Guard with a fine Cuban pistol that Domingo had confiscated from his rightist brother-in-law while in office; the captain kept the pistol. Federico Santis, who had collected taxes for the Socialist Town Council, was found hiding in one of the grain mills and shot against the mill door, where the bullet holes still show. Gregorio Núñez, another ex-councillor and syndicate leader, was traced to a country hut near El Cerro de Andévalo in the mining zone, where he was burned to death when his pursuers set fire to the hut to flush him out. Celestino Munís, the Socialist secretary, was shot at the gateway to the cemetery. Pablo Santis, son of the Socialist mayor and barely 17 years old at the time, arrived at the garrison too late to be sent out with the last group massacred. The Civil Guard confined him overnight and then dragged him out to the cemetery to execute him. He put up such a fight that they shot him along the way against the wall that now marks *El Camino de Todos*, the path of death that all tread sooner or later.

Quirks of fate spared a few leftists. Saturnino Santis, a young militant, was hauled off to prison in Aracena together with other victims of the second mass execution. His brothers, desperately seeking to free him, learned that a doctor they had known years before in Riotinto when the family worked there had been sent to Aracena as a prominent Falangist; they convinced him to intercede for Saturnino. Felipe Ramos, who had run the leftist bar, was saved by the Virgen de Amparo; he had disobeyed orders to bring the saint's image to the river to burn, and when the Falangists found the image in his house, they spared him temporarily. After the second mass killing, Felipe fled to France or Andorra, never to return.

Gregorio Iglesias suffered a less happy end, one of many to die in jail after the war was over. A militant miner, he had been

El Camino de Todos. The path that all will follow; the path to the cemetery is so marked today. (Photo from 1963–64 fieldwork season.)

one of the ten on the list of victims drawn up for the first mass killing, but since he was quite deaf, he did not hear Falangists pound on his front door to round him up. Thinking that he was at his in-laws, the Falangists went off to find him there. Someone tipped Gregorio off, and he fled to the countryside, hiding for two days in an orange tree. Finally, he made his way to Nerva, where his sister hid him for three years in a cubbyhole in her house. He surrendered at the end of the war when amnesty was offered to leftists, but he was sentenced to a 30-year prison term for "armed rebellion" and died in the Segovia penitentiary in 1942.

Several other leftists who escaped killing in the war ended up in jail; some died there. José Antonio Ramos, the first Republican mayor, was taken prisoner after refusing to abandon his wounded son, José Antonio, in a manhunt late in the war. Father and son were imprisoned in Huelva but released to "supervised custody" in Los Olivos in the early 1940's. Shortly after his release, the younger José Antonio died of a foot wound and of an illness contracted in jail. The father lived another ten years in Los Olivos with his daughter.

Other principal leftists who escaped the initial onslaught by fleeing were imprisoned at the end of the war in 1939. Claudio Teodoro Santis, an ex-councillor, was captured in hiding toward the end of the war and sent to prison, where he died of beatings and illness. Pablo Moreno, Socialist ex-councillor and ideologue, fled to Madrid at the time of the Levantamiento and fought for the Republic. At the end of the war, when amnesty was offered to Republican troops who surrendered, Pablo made his way back to Los Olivos and turned himself in. As thousands of Republican soldiers discovered, the promise of amnesty was false. Local Falangists charged Pablo with participating in the siege of the Civil Guard at Higuera de la Sierra and tried to have him sentenced to death. A tribunal jailed him in Huelva, instead, where he served three years of a much longer term. He was released when his mother and sister were able to ransom him by bribing corrupt officials. Pablo dared not return to Los Olivos and lived out his life in Sevilla, instead. Zacarías Gómez, president of the Juventud Socialista, also served a prison term after the war and was eventually released to live in a town in Córdoba, where he married and had children.

A few of the leading leftists escaped death or imprisonment by not returning to Los Olivos at the end of the war. Eusebio Santis, an ex-councillor, fled to France, where he and many other Spanish refugees lived out the war years (see Stein 1979 on Spanish Republicans in France). He returned to Los Olivos only in the 1950's and lived out the rest of his life in the pueblo. Ceferino Santis, the Socialist leader and ex-mayor, also returned to the area after living 15 years near Madrid. By then, his wife and surviving children were living in Fuenteheridos, where Ceferino joined them.

The Plight of the Vanquished

The story of the Levantamiento and the subsequent war years belongs as much (if not more) to the 116 family members who survived (see Figure 8.1) as it does to those who perished at the hands of the Falangists. For these vanquished survivors—if not for other villagers—the humiliation, grief, and fear of the initial reign of terror lasted throughout the Civil War and longer, aggravated by their being forbidden to mourn their dead, by the covering up of the executions, and by the loss of possessions.

As we have seen, the Falangists paraded Socialists' wives and daughters, shorn and incontinent from having taken doses of castor oil, through the town and forced them to clean the charred church. The authorities forced all young men, including those from victims' families, to participate in the imposition of martial rule. Repeatedly, they placed leftist youngsters in front of Falangist squadrons on manhunts in the countryside so that leftist fugitives would not fire on the hunters; indeed, calling young leftists to a batida was the ruse used to round up the second batch of leftists to be executed.

Survivors remember that young men had to dig graves for the victims at the cemetery, often for relatives. Jesús Muñoz was one of the young men that the Town Council minutes record as having been paid for "cemetery service." He probably learned too much about who was responsible for killings since he was among the last batch executed en masse. Another young man went mad after being forced to dig his brother's grave.

Probably more painful than any other humiliation and terror that the women recall was the fact of having turned sons and husbands over to the authorities to kill. It was women who opened the door to Falangist forces, women who had to tell the Falangists where absent husbands or sons were to be found, and women who passed on summonses to their loved ones from the authorities.

María Sánchez heard the Falangists outside her door trying to decide where to take her husband and son to kill them. But she could do nothing to save them because they were in her house, and there was only one exit, the door outside which the Falangists were congregated. Natalia Nogales, wife of the Socialist

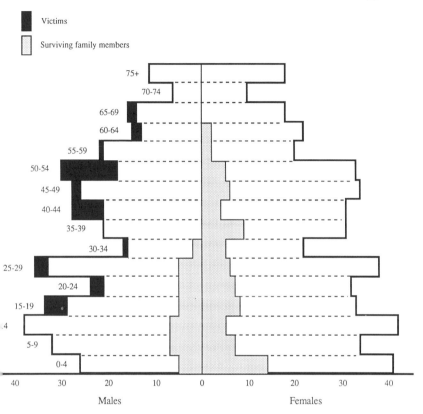

Fig. 8.1. Victims and the Vanquished in the Los Olivos Population. Corresponding to the population of Los Olivos just before the Levantamiento, the pyramid shows the 38 men killed in 1936 in black. The immediate family members of those killed (widows and children of adult victims, parents and younger siblings of victims as yet unmarried) are shaded in grey at the center of the pyramid in this and subsequent figures. The population of Los Olivos in 1936 was reconstructed from census and family history materials.

mayor, was told that her son Pablo was wanted at headquarters to form part of a manhunt. She did not know that men were being rounded up for execution. When Pablo returned from working in the field, she hurried him off to the cuartel without letting him stop to wash up. Pablo was too late to join the batch to be executed, so the authorities jailed him. Expecting him to return, Natalia waited all night for him on her porch. It was only the next day, when she heard the Falangists drag him screaming to the cemetery to be shot, that she realized in horror what was happening. Another woman's husband was out working in the fields when the Falangists came to his house to get him. The Falangists made her come along with them to call her husband, thus making him identify himself to his killers.

Although the war raged far from Los Olivos in 1937, Falangist deeds sustained the terror with which survivors experienced the initial occupation. The province of Huelva had fallen quickly to the Nationalist insurgents and remained in their power throughout the Civil War, but the region experienced systematic terror to discourage resistance. Los Olivos was nowhere near the Nationalist-Republican front, but there were fugitives in the countryside that the insurgents had not hunted out. Some of these fugitives hid out in a cave near the crest of the ridge high above Los Olivos. They dared not build fires to cook or to warm themselves in winter lest the smoke give them away; instead they used charcoal for fuel, stealing it at night from where it was made at the other end of the municipality. They could do so because the insurgents did not fully control the countryside. Indeed, in some parts of the Sierra Morena—proverbial bandit land of which the Sierra de Aracena was a western extension— fugitives held out for more than a decade after the end of the Civil War.

Terror helped the Falangists root out and control fugitives. In effect, they held leftist families hostage to discourage fugitives from undertaking any resistance. Sending young family members out in front of the batidas to hunt down fugitives was part of this strategy. Threatening women and children was another. Falangists never raped or killed women of leftist families in Los Olivos, but they repeatedly violated the integrity of their homes on the pretext of searching for fugitives. One day the captain of the Civil Guard lost himself in the countryside during a manhunt. When night fell and he had not yet returned, leftist women and children were told that they would all be shot if anything happened to him. Librada Moreno remembers spending this night in terror on the balcony of an uncle who might be able to protect her. Fortunately, the captain turned up the next day unharmed.

Humiliations aggravated the atmosphere of fear. The authorities forced women and children, as well as men, to do menial services for them, much as the leftists had forced degrading jobs on rightist men a few months earlier. Guadalupe Nogales, widowed in the final mass execution, told us how she had to work as a maid in the quarters of the Civil Guard. Felisa Mora, the mother of ex-councillor Pablo Moreno and of Felipe, the young truck driver that the Falangists sent to his death in Riotinto, had to work as a servant for the household of one of the Civil Guard. That these women came from once wealthy families added to the gall of doing menial labor for people they saw as killers.

Most aggravating to the vanquished is their perception of how the authorities tried to cover up loved ones' deaths, refusing to let survivors mourn. It was a policy of the Nationalists to hide the bloodbath from the eyes of the world. Authorities conducted executions in out-of-the-way places. Villagers usually learned about executions when they found blood or freshly dug dirt in the cemetery. But the authorities maintained the fiction that certain victims were still alive. They did not register their deaths. They would not allow victims' families to mourn publicly. They continued to "search" for victims in their homes. Draft records from 1937 show that after killing one young man in 1936, they called him up for the draft and declared him a fugitive because he did not appear. They summoned victims to participate in manhunts and harassed widows about their whereabouts. One young woman retorted that the captain of the Civil Guard knew perfectly well where her husband was; the captain then called her in to headquarters to try to force her to sign an affidavit that her husband had died a natural death. Meanwhile, the vanquished had to lead their lives as though nothing had happened, however deep their grief. Many of the deaths were never officially acknowledged. After Franco's death, the widows and orphans of leftist war victims were finally allowed to apply for pensions; only then were some of the deaths finally entered in the Los Olivos civil registry.

Survivors bitterly remember other incidents of official cruelty. Claudio Gómez blamed the Falangists for his sister's agonizing death from gangrene after four days' labor in a breech birth. He claims that the two village doctors refused to operate on her and that local authorities refused to send her to a hospital in Sevilla because her dead father and brother had been leading leftists.

Finally, most of the vanquished lost possessions to other villagers during and after the war. Many household possessions were stolen in the initial looting. But losses soon extended to real property. A Falangist decree of August 18, 1936, permitted the occupying forces to appropriate and sell property of victims to pay for alleged crimes. The decree was amplified and distributed in Huelva's *Boletín Oficial* on September 17 together with advertisements from printing presses offering forms to facilitate confiscations. In Los Olivos, local rightists bought several victims' houses and farmlands under this provision. Wealthy families also took advantage of the plight of the vanquished to buy up additional property. When surviving leftists were jailed after the war, corrupt jail officials allowed their families to ransom prisoners for early release. Some of the vanquished sold most of their remaining property to other villagers to raise the ransom. Meanwhile, the vanquished could do nothing about petty despoliations, about pigs stolen from the sty, potatoes dug out of the garden at night. Even if they learned through gossip who the thieves were, they knew it was useless to complain to the Civil Guard.

Assessing Blame

Villagers clearly attribute major responsibility for the Falangist retribution to outsiders. Although they were guided by Inocencio Moreno, it was Falangists from outside the town who accompanied occupying forces, organized townfolk into squadrons for drills and manhunts, and directed the repression. The mass executions followed higher orders that gave local authorities a quota of people to kill. The Civil Guard, all outsiders, were instrumental in the arrests and executions; one captain is blamed for ten deaths. Villagers know that other towns also experienced harsh repression. Thus, they implicitly recognize that the repression followed from what historian Richard Herr (1971: 190) describes as a deliberate Nationalist policy of terrorizing civilian populations behind the advancing front.

Yet the Falangists had their sympathizers, outsiders their collaborators, within the town. Only villagers could have identified the fathers and brothers of leading Socialists and militant youth for Falangists to round up for the first mass execution. Outside authorities invited and usually acted on the denunciations of villagers; only two "witnesses" were needed to back up one of these accusations. The rightists appointed to the Town Council and court were the ones who drew up the lists of those to be killed when orders to fill a quota came from higher up. Villagers, some of them alive today, summoned fellow townfolk to headquarters and helped in the manhunts. Survivors remember these acts as discretionary acts, even though they were ordered from above. Villagers feel that the executions would not have happened at all in Los Olivos if the rightists had interceded on behalf of other villagers. They cite the example of Los Marines, a nearby town where reportedly no executions took place because leading families interceded every time a villager was arrested.

The vanquished do not blame rightist villagers generally for their plight. Villagers remember incidents in which prominent rightists saved the lives of fellow villagers, and they can identify those who refused to collaborate with the Falangists. Many survivors had rightist kin whose assistance and protection they cherish. Many of these kin shared the hardships of the Civil War and its aftermath.

Rather, blame fell to the handful of those whom they saw as the leading Falangist and Nationalist collaborators, particularly to prominent villagers who refused to intervene on behalf of others whom they had the power to save. In contrast to Patricio López, for example, who used his influence to protect Socialist relatives of his future daughter-in-law, Isidoro Moreno refused to save his chauffeur, a fine young man from one of the mining towns, from execution. Village authorities may have been forced to draw up lists of those to kill to meet a quota, but they exercised discretion in drawing the lists up, ironically casting themselves as saints to those they saved and as devils to kin of those they condemned. Many villagers bless Teodoro Martín, who was mayor when an order to execute 20 villagers arrived, because he drew up a list of only seven. Surviving family members of these seven curse him.

As a consequence, each surviving family tends to identify a

particular villager as a *principal horroroso*, the villain responsible for a loved one's death. Sometimes this person would be shunned: Guadalupe Nogales blamed Teodoro Martín for her husband's execution and told him never to speak to her again; thereafter, she not only refused to look at him when they encountered one another in the street, but even made the sign of the cross "as though he were the devil." Some were openly cursed: Rufina Gómez, who held Francisco Moreno responsible for her husband's death, would drop whatever she was carrying if she encountered him in the street to scream curses at him. Thus, the vanquished were themselves filled with rancor against those whom they blamed for acting out of rancor against their loved ones.

Most villagers were shocked by the war and were eager to put these events behind them, but the vanquished could not. Rather, the vanquished experienced the war and its aftermath as a stigmatized underclass in an enforced servitude that one man compared to the Inquisition, a relentless and undeserved persecution from which there was no escape.

NINE

The Uncontested Reign of Property and the Return to "Normality," 1939-1957

DURING OUR FIRST STAY in Los Olivos in 1963, the mayor described to us some of the town's experiences of the Civil War and its aftermath: "After July 18, 1936, was when the miners from Riotinto came and burned the church. But soon the military came, and it then was a matter of the Communists fleeing before the army. There were no battles here as there were in Santa Ana and Riotinto. Once the military passed through, order was restored, and little by little things have returned to normal since then." Indeed, the "normality" of peasant smallholder life seemed to prevail.

A few years after our visit, a massive emigration to the cities began—to Huelva, Sevilla, Madrid, and above all faraway metropolitan Barcelona—sweeping away the cloak of normality from village life. It was only when we began to reconstruct the exodus and its social history that we learned about the widows and children of Civil War victims, who for the most part had left the village before 1960, and about the part that they had played in the earlier emergence of "normal" village life.

This chapter and the next concern the postwar experiences of the vanquished Civil War survivors. What happened to them is of more than human interest because it sheds light on postwar developments involving the entire pueblo that help to deconstruct the apparent normality of village life in the 1960's. My aim is to show how strongly the postwar years were locked in a negative dialogue with the events of the Second Republic, sometimes inverting, sometimes absolutely silencing, the discourse of class relations that had prevailed. Cultivation of smallholdings alongside that of larger, labor-employing properties revived at the expense of the vanquished in the 1940's and 1950's, reestablishing an uncontested reign of property hearkening back to the past, but with a vengeance negating the developments of the Second Republic. Patronage and other social and cultural idioms of the old, pre–Second Republic order reemerged. But the role of the vanquished was more subservient and politically subordinated than was that of workers in the past because vanquished were easy to stigmatize and to exploit. The vanquished had little opportunity to resist other than passively and much reason to appear to conform to the prevailing norms. Not surprisingly, the vanquished were among the first villagers to emigrate from Los Olivos when circumstances changed, leaving behind a pueblo life that appeared all too normal in the uncontested discourse of the victors.

By following the vanquished forward through the postwar years in the pueblo and in migration, I circumvent one of the pitfalls that can beset efforts to reconstruct the past. Were I to reconstruct the past of the pueblo solely on the bases that nonmigrants could afford me, I would risk not only a one-sided view but also the error of misconstruing the "normal" as traditional. A related error in anthropology is that of projecting the present—the ethnographic present—into the past as "tradition." Historians are wary of the analogous problem of anachronism or the more pernicious "Whig interpretation of history" (Butterfield 1965), the antidote to which is to take the past on its own terms rather than on modern terms. Historical demographers recognize the related error of bias in retrospective sampling, in which the course of events is reconstructed on the basis of those who survive them, failing to take account of the experience of those who do not. By the design of our larger study, in which we take the Los Olivos population of 1950 as a baseline for subsequent family history, we endeavor to avoid this bias. Taking similar pains to follow pueblo Socialists and their family members forward from the Second Republic, some to their death, others through the postwar era both in and out of pueblo life, I seek to cast new light on postwar pueblo experience and to afford a perspective different from that of existing Spanish ethnography.

The Socialists, by attempting to invert the power of proprietors and employees in the Second Republic, had mounted an attack on the very foundations of the social order by calling the ownership of property into question as a legitimate basis for the relations of production. The Nationalists restored the propertied class to power in Los Olivos, and the postwar circumstances and policies of the Franco regime sustained them in that position for at least two decades. The period was one of an uncontested reign of property in several senses. First, the postwar famine and state efforts to revive agriculture to alleviate food shortages favored landowners, especially those in a position to intensify production by employing cowed workers. Labor-intensive farming revived in Los Olivos earlier than elsewhere and actually flourished during the early 1950's. Second, along with the revival, the social relations of production reaffirmed a stratification based on differential ownership of property. While the gap between those who lacked and those who held property grew, egalitarian and hierarchical relations of complementary exchange and patronage reemerged among the latter group, much along the lines that had prevailed before the Second Republic. Finally, the norms of the propertied class, no longer contested through agrarian conflict, reasserted themselves in social life.

The Revival of Agriculture

The importance placed on agriculture in the Franco regime's economic nationalism conditioned its revival in Los Olivos. The Civil War had eroded the production infrastructure; this and droughts in the early 1940's confronted the country with severe food shortages that necessitated massive importation of wheat. Yet Spain's growing isolation during World War II and after the Allied victory precluded a recovery based on international trade. Instead, Franco promoted autarkic development protected by tariffs and import restrictions, stressing agriculture as the key to national economic recovery (see Carr and Fusi 1981: 48–53).

In particular, the regime promoted the style of agriculture epitomized by smallholding Castilian wheat producers, many of whom had supported the Nationalist movement. In a patently negative dialogue with the Second Republic, the regime declared Spain a "state of smallholders" in repudiation of the "republic of workers" it had overthrown. With an ideology that Eduardo Sevilla Guzmán (1979: 141) has termed *soberanía del campesinado* (idealization of the peasantry), it heralded the supposedly natural virtues of smallholding family producers—liberty, wisdom, and peace-loving traditionalism—as against the purported vices of urban workers—decadence, disorder, atheism, depravity, and Marxism.

Various of the regime's economic institutions and programs favored agricultural proprietors. The institution that most directly affected Los Olivos was the *Hermandad Sindical Nacional de Labradores y Ganaderos,* a vertical corporative syndicate for agrarian producers. This national syndical organization established a local branch in every agrarian town to implement state agrarian policy. Conceived along the corporatist lines of earlier social Catholicism, this "brotherhood" (known as the "syndicate" in Los Olivos, but not to be confused with the earlier Socialist union) supposedly integrated the interests of employers and workers, who were represented in separate "economic" (employers) and "social" (workers) sections. But in fact property owners dominated the organization in Los Olivos, as elsewhere. The syndicate was run by none other than Patricio López's son, José Antonio, who also served as acting secretary to the Town Council. When social security was later introduced, José Antonio López administered it through the syndicate. This gave him considerable discretion to designate which villagers were "workers" and thus entitled to social security. On the pretext that they "worked" for their parents, José Antonio signed up the children of many propertied families as workers both under social security and in the syndicate, giving control of the social section of the syndicate to propertied interests—an ironic inversion of what the Socialist syndicate had once stood for. Finally, the syndicate had a formal role, together with household heads, in designating town councillors. This further secured the interests of property owners since most decisions affecting agriculture, such as where to build roads and bridges or how to implement controls on wheat production, were made by the syndicate in consort with the Town Council.*

State institutions monopolizing wheat markets and rationing food to cope with postwar famine also benefited agrarian proprietors by placing a premium on their produce. The National Wheat Service set artificially high prices for grain, intensifying its cultivation in Los Olivos. The law required wheat producers to sell all of their harvest to the agency except for a portion for domestic use. Many landowners retained more than the share allowed by law, milling it clandestinely and baking bread, often at night in small ovens hidden in stables or attics, and hoarding it to feed themselves and their workers. Other locally grown foodstuffs were also at a premium since most staples were rationed until 1952. In Los Olivos, José Antonio López managed the ration cards in his function as acting secretary to the Town Council. Landless villagers could obtain rationed food only at specific stores—one run by a branch of the Mora family, another by José Antonio's brother Patrocinio in the store next to their father's Casino—or from foodstocks kept out of legal circulation by the cultivators in the town.

Although villagers remember the early 1940's as the time of hunger, they also date the revival of agriculture to the decade's later years. Intensive cultivation, in which the vanquished and other poor labored, made possible an expansion in local production that the Franco regime failed to achieve generally until after 1950. In Los Olivos, cropping spread to the crests of the most marginal slopes, and careful masonwork tamed gulleys and irrigated the nooks and crannies of the valley bottoms. Orange, apricot, apple, peach, and pear orchards began to thrive. The fruit business grew apace in the 1950's, and as much as two truckloads a day were shipped to Sevilla during the summer months.

The regime's policies might not have affected local agriculture greatly had not the desperate conditions of the poor and the van-

*See Martínez Alier (1971: 42–47) on the syndical organizations' poor representation of workers' interests in the Andalusian *campiña*. Sevilla Guzmán (1979: 173–76) also discusses these organizations in terms of their subordination of landless workers.

quished made them willing to work the land in return for food and little more than starvation wages. The ranks of the poor had grown in the immediate wake of the Civil War, swelled by refugees from other areas and by the widows and orphans of the slain dissidents. Even wealthier Socialist families became impoverished as the victors despoiled their property. Ration records for 1941 and 1945 show that some refugees came from the mines, most of them families with relatives in Los Olivos. The polluted farmland around the mines produced little, and people were dying of starvation there. Others were former villagers who returned from the cities, where food was also short.

The plight of these poor was pitiful. Famine and disease took a heavy toll in Los Olivos among all age groups (see Figure 9.1), but particularly among the vanquished. In 1940 and 1941, when the state rationed food in tiny amounts and almost no other food was available, families with smallholdings subsisted on a crude bread made of acorns, corn, or chestnuts and on what they grew in their gardens. But many of the vanquished, lacking even gardens, were reduced to more desperate alternatives. At least three widows smuggled contraband coffee from Portugal to sell on the dangerous black market that accompanied rationing. When two of them were caught and jailed, the Town Council supplied funds to help feed their children. Poor villagers, several of them survivors, foraged clandestinely in the countryside; court records show that many were caught and fined by the Civil Guard.

Under these conditions, the poor accepted almost any employment in which they would be fed. Most of the vanquished accepted work from other families as domestic servants and as field workers. Widows sent their daughters to do childcare and housecleaning for families that would feed them. Young boys herded pigs or goats in return for food. Adult women worked in the countryside, at a fraction of a man's wage, doing agricultural chores ordinarily thought appropriate for men. A fair number of the vanquished took up such work in nearby towns. With one exception, the women and children who left Los Olivos during the 1940's went to neighboring towns to work as servants or shepherds for wealthy families. In a few instances, women who had worked as servants in the 1920's before marrying took up

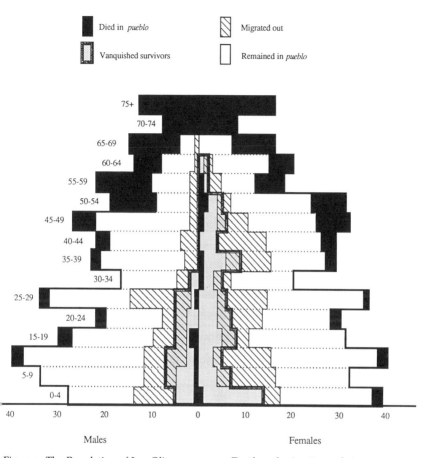

Legend:
- ■ Died in *pueblo*
- ▨ Vanquished survivors
- ▨ Migrated out
- □ Remained in *pueblo*

Age groups (top to bottom): 75+, 70-74, 65-69, 60-64, 55-59, 50-54, 45-49, 40-44, 35-39, 30-34, 25-29, 20-24, 15-19, 5-9, 0-4

Scale: 40, 30, 20, 10, 0, 10, 20, 30, 40

Males   Females

Fig. 9.1. The Population of Los Olivos, 1937–50. Death and migration substantially reduced the Los Olivos population during the war and in the decade that followed. They affected vanquished survivors, shown in the center of the population pyramid, somewhat more than other villagers. Between 1937 and 1950, about 35 percent of the vanquished survivors emigrated, as compared to only 25 percent for the village at large. Vanquished survivors suffered higher death rates among youthful age cohorts, particularly during the postwar famine. (The figure does not show the refugees, 21 women and 24 men, who migrated into Los Olivos during this period.)

service with their former patrons. Several obtained menial work in Fuenteheridos through the patronage of Feliciano Moreno, who had moved there from Los Olivos during the Republic to marry the schoolteacher's sister. That is to say, although removing themselves from the immediate terror and stigmatization of the postwar repression, they left to take up work identical in its servility and in its affirmation of old class relations to work available to them in Los Olivos. Fully one-third of the 102 vanquished survivors had left Los Olivos for nearby towns by 1950 (as compared with about one-fourth of other villagers).

Employment by the propertied class expanded on terms familiar from earlier in the century that reversed the advantages won by workers during the Second Republic. Many smallholding villagers who had not formerly hired domestics or field hands did so after the war. Because some were themselves hard pressed for food, they felt they were helping the vanquished charitably by giving them food in return for work. But the survivors and other poor think back on these jobs as exploitation, as do their counterparts in other areas of Spain (see Buechler and Buechler 1981: 1–13). They describe their work as *esclavitud* (slavery) and the most exploitive of their employers as *negreros* (slave drivers). And they believe that agriculture revived at their expense.

Postwar Stratification

Shortly before 1950, the Los Olivos Town Council established the *Igualatorio Médico*, a fund collected annually to supplement the state physician's salary in order to secure his regular services to the town. The Igualatorio Médico raised 9,030 pesetas for the doctor in its first year; all but 20 of the pueblo's 184 households were assessed on the basis of their ability to contribute, in amounts ranging from 15 to 200 pesetas and averaging 55 pesetas per household.

The variation in these assessments is of interest because it acknowledged stratification in the town, evidently based on property ownership. Statistically, they correlate strongly with the retrospective ranking of households in the 1950 census by wealth that I asked a then–town councillor and later mayor to construct for me (see Table 9.1). They correlate even more strongly with

TABLE 9.1
Intercorrelations of Igualatorio Médico Assessments,
Wealth Rank, and Property Tax, Los Olivos, 1950

	Igualatorio Médico	Wealth rank	Property tax
Igualatorio Médico	1	.68	.77
Wealth rank	—	1	.50
Property tax	—	—	1

NOTE: The intercorrelations of Igualatorio Médico assessments, property taxes, and a retrospective ranking of wealth are indicated by Goodman and Kruskal's Gamma.

property taxes for household heads listed in that year's tax rolls. At the same time, the Igualatorio Médico embodied the egalitarian and hierarchical principles that interpenetrated one another in pueblo public life. Households were the participating entities. Wealthy households, even though likely to consult private physicians in Aracena or in major cities in case of medical need, effectively patronized the fund by contributing substantially more than the poor.

This interweaving of equality and hierarchy exemplified the social order based on property that antedated the Second Republic in many areas of rural Spain and that revived after the war. In this respect, postwar developments in Los Olivos paralleled those in Ibieca (Aragón) before the major agrarian change under Franco in the 1950's, as Susan Harding (1984) has described them. Three realms interpenetrated one another in this social order, the realm of the household, that of egalitarian peasant production, and that of hierarchical capitalist relations of production.

In Los Olivos, as in Ibieca, the household ideally was endowed with enough property to be autonomous. In the case of Ibieca, a stem-family household strove to build up patrimony and to pass it on in dowry and impartible inheritance. Although the household in postwar Los Olivos endured as a conjugal family, it sought similar goals for offspring by building up patrimony for equal-partible inheritance. In Ibieca, as in Los Olivos, "the inheritance system emphasized the hierarchy between parents and children, while the ethic of the good worker stressed action

by all family members for the common good of the family"
(Harding 1984: 111). The autarky of the postwar years, if anything, heightened the significance of self-sufficiency for the autonomy of this entity. Smallholding families in Los Olivos held
their own in these years, sharing in the revival of agriculture and
the gradually increasing prosperity of "normal" life.

Egalitarian relations arose from the theoretical equivalence of
households as autonomous entities within a general stratum.
Reciprocal exchanges of labor among households in peasant
production were perhaps less significant in Los Olivos than
Susan Harding (1984: 87–91) describes them to have been in
Ibieca, although, in both communities, networks of families
shared labor in the annual slaughtering of hogs to stock the
household larder. Rather, households in Los Olivos stressed the
equality of not being outdone publicly by other households in
their general stratum, however much privation within the household this public stance might require. This was a competitive
equality designed to avoid loss of status, reminiscent of the adherence to norms of *honradez* (honor) and *vergüenza* (shame) that
Carmelo Lisón Tolosana (1983: 316–18) describes as guarantee-
ing participation in communal work projects in Belmonte de los
Caballeros (Aragón). Thus, virtually all households collaborated
in such collective endeavors such as the annual fiesta for the
town's patron saint, the activities of the principal religious con-
fraternity, and the Igualatorio Médico.

Hierarchical relations in postwar Los Olivos were not exclusively exploitative. Although they stemmed from the revived
power of propertied elites to control employment in capitalist
relations of production, they also involved asymmetrical exchanges of patronage. John Davis (1977: 132) argues that patronage "occurs whenever men adopt a posture of deference to those
more powerful than they and gain access to resources as a result"; he stresses that clients seek patrons out and that patrons
can allocate honor to clients through their discretion to choose
among aspiring clients. In addition to the gift of work, elites in
Los Olivos and elsewhere in the Sierra de Aracena could bestow
a variety of services and favors, as did their Ibiecan counterparts, such as loans, influence with higher authorities, and access to nonagrarian jobs and education (Harding 1984: 91–93). It

is thus not surprising that even those from families in Los Olivos of more than minimal means sought field and domestic work on patrons' estates and in their households in order to establish and attempt to personalize relations with powerful local and regional elites.

For most citizens of Los Olivos, pueblo stratification balanced autonomy with dependence in this interweaving of egalitarian and hierarchical relations. Stratification was considerably less benign as far as the vanquished and other working-class poor were concerned, however, in that the postwar years deepened the gap between these and other villagers.

The economic divide separating workers from landowners seems to have broadened generally throughout Spain during the first two postwar decades. Although wages rose during this period, living costs outstripped them. Sevilla Guzmán (1979: 175) argues that the slippage in real wages for workers was 40 percent between 1940 and 1950. Carmelo Lisón Tolosana (1983: 126–33) has calculated that living costs for a typical Aragonese landless laborer rose elevenfold from 1936 to 1959 as compared to only a ninefold rise in wages—that is, a slippage of nearly 20 percent in real wages. There is no reason to think that workers in Los Olivos fared any better. The real income of Aragonese small-holders, meanwhile, rose at least 45 percent, and that of holders of more sizable properties rose more than 73 percent.

The marginal and deteriorating economic position of the vanquished as working poor is reflected in the Igualatorio Médico. There were as yet 21 households of former Socialists' widows and orphans living in Los Olivos in 1950. Thirteen among these were concentrated at the bottom of the fee scale (see Figure 9.2), and the remaining 8 made no contributions to the Igualatorio Médico at all. (Most of the other 12 noncontributing households were landless.)

The vanquished were evidently conscious of their deteriorating position, experiencing it in terms of diverging life opportunities for their offspring relative to those for other villagers. Echoing an older discourse of class relations in terms of access to education, several of them told us that one consequence of their plight was that many school-age children of the vanquished families went uneducated, prevented by chores from attending

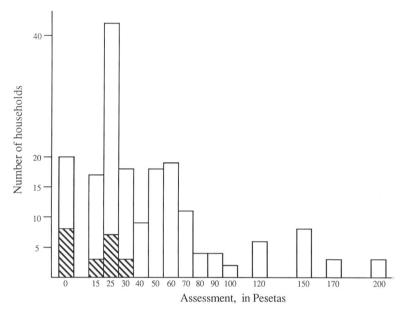

Fig. 9.2. Igualatorio Médico Assessments, 1950. Assessments ranged from 15 to 200 pesetas per household. Crosshatching marks fees paid by households of vanquished Civil War survivors.

school. By contrast, most age mates from propertied families studied at least through the elementary years in Los Olivos, some of them going on to high school and further study outside the town. Many hold Franco responsible for the crime of withholding education from working-class youth.

The vanquished experienced hierarchical relations in pueblo life much more in terms of exploitation than did other villagers, who sought advantages through ties to patrons. Although the vanquished sometimes gained real protection and ultimate advantage through patrons elsewhere (particularly after entering migration in the 1950's, as described in the next chapter), they were in many instances more hindered than helped by local elites. For example, some of the vanquished we interviewed accuse certain former local authorities of withholding the rights and benefits due them as citizens. This they attribute to vengeance for what the Socialists had done years before. Every municipality had a *beneficencia muncipal* to pay for the medical fees and medicines of indigent townfolk, but Patricio López's son José Antonio, the acting town secretary, told Guadalupe Gonzáles, who had six elderly relatives to support as well as two children of her own, that she was not poor enough to receive these funds. As acting secretary of the Town Council and the syndicate, José Antonio López managed the inscriptions through which villagers could get medical and retirement benefits under social security. Whereas many villagers bless José Antonio for obtaining these benefits for them, certain survivors charge that he acted corruptly, allowing close kin and the well-to-do to sign up illegally while excluding many survivors' family members. When Gumersinda López, widowed and with a family of nine to support, tried to sign up for social security as a worker, as other villagers did, she was told she could do so only as a self-employed person, a much more costly way to enroll.

Worse yet, according to some, the town authorities used their power to hinder the efforts of the vanquished to recover and advance. Although many of the vanquished migrated to find better lives, they could not always leave behind the stigma of their political background. Under Franco's dictatorship, the local authorities' certification of a person's good behavior entered into employment and career advancement. The captain of the Civil Guard and other local authorities repeatedly refused to certify the good behavior of a young survivor who joined the army, thwarting his promotions.

Seen from the perspective of the vanquished, stratification in postwar Los Olivos was more intense and more exploitative than it has usually been portrayed in the ethnographic literature on Spain. The vanquished did not share in the gradual improvement of life after the famine years. They found themselves increasingly marginalized with respect to communal institutions and scorned within the networks of local patronage through which others sought to ameliorate their own lot.

Norms and Conformity

More than simply resuming economic dominance in the postwar years, property owners, backed by the Franco regime, articulated village life on their own terms. In doing so, they set the acceptable terms of public social discourse for other villagers as well, limiting how the vanquished could resist and establishing norms to which they had to conform in order to live in the village.

Politics had voiced leftist challenges to the reign of property during the Second Republic. The utter silencing of politics in the postwar years negated the past and shielded propertied elites from opposition to their reign. Initially, the Levantamiento and the Nationalist takeover muted all active leftists and almost all of their allies. Some 50 men in a population of less than 900 in Los Olivos were killed or jailed; only two protagonists escaped by fleeing. As happened in town after town throughout Andalusia, the insurgents eliminated all those "who had ideas." No one remained in the village who dared to articulate what the Left had struggled for.

Subsequently, the regime impugned political activity, while justifying its own corporatist ideology, by holding the politics that led to the Second Republic responsible for Spain's past and present ills. The schoolbooks and sermons of the 1940's and 1950's vilified the "reds" and blamed the Republic on nefarious subversive and foreign influences. The church sent catechists to Los Olivos to preach hellfire to women and children in the cemetery and likened the Levantamiento and Franco's Movimiento Nacional to a crusade. Grade-school textbooks, like the one used in Los Olivos during the late 1950's, traced the evils of the Second Republic forward from the nineteenth century,

when Spain was invaded by foreign ideas, suffered defeat and lost its universal preeminence. . . . During the five years of the Second Republic, Spain's ills worsened. Spaniards were divided up into many political parties; [regional] separatism was preached; Catholics were persecuted, churches and convents burned, the Crucifix was taken out of schools and the teaching of catechism in school was prohibited; class war assumed alarming proportions; no one had personal security because violence was the order of the day; industry and commerce verged on ruin.

It was then that the Falange was born, to save the *Patria*. (Hijos de Santiago Rodríguez 1957: 787–88)

Apathy, cynicism, and fear regarding matters political envel-
oped Spaniards generally, not just those who had had ties to the
Left. Repression and economic hardship so cowed urban workers, according to Carr and Fusi (1981: 88), that they took no risk
of being sacked as "reds" over disputes concerning work or
wages. During the 1940's, repression and the struggle to survive
were such that Spaniards avoided the topic of politics altogether.
Such attitudes continued even in the 1960's. When we asked a
close friend and neighbor about politics several months into our
first stay in Los Olivos, she told us that villagers did not talk
about it any more because people kill one another over politics.
For some, the terror of the repression had been so intense that
they extended a veil of silence over what had happened to them,
hiding the truth even from closest family members. Guadalupe
Nogales, for example, did not tell her daughters how their father
had died; their aunt revealed the truth to them many years later.

Similar attitudes prevailed in many rural areas, for example, in
Galicia, where the Buechlers encountered evasiveness, apathy,
and scathing criticism of politics in their interviews of the early
1970's (Buechler and Buechler 1981: 120). Carmelo Lisón Tolosana (1983: 189–90) found in the 1960's that most of the generation that had suffered losses in the Civil War held politics in absolute discredit, regardless of prior loyalties. The Castilians
studied by Stanley Brandes (1975: 29) in the 1960's in Becedas,
where Falangists purged Republicans in the Civil War, remembered the tragic divisiveness of the era but denied any association with its politics, stressing instead the economic hardships
brought on by the war. In her study of Ibieca just before and
after Franco's death in 1975, Susan Harding (1984: 181) witnessed
the gradual opening up of political discourse among villagers
who had previously been apolitical and apathetic, watching their
words and censoring what they said about government and politics. Even workers in the Andalusian *campiña*, whose political
and class consciousness during the 1970's has been emphasized
by David Gilmore (1980: 79–89), spoke out or acted politically
only with great reluctance or ambivalence during the early 1960's,
according to Juan Martínez Alier (1971: 221–34).

Propertied elites, in the meantime, managed local government

and other community-level institutions such as the vertically organized agrarian syndicate, the ration system, and the religious
confraternities virtually unchallenged.

The enforcing of Catholic religious practice was another way
in which the reign of property asserted the norms of village life.
In the Sierra de Aracena as throughout much of central Spain,
the church and landowners had joined in Catholic agrarian syndicates under Primo de Rivera. Common opposition to anti-
clerical and reformist agrarian legislation during the early Second Republic had reinforced the link. When Franco restored
church jurisdiction over births, marriages, and deaths and over
education, agrarian proprietors helped reestablish devout practices at the local level.

In Los Olivos, the alliance of the propertied class with the
church was quite strong. A church canon was one of the town's
wealthy proprietors, and he linked devotion to agrarian employment. Because of his influence, other proprietors required their
employees to attend church. During the Republic, Socialists had
attempted to enforce Sunday as a secular day of rest. Under
Franco, proprietors inverted this practice by requiring workers
to attend Sunday mass as a condition of employment.

In the postwar period, the propertied class's norms penetrated
yet another area of village life—marriage—bringing greater uni-
formity where previously there had been diversity. Before the
war, there had been considerable flexibility in courtship and
marriage in Los Olivos, with poor women marrying younger
than rich women. After the war, the practices of courtship and
marriage converged to those of the propertied class. This was
more than a minor change since courtship and marriage struc-
tured the entire life cycle and defined idioms of honorable personhood. By exemplifying these practices, the propertied class
affected how other villagers lived and experienced their intimate
lives as well as their public lives.

Marriage at an advanced age after lengthy courtship fit the
frame of a conjugal family system constituted by property. When
they married, a couple had to be ready to assume the obligations
and full responsibilities of managing an independent household. This was because they had to be able to defend and aug-

ment the patrimony brought into marriage on behalf of their legitimate offspring and heirs. Extending courtship and delaying marriage gave a couple time to accumulate the assets a household required to function independently. For some of these assets, a young couple might have to await inheritance; others might be earned. Either course tended to delay marriage. In turn, long courtships postponed the obligations and responsibilities of marriage. In the heyday of late marriage in Los Olivos after the war, courtships might extend from adolescence into the late twenties or early thirties. Courtship was in itself relished as a life-cycle phase free from adult burdens and cares, as Richard and Sally Price (1966*a*, *b*) found when they followed us in field research in Los Olivos in 1964.

Long courtships, in addition to postponing the responsibilities of marriage, demonstrated the personal honor and virtue requisite in a family system constituted by property. Chastity and fidelity in a wife guaranteed the legitimacy of offspring entitled to inherit the family patrimony. Masculine honor protected female virtue within the household. A courting couple demonstrated these attributes in faithfulness to one another through the successive, formally recognized stages of courtship, enacted publicly in evening walks and privately in chaperoned home visits. Courtships that broke up, by contrast, tarnished participants' reputations, particularly the woman's, jeopardizing her ability to marry.

In the decades leading up to the Civil War, there had been considerable variation in marriage by class and party, to an extent that suggests concepts of the family among workers distinct from those of property holders. Poor people experienced marriage differently from the rich, often marrying with only wages to support themselves, whereas richer couples married with established household properties. Just after the turn of the century, poor women born in the 1870's and 1880's were shouldering the obligations of married life up to five years younger than their wealthier agemates (see Figure 9.3). As throughout much of Spain, the age of marriage had been advancing after 1900 (in contrast with the situation elsewhere in Europe where John Hajnal's [1965] "Western European" late marriage had disappeared

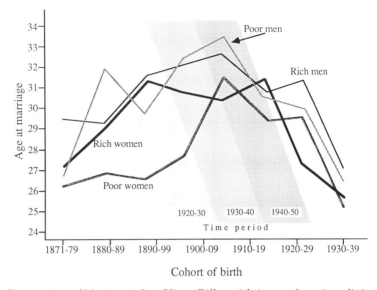

Fig. 9.3. Age of Marriage in Los Olivos. Differentials in age of marriage distinguished wealthy and poor women before the war, with poor women marrying at considerably younger ages. There was no significant differential among men, who married at a slightly higher average age than did women. After the war, the marriage age of poor women converged to the late ages of marriage of wealthier women.

or was receding), but the advance among Los Olivos women was mostly among the rich. By the time of the Second Republic, women from propertied families were prolonging courtships into their early thirties, whereas poor women, particularly those from Socialist families without a history of migration into or out of the town, had continued to marry in their early twenties.*

For men, marriage had varied by class in a different way before the war. Rich and poor men did not differ significantly in the age at which they married before the war, although their age at marriage had gradually risen to above 30 years. But Socialists had been twice as likely as rightists to enter marriage with a pregnant wife near term, possibly thus heralding the ideology of free love of leftists of the era.

*I draw here on a systematic reconstruction of trends in marriage made possible by linking the Los Olivos vital registries of births, marriages, and deaths together with household census and other data.

Matters changed during the postwar reign of property. Marital practices of the left-leaning and the poor converged to those that had become normative for the propertied elite. This falling into step with the propertied class was especially notable in the delaying of marriage among poor women to the same late age as wealthier brides. To be sure, poor women who lost their *novios* (fiancés) in the bloodbath of 1936 and couples awaiting the amelioration of postwar famine before marrying had little choice but to marry late. But the poor of subsequent cohorts of the younger generation continued to conform to the later marriage pattern of the rich.

This generalization of propertied class norms shaped how generations maturing after the war evaluated their members. Idioms of honorable personhood replaced the language of politics and conflict in this discourse. In the 1960's, for example, villagers whom Richard and Sally Price interviewed (1966*a*, *b*) attributed the nonmarriage of certain women to domineering behavior or to purported shameless sexual laxity that broke or prevented courtship. In the case of certain men, villagers attributed nonmarriage to shyness or homosexuality. Scrutiny of the Prices' interview materials shows no evidence that villagers ever mentioned Second Republic politics or Civil War events when explaining nonmarriage or celibacy. Yet an analysis of persons so stigmatized shows that a disproportionate number of them were from former Socialist families. One purported homosexual was a Socialist whose father and brother had taught him to forswear alcohol and tobacco; he did not frequent the bar as other men did in postwar years. Three "domineering" women were sisters who had had to support their mother after their father died and their only brother was shot in 1936. Several "loose" women were closely related to the Iglesias family that the propertied elite had removed from power in 1920 and had purged together with other Socialists in 1936; this family included Socialists whose wives had entered marriage pregnant. Had interpretation in terms of postwar norms of honorable personhood obscured the political dimension of these men's and women's life circumstances or stigmatized them?

Since the 1960's, smallholding agriculture has been marginalized and many villagers have emigrated to cities, bringing an end to the reign of property in Los Olivos. Age at marriage has declined, reflecting the breakdown of a social and moral order constituted by agrarian property. These are part of the next chapter's subject matter.

How did the vanquished respond to the normative pressures of the postwar reign of property? Some villagers clung resolutely to their convictions. One of the few to talk about her past in the 1960's, Leocadia Infante held out against efforts to bring her back into the church. She blamed priests for their complicity in events resulting in the death of her son in one of the 1936 massacres, and she refused for years to attend mass except once yearly at the obligatory Easter rites. She was outraged when the priest persuaded her sister to confess and receive last rites on her deathbed. Like leftist survivors elsewhere, Claudio Gómez, another staunch holdout, waited in vain for vindication to come from the Allies in World War II, then from a hoped-for collapse of the dictatorship, from the return of democracy, and finally from the Socialists' electoral victory. When I interviewed him in 1983, he asked, "Why have the Socialists not sent someone to investigate what happened in this town, as you are doing?"

Other survivors fell prey to postwar propaganda. Tragically, we found that several of the widows and orphans we interviewed had come to believe Franquista vilifications of the Second Republic Left, although they did not include loved ones among the Socialists so scorned. One orphan, for example, although proud that his father had helped build the entrance road to Los Olivos, told us that his father was not a bad man, even though he had been a Socialist. And many widows took pains to tell us that their husbands had not taken part in the church burning, each saying that her husband had been working in the countryside at the time the burning took place.

Additionally, there were the vanquished who attempted to put the past behind them, reinserting themselves and their families as best they could into the social life of the pueblo. Guadalupe Gonzáles made peace with the family of the man she held responsible for her husband's death by attending his funeral, thus rejoining the network of women mourners she had shunned for years; thereafter she and her daughters sustained good relations with that family. In a similar vein, Librada Moreno reestablished ties with a neighbor's family after the death of the man who had wronged her kin in the war. There were, finally, the vanquished who left the pueblo as soon as emigration became possible in the postwar years. These émigrés are the focus of the next chapter.

TEN

The Transformation of Los Olivos
Since the 1960's

IN THE YEARS since our first visit, Los Olivos has been transformed by changes that have altered the face of rural Spain. Much of its agriculture, beginning with fruit and extending to other labor-intensive production, has been abandoned. Many laborers, peasants, and even some landed proprietors have emigrated, leaving behind a diminished and considerably altered community. In bringing to a close my account of Second Republic Socialists, I consider in this chapter the role of their surviving widows and children in these recent transformations.

Their role has been twofold. First, the vanquished began to emigrate to other parts of Spain as early as the 1940's, and they continued to do so as wages rose nationally in the 1950's and owners of large estates began to lay off employees. In some respects, the vanquished paved the way for others to follow in an exodus that swelled to major proportions by the end of the 1960's. Second, property owners who did not emigrate have had to face a loss of status relative to migrants because of the recent marginalization and abandonment of Sierra de Aracena agriculture. Like other migrants, certain of the vanquished retain ties to the pueblo, and they bring a distinct consciousness of the irony of this inversion of status into villagers' sense of their history.

Emigration and Agrarian Change

Scholars of Spain generally agree that the *éxodo rural* of the past 20 to 30 years has differed from earlier migration in scope, causes, and long-term significance for the countryside (e.g.,

Aceves and Douglas 1976; Gregory 1978; Pérez Díaz 1966). Little need be said here about the magnitude of the exodus; in Los Olivos as virtually everywhere, departures from the countryside swelled to a flood sometime in this period. As to the causes and lasting consequences, they involve fundamental transformations of agrarian production engendered by state policy.

Major state policy changes beginning in the mid-1950's lifted the protective isolation of autarky and opened agriculture to capitalist development. The 1953 Pact of Madrid between Spain and the United States initiated the changes. In the wake of the treaty, U.S. aid helped finance imports of farm machinery, and U.S. agricultural experts brought chemical fertilizers into wider use. Producer cooperatives disseminated some of the innovations. The Institute of Colonization began important irrigation projects, and the forestry service initiated erosion control and reforestation programs. These measures received major impetus after 1957, when Franco brought technocrats into the government to coordinate economic policy. Responding to a balance-of-payments crisis, the technocrats lifted autarkic tariffs and opened the country to foreign investment to integrate Spain into the world capitalist economy. Expanded credits hastened capitalization of the agrarian sector (Herr 1971: 247–52; Aceves 1976; Barrett 1974; Carr and Fusi 1981: 55–57).

Urban and industrial growth during the 1950's and 1960's increasingly drew Spanish laborers from the countryside. Construction absorbed large numbers of unskilled workers from different rural areas. The state's first four-year development plan (1964–67), which targeted specific regional centers for capitalist development (among them Sevilla and Huelva), specifically planned for large-scale transfers of labor from the countryside to cities, and subsidized the construction needed to house migrants (Herr 1971: 21; Sevilla Guzmán 1979: 205).

The interaction between migration and the capitalization and commercialization of agriculture varied from one setting to another. In some areas, the tractor was the pivot for all other productive changes, throwing occupational specialists such as blacksmiths, muleteers, and reapers out of work, eroding the asymmetrical dependencies between landed proprietors and their employees, and inducing those who lost work to migrate.

Such seems to have been the case in David Gregory's Estepa (Sevilla) (1972: 317) and Carmelo Lisón Tolosana's Belmonte de los Caballeros (Aragón) (1983: 123–24), communities whose large holdings invited mechanization. Alternatively, as wages rose nationally, rural workers emigrated from regions where employers could not match current wages. Their departure forced producers to mechanize and facilitated consolidation of vacated land into parcels of sufficient size to farm with machinery. Such seems to have been the case in settings of small and medium holdings, such as Stanley Brandes's Becedas (southwestern Castile) (1975). Where land was more marginal, as in Los Olivos, the rural exodus left much land abandoned.

Irrespective of the causal linkages between migration and agrarian development, major changes accompanied them in the material and social relations of agrarian production. Large-scale producers laid off most of their laborers where mechanization was feasible. Machinery and new infrastructure for transport rendered many conventional tools and practices obsolete. Motor vehicles began to displace beasts of burden. Various occupational specialists lost their livelihoods with the advent of commercial products to replace their wares and services. As Susan Harding (1984: 161–63) and Carmelo Lisón Tolosana (1983: 123–24) have stressed, the demise of autarky stripped the autonomous peasant household of much of its meaning (see also Douglas 1975: 162–77). Labor-intensive multiple cropping became uneconomic, stripping households' family labor and ecologically diverse holdings of their value. Even the relation between heirs and legators shifted as youthful members left agriculture to take up new occupations. The capitalization of agriculture tended to shift farming away from the traditional household arena, requiring new kinds of interdependencies to share machinery, land, and labor.

Los Olivos entered the 1960's with a history of relatively steady net outmigration dating from early in the century, but after 1960 such migration swelled substantially. There are several ways of documenting this net outflow and assessing its pace. Military conscription requires local authorities to determine the whereabouts of every young man born in the town who has reached the age of conscription. Those of an enlistment cohort, or *quinta*, who reside elsewhere may enlist there, but officials there must report such a person's whereabouts to authorities in his natal pueblo. The records for Los Olivos, which are continuous from 1905, show that, with the exception of the war years, approximately 15 percent to 25 percent of pueblo-born youth had emigrated prior to enlistment from 1900 through the 1950's (see Figure 10.1). Thereafter the percentage rose to over 50 percent.

More detailed records substantiate similar trends for other segments of the population. Household registers from before 1950 do not survive in the Los Olivos archives. But ration records, in which a card was filed for every person, do exist for 1941 and 1945. The 1945 file was continuously updated through 1952 (when rationing stopped) to show the destinations of those who moved elsewhere and the origins of those moving into the town. The *Padrón de Habitantes*, a household registry compiled anew every five years and updated annually to show changes in civil status as well as additions and deletions because of temporary or definitive change in residence, is an additional resource for documenting emigration. Household registries from 1950 onward are archived in Los Olivos. The civil registry is also a source of information on migration, insofar as birth entries are

Fig. 10.1. Outmigration of Los Olivos Males of Recruitment Age, 1906–80. The figure shows the proportion of village-born males known to have resided elsewhere at the age of military recruitment (20). The materials are drawn from the Los Olivos recruitment records.

annotated to show dates and places of marriage and death when these occurred elsewhere and were made known to Los Olivos authorities (as was supposed to happen routinely). These data, together with interviews to iron out ambiguities, make it possible to track Los Olivos emigration continuously from 1945. They reveal a pattern similar to that suggested by data on migrant military conscripts; namely, a relatively steady exodus of about 1.6 percent of the pueblo's population per year before 1960, rising to nearly double that rate for a period after 1960 (see Figure 10.2).

Net emigration thus dated from before the postwar years and was endemic to Los Olivos's twentieth-century experience (as declining census tallies suggest was true through much of the Sierra de Aracena). During the 1940's, as discussed in the last chapter, most emigrants went to other Sierra de Aracena towns. For the most part, emigrants took up menial jobs such as domestic service or herding. In proportion to their numbers, more of the vanquished Civil War survivors emigrated than did other vil-

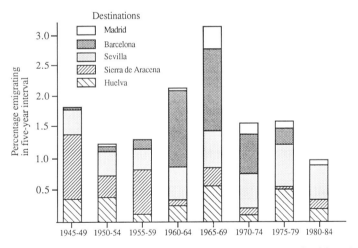

Fig. 10.2. Principal Destinations of Los Olivos Migrants, 1945–84. Migration from Los Olivos to Catalonia swelled in the 1960's and then diminished as economic growth tapered off. Each bar corresponds in height to the proportion of villagers migrating out per year in a given five-year interval. Segments in a bar correspond to the first destinations of these villagers when they migrated.

lagers; most of them never returned. Some of the women who worked for former patrons later followed them to Sevilla.

In the 1950's, urban-industrial development had more of an impact on Los Olivos than did changes in agriculture in that the prosperity of the cities attracted poor villagers even though agriculture was thriving. The exodus from Los Olivos continued, particularly among the vanquished, with more emigrants moving to the provincial capitals of Huelva and Sevilla than before. Migration to more distant urban places also began in the 1950's, in some instances to places young men had come to know in military service. For example, some pueblo youth went to work in Catalonia, unwittingly anticipating the future. Migrants leaving Los Olivos in this decade were youthful for the most part (see Figure 10.3); both women and men in their twenties and early thirties established themselves in jobs and lodgings before calling other family members to join them. The vanquished joined this exodus at twice the rate of other villagers, and by 1960 about two-thirds of the pueblo's war orphans and widows (who with but one exception did not remarry) had left.

Developments in agriculture stemming from state policies began to have undesirable consequences for Los Olivos during the 1960's. Fundamentally, much of the Sierra de Aracena was too rugged to be farmed other than labor intensively. Although motorized transport grew, many farming tasks could not be mechanized. Agrarian development in other regions thus tended to marginalize agriculture in the Sierra (Durán Alonso 1985; see also Roux 1975; statistics from the province, e.g., Instituto Nacional de Estadística 1964, 1974, and Organización Sindical de Huelva 1975, reflect these trends).

One of the enterprises to suffer was the local olive mill, owned by the López family. Using newly available bank credits, a group of entrepreneurs set up a cooperative hydraulic press in Aracena. Three Los Olivos truckers joined the cooperative as middlemen, purchasing olives at harvest time from other villagers to ship to the cooperative for milling. This threw the outmoded local olive press out of business, putting several employees out of work.

The fruit business followed the olive press into ruin because of

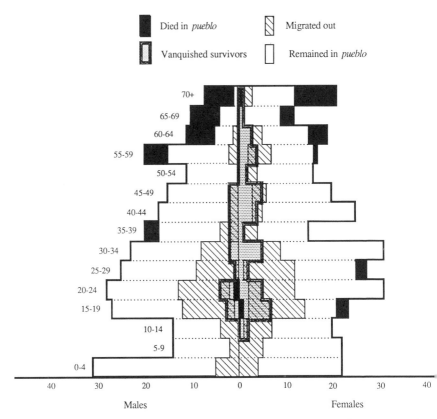

Fig. 10.3. The Los Olivos Population, 1950–60. Young men and women constituted the bulk of those who migrated in this decade, often establishing themselves in work before calling other family members to follow in later migration
(see Figure 10.4). Migration drew on a higher proportion of surviving vanquished villagers (45 percent) than of other villagers (22 percent) in this decade.
Together with those that migrated before 1950, the vanquished paved the way, in
some respects, for others to follow. (As in previous figures, the Civil War vanquished constitute the central segment of the pyramid. Crosshatching identifies
migrants, vanquished or otherwise.)

competition from other regions. Vendors found that larger and
unblemished fruits were crowding Los Olivos produce out of the
Sevilla market to the point where, one sad day in the late 1960's,
two truckloads of Los Olivos fruit could not be sold at any
price—the truckers had to pay to unload their fruit at the dump.

One immediate consequence for Los Olivos of the development plan for 1964–67 was the shifting of substantial tracts out of traditional cultivation and into eucalyptus plantations. Huelva's paper industry was given substantial impetus by the development plan, necessitating sources of supply for wood pulp. At the same time, minimum wages had risen nationally, and this induced landed proprietors to shift land out of labor-intensive production. The result was that huge tracts of the province of Huelva, including the southern portion of Los Olivos, were given over by their proprietors in long-term leases to the paper industry, which bulldozed existing vegetation away and planted eucalyptus. Subsequently, the proprietors of some of the largest holdings in Los Olivos closed their pueblo houses, laid off their regular workers, and moved elsewhere.

These and other setbacks for local agriculture threw many laborers out of work and threatened many smallholders with the loss of a reasonable livelihood. As a result, the 1960's brought a substantial increase and qualitative shift in migration away from Los Olivos. For the first time, people of every age emigrated (see Figure 10.4), and at unprecedented rates. Between 1960 and 1970, Los Olivos lost 35 percent of its population to migration, particularly to employment in Catalonia in the ring of cities around Barcelona (a small number of families migrated to guest-worker jobs in France, Germany, and Switzerland).

It was at this juncture that villagers followed in the paths that the vanquished Civil War survivors and other earlier emigrants had opened. More often than not, ties of matrilateral kinship linked the migrants. We learned of one such case while interviewing former villagers presently living near Barcelona.

Primitiva Santis and Manuel Navarro were engaged when the Civil War broke out. Both were closely related to war victims. Manuel's older brother, one of the Socialist town councillors, died in jail when Manuel was 26. Primitiva's sister Emiliana lost her husband in one of the massacres just days after their daughter Teresa was born. Primitiva married Manuel in 1943, just a year before Emiliana remarried and her brother José María married Gumersinda López. All three couples lived in the pueblo and bore offspring there (see Figure 10.6 below).

Around 1957, Manuel found employment in the Riotinto

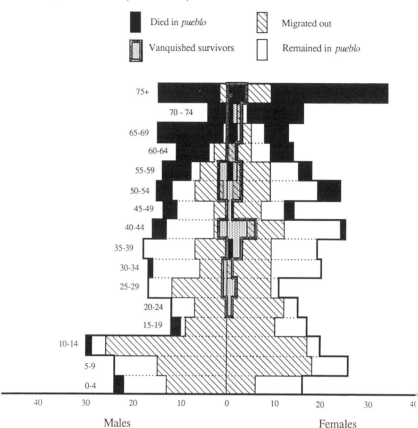

Fig. 10.4. The Los Olivos Population, 1960–80. A massive exodus encompassed all age ranges and depopulated Los Olivos in this period, leaving behind virtually no Civil War vanquished.

mines, and Primitiva and their six children joined him there. When the mine closed down, the family migrated to Catalonia, taking up work and lodgings in Cornellá. They were the first of the pueblo to arrive there.

Employment was excellent in Cornellá at the beginning of the 1960's, and shortly after arriving, Primitiva and Manuel called on Emiliana's elder children to come to Cornellá, which they did, sharing lodgings with their cousins. Emiliana and her husband followed their children six years later, in 1967. At about that time, Emiliana's brother José María died in the pueblo. Gumersinda López, his widow, and his elder children took up work in the pueblo to pay off debts. Primitiva wanted them to emigrate to Cornellá. And when her daughter, Micaela, visited Los Olivos on her honeymoon, she prevailed on Gumersinda's eldest daughters to return to Cornellá with her. One by one, three more of Gumersinda's children came, as did Gumersinda herself in 1972 (see Figures 10.5 and 10.6).

This was not the end of the emigration to Cornellá by any means. Gumersinda helped her son-in-law's sister establish her family in Cornellá a few years later.

Primitiva's children and their cousins, meanwhile, matured in Catalonia and have married, in some instances to Catalan na-

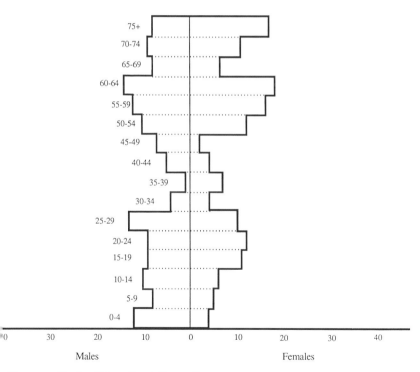

Fig. 10.5. The Los Olivos Population, 1980.

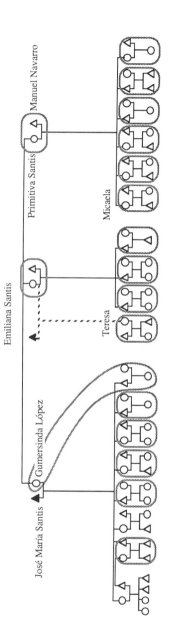

Fig. 10.6. Family Migration from Los Olivos to Cornellá. The genealogy shows the relationships among kin who followed Primitiva Santis and Manuel Navarro from Los Olivos to Cornellá.

◯ Marks households living in Cornellá or one of its neighboring cities in 1983.

tives. They now live in Cornellá, Hospitalet, Sants, and St. Boi. They and their spouses work in electrical assembly, carpentry, construction, welding, accounting, textiles, typesetting, and barbering. One is a deliveryman, and one is a municipal policeman. Every Sunday, if the weather is not too unpleasant, they picnic together in the environs of Cornellá.

The Overturning of the Old Order

Petra Ramos was one of those who left Los Olivos in the 1960's as a teenager, first for study in Huelva, then for professional training and employment in Sevilla. In 1969, she sent us a poem she had written, entitled "Los Emigrantes":

Los Olivos se queda solo
    sin poderlo remediar.

El campo nadie lo quiere
    todos temen trabajar.

Todos se marchan corriendo
    sin volver la cara atrás
    unos para Barcelona
    otros para Llobregat. . . .

El zapatero se fué los demás
    iban detrás sin darle
    ninguna pena pasar
    pa' vendimiar aunque
    estaban los naranjos
    muy cargados de azahar
    el corcho recién sacado
    y las uvas para pisar.

La panadería se cierra
    la luz tendrán que cortar
    las tiendas sin un garbanzo
    y la barbería fecha'.

Los ricos parecen pobres
    cansados de trabajar
    porque el sábado no quieren
    pagarle a nadie un jornal.

Los Olivos is left alone
    with nothing to do for it.

No one wants the countryside,
    no one dares to work it.

Everyone is running away
    without looking back,
    some going to Barcelona
    and others to Llobregat. . . .

The shoemaker left, the rest
    followed without giving
    a second thought
    to harvesting, even though
    the orange trees were
    burdened with blossoms,
    the cork recently stripped,
    and grapes ready to crush.

The bakery is closing down,
    electricity will have to be cut,
    the stores are without a pea,
    and the barbershop closed.

The rich seem like poor people,
    exhausted by work,
    since on Saturdays they won't
    pay anyone a worker's wage.

Por eso y cabreados se marchan
  a la ciudad cambiando su
    vieja
vida por otra de bienestar
    aunque
vendan abellanas si la cosa
    les va mal.
	That's why workers, fed up, go
	  to the city, changing their
	    old
	life for one of well-being
	    even if
	they may have to sell
	    hazelnuts if things
	    go badly for them.

As the poem makes clear, the villagers were experiencing migration in terms of changing class relations. Unwilling to pay workers a salary, agricultural proprietors of a younger generation had to toil in the fields themselves. Workers who left Los Olivos expected to better themselves, at least for a while.

Fifteen years have partly borne out Petra's prescience. Although the village has not closed down by any means, the old order that agricultural proprietors dominated has been overturned. The migrants of the 1960's did prosper, although recession has limited their affluence in recent years. Those who sustain a relation to the pueblo, the vanquished among them, nonetheless recognize in their own improved circumstances the ironic inversion of old statuses.

Agriculture has not been totally abandoned in Los Olivos in recent years, but the proprietors who have chosen to continue in agriculture have had to scale it down to adapt to unfavorable market conditions. One adaptation has been a resort to family labor by those who once were able to employ agricultural workers. With but a few exceptions, proprietors do not employ regular workers because minimum wages exceed a worker's productivity on Los Olivos's marginal land. For example, at the selling price of approximately 23 pesetas per kilo, proprietors could not afford to hire workers at 1,000 pesetas per day to harvest a bumper crop of olives in 1983. On the other hand, youthful family members could not find employment because of the recession and had to work for their parents. Proprietors harvested only what they could with family labor, but they left many tons of olives to rot.

Proprietors have restricted cultivation to only the best land close to motorized transport, allowing vast expanses of pueblo territory to revert to scrub and thicket. For the most part, the land they keep in cultivation is the irrigated land close to the village, which yields plentiful truck garden crops to consume at home or to market within the region.

They have changed animal husbandry considerably. According to censuses of animals taken by the Town Council, beasts of burden (mostly donkeys and mules) diminished from 148 in 1958 to only 68 in 1974 because they were no longer much needed in transport. (Some old men keep them as pets!) Goats had increased, meanwhile, from 66 to 960 because goats can forage on the scrub and thicket to which the countryside has reverted. Hogs diminished in number and shifted in variety. Since swineherds are no longer available to tend the *cerdo ibérico* (the native Iberian pig) in oak groves, families raise smaller numbers of them in pens close to the pueblo and gather acorns to fatten and flavor them in the last weeks before slaughter. A white pig, fed on garbage and feed and butchered for fresh meat rather than to be cured, is replacing the cerdo ibérico in the pueblo.

These adaptations notwithstanding, proprietors who have stayed in agriculture acknowledge that they have come down in the world from the days when they or their parents could afford to hire workers. They and their family themselves accept occasional wage work when it is available. For example, certain young women in the pueblo take piecework from a clothing manufacturer who has supplied them with industrial sewing machines to use in their homes, but the availability of this work is erratic. In slack periods, many men turn to public-works jobs paying a minimum wage provided by the state to aid agrarian unemployed. Thus, recent developments have tended to proletarianize former proprietors, as Eduardo Sevilla Guzmán (1979: 221) has pointed out.

Although agricultural proprietors have retrenched, new sources of wealth keep Los Olivos's bakery, stores, and barbershop open. Social security benefits make it possible for retired people to live quite well in the pueblo. Many of those who signed up for social security in the 1950's and 1960's are now receiving those benefits. More important, migrants bring wealth back to the pueblo. Those now living in Sevilla and Huelva frequently spend weekends in Los Olivos. Summer vacations draw those currently living in distant places such as Madrid and Barcelona back to the pueblo with enough money in their pockets "to live like kings," as one envious villager put it.

There are instances in which former migrants have returned to Los Olivos to invest in businesses. Enrique Ramos returned from work in Germany to run the family store when his parents died; he invested his earnings in a facility for butchering hogs and curing pork in the traditional manner for which the Sierra de Aracena is famous. (These products command excellent prices from metropolitan bars, which burgeoned with the rural exodus.) The meat-packing facility gave several local men and women seasonal work and was profitable. Francisco Gómez returned from Barcelona after having been indemnified for being laid off from a permanent job. When his wife inherited the bakery, he used his indemnity money and a bank loan to modernize it, installing a modern gas oven and extending his sales to nearby towns.

The expenditure of this new wealth in Los Olivos manifests Spain's shift from autarky to a consumer society in recent years (Carr and Fusi 1981: 49–78). Automobiles are very much in evidence; villagers owned 11 trucks and 30 cars in 1982 as compared with 3 trucks and 11 cars in 1974 despite the decline in population in that period. Store-bought goods are much more current than they were in 1963. Furthermore, retirees and migrants have spent heavily to remodel homes and summer lodgings, which they equip with modern kitchens and bathrooms and furnish with such conveniences as televisions, appliances, and gas or electric heaters.

Los Olivos, in short, has ceased to be a place in which the owner of agrarian property reigns supreme. More than likely, he has abandoned most of his parents' land, has applied for public-works unemployment relief, and has joined one of the crews rebuilding a retired person or émigré's pueblo home. Meanwhile, the former landless worker or poor smallholder who left for blue-collar work in the city more than likely has visited the pueblo to talk about his bettered fortunes. He may even be one of those who employs the sons of those for whom he and his parents once labored. In the course of a generation, history has inverted the postwar order.

Vanquished Civil War survivors and working-class emigrants appreciate the irony of this inversion. Old-timers among them contrast the overgrown abandon of pueblo farmland today with its flourishing state 50 years ago under the regime of Socialist labor organization. Like their counterparts elsewhere in Andalusia, they lament that so much land should be held in an unproductive state (Martínez Alier 1971: 117; Suero Sánchez 1982: 146). They believe history has borne out that they were more competent in production than the landowners themselves.

For the most part, the 1970's and 1980's have brought ostensible improvements in the lives of those of the vanquished who are still alive, whether they migrated or not. With the passing of the Franco dictatorship, widows have been able to get pensions due them as war victims. Like other migrants we have interviewed, the vanquished and their families enjoy the better wages, education, and social services of contemporary metropolitan Spain. Some have bought apartments. Most of those who were children in the war expect to retire with pensions. They are consumers of television and of leisure. Some have fixed up modest quarters in the pueblo as vacation and future retirement homes.

The vanquished have a sense of their shared history. We learned that they pooled experiences to piece together the roles of specific Falangists responsible for their misfortunes. Through the years, they shared one another's minor triumphs in outwitting local authorities, in affronting an oppressor with a well-turned retort. They advised one another about how to obtain the pensions due to war victims. They have sustained contact in the face of migration.

Lacking vindication, the vanquished take a certain comfort in the misfortunes that time and fate have dealt their oppressors. Guadalupe Nogales relished the incident in which a mule bit and nearly severed the hand of Teodoro Martín, one of those whom she held responsible for her husband's death. Survivors agree that divine justice meted out agonizing illness and death to José Antonio López, acting secretary of the Town Council in the postwar era, and others of the leading Falangist collaborators; one man felt sure that God had kept him alive so that he could witness these deaths. Survivors also believe that the villagers view Falangist collaborators with hidden disdain, refusing to look at them forthrightly, *con buena cara* (with a good face). Like other working-class migrants, if not more so, the vanquished relish witnessing the plight of village landowners—the former elite—who have been reduced to working their own land while onetime field hands have cash in their pockets to spend.

Like other older villagers, the vanquished gravitate back to Los Olivos for vacations. In some instances, they have decided to make their peace with villagers who may have wronged them, as Guadalupe Nogales did with the family of a Civil Guard by attending his funeral. Certain of the vanquished wish to retire in the pueblo. One man explained that only among villagers with whom he had grown up did he feel truly at home, and it was for this reason that he planned to retire to the place in which he had experienced so much suffering. Perhaps history, by uplifting workers while lowering those who once lorded it over them, has made such reconciliation easier.

ELEVEN

Understanding the Past

AT FIRST GLANCE, the Socialists of Los Olivos might well seem an improbable focus for shedding light on the study of history. A rural place of little significance, its population dwindling steadily during the century, Los Olivos spawned no figures of national note. It was no Casas Viejas. Yet scrutiny of its Second Republic Socialists has allowed me to investigate the character and legacy of socialism in rural Andalusia while exploring issues of relevance to any endeavor at ethnohistorical interpretation.

Redefining the Ethnographic Subject

In studying the Socialists of Los Olivos—how they organized after 1929, what they struggled for during the Second Republic, and what legacy they left their pueblo in the postwar years—I have departed from conventional ethnography in its definition of problem. The unanticipated salutary results warrant consideration by all anthropologists. Unlike the ethnographer who studies those living in the present as an effective, collectively acting group, I have concerned myself with pueblo dissidents, men who coalesced as such a group half a century ago. It is true that I have combined ethnography and history to reconstruct these men's past, their goals, their accomplishments, and their repression, radicalization, and ultimate defeat. But by fixing my vision on pueblo Socialists and focusing on their legacy, by following their vanquished heirs in repression as well as in migration, I have repositioned myself with respect to the ethnographic subject. Rather than reconstructing the past of a present-day people and place, I have followed a particular group as their fate unfolded in time and through space. Without losing sight of Los Olivos as a community for study in its own right, I have situated it in the background of an analysis centered on the proletariat that once lived there. As a result of this definition of problem and selection of vantage point, I have circumvented the bias inherent in the more usual practice of studying a people and place retrospectively from the standpoint of those who currently live there. By giving other perspectives equal if not greater weight, this study has, I think, arrived at an original and deeper understanding of the pueblo, its people, and its past.

This approach, valuable in its own right, has proved indispensable for overcoming the methodological difficulties confronting the study of the Second Republic and the Civil War. The era is no longer one of lived experience for most Spaniards. Moreover, many Republican political activists were executed during or immediately following the war, and others fled or later moved to large industrializing cities to start a new life in the anonymity of the urban environment with better jobs than those available in the countryside. Only by following the vanquished and their heirs to such settings could I hope to recover the experience and legacy of Los Olivos's Socialists.

Political Economy and Cultural Analysis: Politics, Honor, and Autonomy

Every analytical paradigm illuminates a distinctive range of problems through the questions that it poses. Anthropologists are increasingly resorting to political-economic analysis to study conflict and change, to understand the embedding of local worlds in larger systems, and to correct the ahistorical character of earlier ethnographic writing (Marcus and Fischer 1986: 77–78). The political-economic perspective requires that one look beyond the community for a fuller understanding of the forces that shape and move it. It is concerned with both internal and external dynamics. In a general way, it frees us from a concept of society and culture as something stable, and of people as living in unchanging routines year after year. This study amply illustrates the value of political-economic analysis for such purposes.

I have been particularly concerned to explore how the relations of production entered into the establishment and maintenance of political forms in rural Huelva and thus to attend to the articulation of local politics with the broader context. In doing so, I have had to establish the historical context of Second Republic politics. In the nineteenth century, a landed gentry consolidated oligarchical control of rural Huelva by delivering the vote of its reserve army of irregularly employed farmworkers at the behest of national powerholders. Celestino López inherited his power as Los Olivos's cacique from this legacy, and it was against this legacy that the Socialists struggled. I also have had to explore the regional and national character of local political developments. It was in tandem with Socialist party campaigns—to organize Huelva mineworkers and shortly thereafter farmworkers in surrounding agrarian zones—that the dissidents of Los Olivos first coalesced as a political faction. When, as Socialists, they challenged López and the rural order that he represented, they joined their union's and party's national leaders in Second Republic efforts to gain and master the apparatus of the state.

In Los Olivos, the Socialists wrested control of local government from the landlords and instituted revolutionary changes in the relations of production, but they did so just as control of the state slipped from their party's tenuous grip nationally, undermining what had been accomplished locally. In the radical confrontation that ensued, insurgent Nationalists restored the landed oligarchy to power. Backed by the insurgents, Los Olivos landlords proved that, to the extent that widows and orphans were available to work, they could dispense with dissident male farmworkers. The order that Celestino López represented retrenched and revived in the first two postwar decades, abetted by national agrarian policies. Only as the state transformed agriculture through capitalist development beginning in the late 1950's was the old order overturned. Time and again, local affairs drew on the dynamics of the broader national political-economic context and occasionally contributed to them.

A second central endeavor of this study has been to advance the wedding of interpretive approaches to the analysis of political economy begun by such scholars as Pierre Bourdieu (1977). I have done this by attending to the cultural terms in which the people of Los Olivos experienced the political-economic context of their lives and, in turn, formulated their discourse of struggle. Analyzing the character of political "rights" in the discourse of contemporary democracy and capitalism, Samuel Bowles and Herbert Gintis (1986: 153–55) have argued that discourse is a "set of tools" that people use "to forge the unities that provide the basis for their collective social practices." As deployed in discourse, words—as well as flags, uniforms, and other symbols— "have uses that are transformed through practices and transported from one arena of social life to another in the course of social conflict." Meanings turn on how discourse is used to galvanize collective action and on the way discourse itself "becomes the object of social struggle." Much the same can be asserted of key concepts in any political-economic context. If we are to understand conflict, it is incumbent on us to attend to how meanings borrowed from the experience of everyday life are further forged and put to use in the struggle of collective action.

Attentive to such concerns in this study, I have explored how the concepts of "honor" and "autonomy," so characteristic of agrarian societies of the Mediterranean, entered Second Republic politics in Los Olivos. I am not the first to have related honorable personhood and personal autonomy to the lived experience of the stratified agrarian property relations characteristic of the societies of the Mediterranean (cf. Peristiany 1966; Pitt-Rivers 1966; Schneider 1969). But whereas holders of property and power usually used these concepts to legitimize their status, the Socialists of Los Olivos deployed the concepts to undermine property relations—to subvert rather than to uphold the status quo. The radical character of labor reforms that the Socialists of Los Olivos imposed on landlords becomes intelligible only when we understand how farmworkers drew on the repertory of customary usages and practices of farm work to invert relations of power in employment. They thereby stripped proprietors of their autonomy as owners of capital and of their honor as men. A similar analysis elucidates the postwar repression and the retrenchment of the old order, in which the victors imposed their norms even on the private lives of the working-class vanquished. They stigmatized as sexually aberrant or lax those former Socialists who did not conform to their own norms and practices of courtship and marriage. In veiled negative discourse with the preceding Second Republic era, the victors thereby reaffirmed their own construction of honorable personhood in a poignantly political manner.

The Nature of Rural Socialism

These approaches allow me to come to grips with several substantive problems in the study of rural Spain. One general range of problem illuminated by my approach to Los Olivos concerns the nature of socialism in rural Andalusia. For a variety of reasons, the anarchists have usually been credited with a dominant historical role in Andalusia, more so than seems just, in light of my appraisal of socialism in Huelva. It must be remembered that only in Spain did anarchism develop into a mass political movement and that anarchist ideals have appealed to many writers on Spain. A certain redress is in order, and I have taken a step in that direction.

Most important, I argue that the Socialists accomplished considerably more than historians have credited them in reforming and revolutionizing agrarian labor. The Socialists of Los Olivos devoted their full energies to the arena of employment, and they had reason to be proud of their accomplishments. Land reform, for which Socialist party leaders struggled in the Cortes and on which historians have placed so much emphasis, was of lesser interest to the men of Los Olivos. Clearly land reform *was* of importance in the Andalusian and Extremaduran plains. But have analysts underrated the significance of the arena of agrarian employment for workers' struggles by failing to take full cognizance of the terms in which workers formulated them? If so, then the dynamic interaction between the Socialist rank and file and party leaders during the Second Republic deserves reconsideration. Paul Preston (1978, 1984*b*) and others (e.g., Malefakis 1970) have demonstrated that pressures from rank-and-file members, particularly of the FNTT, radicalized party leaders during the Second Republic. But did the fervor of this pressure derive from rank-and-file frustration with the pace of land reform, as most analysts have suggested? Or was it whetted by victories won in the revolutionizing of employment relations, as the example of Los Olivos suggests?

Other interrelated issues are the origins of Socialist organization and the relations among Socialists, anarchists, and Communists. As for rank-and-file proletarians, I agree with the conclusions of Antonio Calero (1976) that there was less divergence among them than among their leaders and that even the line between these groups and peasants influenced by Catholic mutualism was sometimes hard to draw. As far as I have been able to determine, socialism and anarchism were not clearly differentiable among the rank and file in the Sierra de Aracena until the 1920's. Socialism gained the upper hand in organizing first mine workers and then agrarian workers in Huelva during the dictatorship of Primo de Rivera, absorbing many former anarchist and Communist mine- and farmworkers into its trade union membership. Leaders *did* argue differences of ideology and strategy when confronting one another in organizing campaigns or when jailed together in the bienio negro. But as far as the rank and file, at least among Los Olivos Socialists, were concerned, abstention from drink and tobacco, anticlericalism coupled with ongoing participation in the *hermandades* and with the notion that Christ was the first anarchist, and calls for libertarian communism were all compatible. What united these eclectic strands in Los Olivos was not the notion that seizing control of the state or abolishing it should be the first step in a proletarian revolution, but rather the common endeavor to turn relations of power in local employment on their head.

The example of Los Olivos thus suggests something about the nature of peasant revolutions. Such movements must be understood on their own terms as well as in relation to broader revolutionary dynamics. As Theda Skocpol (e.g., 1982) has argued in a number of contexts, agrarian workers may be inspired by outsiders; they may find possibilities for revolution in the collapse of the state; and they may utilize others' rhetoric. But when they act, I would add, they do so in terms that both grow out of and most directly affect life as they experience it, particularly in relations of production. This study has established how Socialist leaders *did* reach down to mobilize peasants through the FNTT and how, in the context of the breakdown of the Second Republic, rural Socialists became revolutionary. At the same time, it has shed light on the specific ways in which peasant Socialists, as distinct from party leaders, conceptualized their revolutionary involvement in the same terms that they used to make sense of the concrete experience of the relations of production in everyday life.

Reassessing Postwar Spain and the Ethnographic Present

By studying the past in terms of political economy and related interpretive practices, I have arrived at a different and deeper understanding of the present. The Los Olivos that Jane Collier and I first came to know in the 1960's has been cast in a new and different light by our investigation of the legacy of prewar stratification and class conflict for the postwar years. We have seen that the postwar terror and propaganda silenced working-class politics in Los Olivos while state agrarian policies enabled the old order to retrench and reinvigorate itself at the expense of the vanquished. The uncontested reign of the propertied class pressured the working-class poor to conform to propertied villagers' norms, even in their private lives. Not surprisingly, the vanquished were among the first to emigrate from Los Olivos when it became possible to do so. They left behind a village more sociocentric and homogeneous in the appearance of its peasant lifeways than is now credible in view of our knowledge of the pueblo's past.

The conclusion adds weight to the growing recognition that much existing ethnography of Spain needs to be reconsidered. Martínez Alier (1971: 23, 166, 222, 233, 298–315), who criticized Julian Pitt-Rivers' static bias, his misinterpretation of working-class constructs, and his failure to appreciate the class conflict inherent in peasant politics, paved the way for such reconsideration. In *The People of the Plains* (1980), David Gilmore generalized Martínez Alier's critique, attributing ethnographers' stress on homogeneity and sociocentrism in Spanish pueblo life of the 1960's and 1970's to two methodological predispositions of that time. On the one hand, Gilmore argued, analysts overlooked class because their analytical model saw Spanish patronage relations harmonizing status-group differences. On the other hand, concentration on the smaller, peasant pueblos of the sierras and of Castile drew investigators' attention away from issues of class and conflict because these populations lacked a significant rural proletariat or elite. Henk Driessen (1981) extended the criticism further, taking even Gilmore to task for failure to consider historical and regional contexts in Spanish community studies. Taking my own experience as an object lesson, I think it likely that theoretical predispositions and lapses colored other investigators' interpretations as they did my own in the 1960's.

But the reconstruction of Los Olivos's twentieth-century history from the perspective of a different paradigm casts even more complex doubt on the validity of ethnographic findings of the 1960's and 1970's. Although it was a small sierra town, prewar Los Olivos had a proletariat that engaged the local elite in class conflict. During and after the postwar repression, however, workers began to emigrate, leaving smallholders and agrarian proprietors behind; the pueblo became more homogeneous in the 1960's than it had been before the war. The postwar repression made it difficult to investigate or appreciate the nature of this transformation. On the basis of my present grasp of the history of class relations in Los Olivos, I can understand why other pueblos may have been described in terms of sociocentrism and solidarity in the 1960's and 1970's, although I question whether such pueblos would prove on appropriate scrutiny to have lacked a similar legacy of stratification and class conflict. A reappraisal of postwar Spain from our current perspective must thus be sensitive to how the problems that ethnographers of that era posed as central to their analysis interacted with changes in the composition of the populations they studied.

Political Consciousness and Identity

But as if two shifts—one in theoretical paradigm, the other in the composition of study populations—were not enough complexity, a third shift, in postwar political consciousness, must also be weighed in the balance of reappraisal. One of my purposes in setting forth the political history of Los Olivos has been to appreciate how Spaniards even in such places as Los Olivos carried on the vigorous political discourse of the Second Republic. This is a matter that bears directly on how we should interpret the social organization and values of rural society and the role of politicization within it. Most of the classic ethnographies of Spain evoke an image of essentially pre-political societies. I have argued that this is in some degree a matter of ethnographic context, but it is also a matter of changes in politicization. Field researchers in Spain after 1950 encountered a society that had been *de*politicized, but in ways that were not readily apparent. Many Spaniards avoided discussing politics, and ethnographers failed to seek or acknowledge evidence of a more politically active past. Their focus on relatively smaller communities may have made it easier to ignore the political dimension.

By contrast, I have reached the conclusion that rural Andalusia before the Civil War had a high degree of political mobilization and articulation with the wider society. Thus, I have attuned my analysis to the terms in which leftists, who considered themselves men of ideas, made common cause with their comrades in a struggle against those whom they perceived as the tyrants of capitalist agrarian production and their lackeys. These men recognized themselves as a proletariat and took part in a spirited class analysis of their own. They distinguished market production on capitalist agrarian property from peasant production on smallholdings. They perceived that economic conditions forcing their children to work precluded the schooling they would need to defend their class interests. These men had high hopes for the republic of workers in whose name they conducted their struggle against capitalist agrarian proprietors. Why then did the postwar ethnography of rural Spain not acknowledge their keen political consciousness and vigorous discourse, much less consider whether and how it had been lost? I believe that the answer has in part to do with changes in postwar political consciousness and identity among the villagers themselves.

These changes became apparent to me in interviews with vanquished survivors of the repression. Despite the self-evident consciousness of class that the Socialists of Los Olivos and nearby places had voiced in their deeds and rhetoric, as recorded in contemporary newspapers and documents, their heirs, particularly widows of younger Socialists killed in 1936 and others of their generation, interpret the past in different terms.

Their vision of the past discounts class as the significant axis of Los Olivos's polarization during the Second Republic and interprets the tragic events of the Civil War in terms not of the crushing of dissident proletarian men but rather of *rencillos*, personal quarrels embedded in a matrix of kinship and patronage whose rancor and vindictiveness flared momentarily beyond their control.

Those who discount the class basis for Second Republic conflict argue that Los Olivos was essentially a town of rightists and that most of the town councils of Los Olivos (and other Sierra de Aracena towns) were composed of rightists during the Republic. Even the leading Socialist councillors came from rightist families. And after the war, the town continued to be rightist.

Kinship ties crossing political divisions are one basis for their assertion. They point out that rightist councillor Francisco Santis (acting mayor in 1932) was the brother of Socialist Mayor Ceferino Santis. The young Socialist ideologue, Pablo Moreno, had uncles on the Right, and his father, though later sympathetic to the Socialists, had been a monarchist mayor in 1928. Youngsters from families involved in Town Council politics during the Second Republic remember dancing together just as youth had during the monarchy. As several people who were adolescents at the time have put it, the pueblo was "one large family" during the period leading up to 1936, and it continued to be so when "normal" life resumed after the war.

Thus, survivors remember the polarization of the town leading up to the debacle of 1936 as neither fundamental nor enduring. They emphasize that the personal animosities involved in the polarization both antedated and outlasted the Republic. The quarrel between Socialist Mayor Ceferino Santis and his brother Francisco was initially a family affair. Such family feuds often had their basis in resentment or jealousy about the division of family inheritances. The brothers had once been close enough for Ceferino to give Francisco, whose wife was barren, his son Pedro Luís to raise. But some time after their father died in 1925, the two brothers quarreled bitterly, carrying their antagonism into the arena of town government, particularly in and after 1932.

Other feuds had to do with business affairs. Isidoro Moreno, the trucker, feuded bitterly with Pedro Moreno and Pedro's sons,

Pablo and Felipe, in competition for the town's transport clients. Pedro owned a truck in conjunction with his businesses and hauled goods, though his permit to do so had lapsed. Isidoro tried to have Pedro's truck impounded. Pedro and his sons retaliated with civil suits that dotted the court record during the Republic. Villagers claim it was thus not surprising for Falangists to requisition Pedro's truck after appointing Isidoro to the Town Council in August 1936 and to order Felipe to drive it to Riotinto, where other Falangists seized and killed him.

Other animosities stemmed from personal resentments against officeholders for the favoritism they showed in the exercise of authority. Incumbents in office were found to make decisions that favored some and hurt others. Pedro Moreno had been mayor in 1928, and so it was hardly surprising that he had made enemies who later opposed the Socialists, among whom his sons were prominent. Similarly, José Antonio Ramos, who had served as mayor in the months before the declaration of the Second Republic when Socialist unionizing was going on in Huelva, had made enemies who later branded him a socialist. Moreover, both men had grounds for resentments of their own; after leaving office, both were prosecuted for misuse of public funds, charges that did not surprise villagers, who expected officeholders to act out of self-interest. Favoritism and self-interest enter into the widows' explanations in another way. Insurgent decrees made reparations for supposed damages to the state a pretext for confiscating the property of left-wing activists. Several widows claim that authorities helped other villagers who were greedy for their possessions to victimize them on this pretext. More generally, they remember the partiality that prominent villagers showed in village life after the war.

These war widows do remember that the Republic pitted workers against property owners in Los Olivos, but they describe the consequences of this in personalistic terms rather than in terms of class conflict. Property owners reacted "like lions" to being forced to hire workers they did not want, and they vented their rage on leftists after the Levantamiento.

To understand how surviving widows and other villagers see *rencillos* rather than class conflict as motivating the events of the Second Republic and Civil War, we must come to terms with how their generation interpreted the realities of village life as they lived it. We must also attend to how they used the discourses available for them to reinterpret their lived experience in the postwar years.

Political Consciousness and the Discourses of Patronage and Kinship

I have endeavored from the outset of this book to analyze the relations of class that underlay pueblo stratification and social relations. It is within these relations between those who needed labor and those who needed jobs that conflicts rose to the surface during the Second Republic. As my analysis has shown, surviving Civil War widows and others of their generation of villagers are basically correct in remembering Los Olivos as a town whose propertied stratum exercised patronage while grasping the reins of Town Council politics before and after the Second Republic, as well as for much of its course. They could do so in part because agrarian stratification remained fundamentally unchanged, leaving proprietors with the power to reassert their patronage in the discourse of social relations. Both before and after the Second Republic, agrarian proprietors who had land and needed labor could do well by exercising patronage both in private employment and in the public employment that resulted from their control of town affairs. This does not mean that patronage was inflexibly anchored to a political-economic base. Patronage was a form of political discourse and contention. Socialist leaders, who were themselves men of property, wrested control of the Town Council away from agrarian proprietors in order to exercise patronage on behalf of those that lacked land and needed work. It is true that their insistence on strict adherence to the fair employment practices spelled out in bases de trabajo would eventually have undermined the basis of patronage, but initially it did not.

Villagers are also correct in identifying kinship as one of the enduring realities of pueblo life. Kinship was a dominant idiom for social relations in an agrarian society stratified in terms of property. The property inherited and held by members of a domestic group in such a society invested cognatic kinship with the deep solidarities of family members who live in shared pursuit of well-being. The language of kinship thus could be used as a basis for legitimating and explaining solidarity in other domains of discourse.

But property also evoked acerbic quarrels among mature siblings on behalf of their own progeny over division of a parental estate. Inheritance thus provided an explanation for conflicts among kin. Before the war, Los Olivos was an agrarian society in which cognatic kinship was constituted by property in precisely these ways. Although the Socialists challenged the meaning of property by calling into question the ways in which employers could put it to use, they never questioned the legitimacy of cognatic kinship as the basis for ownership (as they might have, had the Second Republic endured long enough to bring into focus the contradictions between inheritance practices that Socialist smallholders shared with proprietors and Socialist challenges to the meaning of property).

Kinship continued as a dominant idiom of property relations after the war, especially insofar as immediate postwar economic nationalism revived agriculture while it hailed the supposed virtues of smallholding family producers. Its foundation in property relations remained secure, at least up to the late 1960's when economic developments throughout Spain marginalized rural agriculture in Huelva.

Kinship and patronage thus had meanings deeply embedded in the prevailing property system yet flexibly available to villagers as discourses for experiencing and explaining both solidarity and conflict. In *Social Origins of Dictatorship and Democracy* (1966), Barrington Moore distinguishes between "conservative" solidarity—in which peasant laborers, tenants, and smallholders are controlled by proprietors through their power over resources and village institutions—and "radical" solidarity—in which peasants and workers achieve control of resources and village institutions and set them against landed proprietors or the state. Kinship and patronage contributed to the radical solidarity that Socialists achieved during the Second Republic. Before and after the Second Republic, the propertied class used kinship and patronage to build and maintain conservative solidarity. The generation of villagers we interviewed, which included war widows who had married just before the war, had experienced the Second Republic as adolescents in the relatively carefree company of village age mates. They remember the solidarities of that experience as living in a village that was "one large family." This same generation experienced the postwar years as adults among whom resentments—over wartime injustices and over the favors that the powerful bestowed or withheld in its wake—exacerbated divisions between kin inherent in family feuds. Yet these realities of village life and lived experience in no way controvert the underlying reality of a system of productive relations in which landless workers labored at the mercy of agrarian proprietors backed by the state.

The Negative Dialogue with the Past

One of the main accomplishments of this study has been to substantiate the postwar period's sustained negative dialogue with the Second Republic era, and I believe that the loss of the discourse of class conflict within this generation becomes understandable in these terms. To begin, one must consider how effectively the incipient agrarian revolution was crushed. The Levantamiento silenced all active leftist males in Los Olivos and almost all of their allies. Over 50 men in a population of less than 900 were killed or jailed; only two protagonists escaped by fleeing. As happened in town after town throughout Andalusia, the Insurgents eliminated all those "who had ideas." No one remained in the village—or anywhere in the nation—who dared to articulate what the Left had struggled for. The discourse of class conflict that had been so vigorous in the Second Republic was, if not definitively buried, at least driven underground.

The Falangists not only did away with the revolutionaries; they also reasserted the class relations of the old order, and they won control of people's minds. The state backed the landed proprietors whose families had held power in the pueblo before the Second Republic, and "normal" village life resumed under their control and on their terms. At the same time, catechists and propagandists inculcated Nationalist doctrine from the pulpit and in school texts. Tragically, we found that many of the widows and orphans whom we interviewed were deeply shaken by this propaganda. Knowing that the Socialists had been depicted as categorically evil, they took pains to point out how their loved ones, at least, were not. One man, for example, however proud that his father had helped build the entrance road to Los Olivos, took special pains to tell us that his father was not a bad man, even though he had been a Socialist.

Their loved ones lost and vilified, their property despoiled, the vanquished nonetheless had to go on living. They had little alternative but to reintegrate themselves into postwar village life in which the familiar discourses of kinship and patronage revived and thrived in a seemingly depoliticized guise, even as the discourse of class conflict withered.

To return to my point of departure, these changes in political discourse and identities are yet a third major shift of which we must take cognizance in reappraising the postwar era. We have traced the evolution of politics in an arc of contention extending through time as the Civil War victors engaged in a one-sided but protracted negative dialogue with the Socialists who had once challenged them. We have seen discourse and identities shift within the political-economic framework that survived the Socialists' challenge until undercut by major economic change late in Franco's reign.

Does this mean that politics is in some way anchored more loosely than class to a base structure of productive relations? Is politics somehow more free-floating than kinship and patronage? In their treatment of political discourse as involving meanings borrowed from other domains but deployed in social action, Samuel Bowles and Herbert Gintis (1986: 153) argue against any strict correspondence between political discourse and shared class consciousness or ideology. In doing so, they take a position on this issue different from the alternatives espoused by contemporary Marxism. Instead of treating consciousness as a direct or even an indirect or false reflection of peoples' experience of relations of production per se, they treat consciousness "as an aspect of the forms of discourse appropriated in social practice" (1986: 231). Their argument is in some ways similar to that set forth by Charles Bright and Susan Harding in their introduction to *Statemaking and Social Movements* (1984), in which they try to mark out a position for some structural independence and autonomy for both politics and kinship vis-à-vis economic relations.

Although I cannot resolve this issue on the basis of my analysis, my empirical findings suggest that any solution must take account of the manner in which the dialectics of kinship and politics can span generations. In a negative dialogue with the past, the politics of postwar Spain spanned nearly half a century, based on a lopsided dialogue between the victors and the vanquished as they lived out their lives in the postwar years. The dialectic of politics is thus akin to the process of kinship as it changes in a protracted dialogue between the generations throughout life, as Sylvia Yanagisako has described it in *Transforming the Past* (1985). It is akin to what David Plath describes in *Long Engagements* (1980) as the discourse of maturity as it develops among groups of people who shape one another's lives in a mutual experience of history and cultural heritage throughout the life course. These findings, and others like them in the anthropological literature, seem to invalidate any narrowly synchronic conception of the relation of kinship and politics to a base of productive relations. Perhaps both kinship and politics must be investigated in part in relation to the structure of their own history. It is precisely this that I have attempted in my reappraisal of Los Olivos in the 1960's, acknowledging shifts in the villagers' political identities and consciousness along with changes in the composition of pueblo strata and in my analytical paradigm.

Recovering the Past

Today, even the political-economic framework of pueblo life has changed. Civil War widows and many other former working poor of their generation now live in urban Spain in the company of their children. Many of their children, now adult, who left Los Olivos before or during the massive rural exodus of the 1960's, attained maturity in the world of urban-industrial blue-collar work. These men and women are for the most part conversant with the working-class political discourse that has resurfaced in the post-Franco years. Many of them interpret the exploitation that they and their parents experienced in postwar

Los Olivos more explicitly in terms of class than does their parents' generation.

Yet few are aware of the full dimensions of the class conflict that so profoundly shaped their lives. Their understanding of the conflict came to them only through reminiscences colored by life as the vanquished had to live it in the postwar period. Going beyond reminiscences is the task of the analyst; in doing so in this book, I have sought out the history of Los Olivos's Second Republic politics in the texts and records of the people involved in municipal affairs. Using systematic methods drawn from both history and anthropology to analyze those sources, I have related local politics to the contexts of family history and pueblo stratification. And I have attempted to place those affairs and the conflict they embodied in a broader political and economic context. By emending and augmenting their reminiscences, I have sought to return the villagers' history to them and to other inhabitants of rural Spain.

Appendix

Chronology

Events in Los Olivos	Events in Spain
1888	
Several protagonists of Los Olivos's 1933 Socialist Town Council born.	Socialist Unión General de Trabajadores founded.
1909	
Key future Socialist protagonists undertake military service.	Barcelona's Tragic Week.
Unrest in nearby Aracena.	
1915	
Villagers in Los Olivos kill hated cacique's wife.	Labor unrest in Riotinto mines.
1918–20	
Lópezes bring in Civil Guard to suppress Iglesias family as "bandit" gang.	*Trienio bolchevista.*
1923	
	Primo de Rivera's coup.
1929	
	Socialist UGT unionizes Huelva mines.

Events in Los Olivos	Events in Spain
	Socialists begin to unionize farmworkers in Huelva.

1930

FNTT campaigns in nearby Huelva countryside.	Jan. 28: Primo de Rivera's rule ends. Alfonso XIII tries to form government without constitution.
Feb. 25: Town Council formed by decree of Feb. 15. José Antonio Ramos presides as mayor.	
Mar.–Dec.: Repeated changes in Town Council membership because of resignations. José Antonio Ramos solicits provincial public-works moneys for a new entrance road to the town.	

1931

	Apr. 12–14: Republicans win municipal elections. Alfonso XIII abdicates. Republic proclaimed; Provisional Government formed.
Apr. 19: New Town Council, led by Celestino López and Patricio López, formed without election under Article 29 of Electoral Law.	Apr. 28–July 13: Provisional Government decrees agrarian program: mixed labor-employer commissions to regulate rural employment; lease evictions limited; agrarian unions given right to strike; eighthour day; preferential

Events in Los Olivos	Events in Spain
May 3: Celestino López cancels road construction project.	hiring of local workers; confiscation of unused land.
May 24: López plans street paving as public works to alleviate the *crisis obrero.* Funds are sought and obtained from the Diputación Provincial.	Constituent Cortes begin to draft Constitution.
Early summer: Socialist Syndicate of Agrarian Workers of the UGT, led by Ceferino Santis, tries to designate workers for public works.	
Aug. 29: Council draws up its own list of "needy" laborers to employ in public-works employment.	
	Sept. 20: Dionisio Cano López takes office as governor of Huelva.
Sept. 23: Socialist syndicate disrupts Town Council.	
Sept. 24: Governor Cano's delegate evicts Celestino and Patricio López from the council but leaves their allies in office; he appoints a secretary, forms junta de policía rural, and legitimates role of Socialist syndicate in regulating employment in the municipality.	

Events in Los Olivos	Events in Spain
Autumn: Uneasy compromise of syndicate and council in seeking state support for public works. Councillors petition governor to be allowed to resign.	Oct.: Azaña becomes prime minister. Law for Defense of Republic passed. Dec. 9: Constitution promulgated.

1932

	Jan. 1: Castilblanco murder of Civil Guards.
Feb. 6: Francisco Santis, brother and opponent of syndicate leader Ceferino Santis, assumes presidency of Town Council. Tensions between syndicate and council rise.	January: Jesuits dissolved; divorce law enacted; cemeteries secularized. Francisco Rubio Callejón takes office as governor of Huelva.
Feb. 13: Cemetery secularized. Street names changed to honor Spanish intellectuals.	
Spring: Syndicate directs protests against council to Governor Rubio.	
June: Syndicate denounces council to governor for provoking labor violence by illegally using public forces in religious procession. Governor Solsano asks the council to respond to the charges.	June 18: Braulio Solsano Ronda takes office as governor of Huelva. July 28: Ley de Orden Público promulgated. Aug. 10: Sanjurjo military uprising put down.
Dec. 24: Council, strictly following the law, fines	Aug. 30: Rafael Montañez Santaella takes office as

Events in Los Olivos	Events in Spain

Celestino López and his sister for violating the bases de trabajo.

governor of Huelva.

Sept.: Agrarian Reform Law, Catalan Statute passed by Cortes.

1933

Jan. 24: Under the government's decree dismissing councils not formed by popular election, council is replaced by an interim commission headed by schoolteacher Niceto Ortega, pending municipal elections.

Jan.: Abortive general strike and anarchist riots in Catalonia. Casas Viejas massacre.

Spring: Niceto Ortega budgets and implements improvements in schools.
  Socialists open Casa del Pueblo in house rented from town.

May 10: Leaders of the Socialist syndicate assume office as elected town councillors. Ceferino Santis, as mayor, raises local wages and assesses property owners for public works to create jobs.

Apr.: Municipal elections in towns with nonelected councils; results mostly favor rightists and monarchists.
  Growing dissatisfaction with Azaña government.

June: Socialist council asks governor for road construction funds. Council orders houses whitewashed and plans school construction

Events in Los Olivos	Events in Spain
with funding from Ministry of Public Education and Fine Arts.	

July: Council authorized to begin yearlong road construction project employing union members. Large numbers of men join union for access to jobs. Council initiates unusual budget transfers to pay laborers.

Aug.: Militants burn harvests in Extremadura.

Sept. 21: Enrique Malboyssón Ponce becomes governor of Huelva.

Nov. 22: Francisco Javier Núñez, secretary, holdover from previous council and opponent of the Socialists, resigns.

Oct. 9: Constituent Cortes dissolved.

Nov. 19: CEDA electoral victory. Lerroux becomes Prime Minister. Bienio negro begins.

   In the wake of CEDA's victory, property owners begin civil suits against leftists for eviction and for debt. These suits continue throughout 1934 and 1935.

Dec. 8–11: Anarchist uprisings put down in Catalonia and Aragón.

1934

April: Civil Guard helps 10 property owners acquire firearms, while confiscating weapons owned by others.

May 1: Socialists declare Frente campesino.

May 2: Governor Malboyssón suspends Mayor Ceferino Santis. Alfredo González takes his place as mayor.

June 5–11: Field workers strike in Andalusia and Extremadura. Jerónimo Fernaud Martín takes office as governor of Huelva. Ar-

June 20: Alfredo González

Events in Los Olivos	Events in Spain
arrested and jailed for 30 days.	rests of labor leaders and of Socialist deputies to the Cortes.
Oct. 8: Reinforcements sent to Civil Guard, who begin night watches of church in collaboration with property owners.	Oct. 6: Uprisings in Catalonia and Asturias. State of war declared. Town councils suspended; imprisoning of leftist councillors and union leaders.
Oct. 22: Governor Fernaud closes the syndicate and Casa del Pueblo, dismisses the entire Socialist council and designates Celestino López and other property holders as new councillors. Tomás Nogales presides.	
Council replaces all public employees, restoring Francisco Javier Núñez as secretary.	
Nov. 12: Governor Fernaud designates a delegate to investigate accusations of fraud and malfeasance against former Socialist councillors.	

1935

Jan. 12: Governor Fernaud's delegate confirms evidence against former Socialist councillors, initiates criminal proceedings against them.	State of alarm, suspending civil rights, continued throughout year.
Jan. 26: At request of the	Early Republican agrarian and labor legislation ignored or repealed.

Events in Los Olivos	Events in Spain

provincial commander of the Civil Guard, the Town Council acts to enlarge the local garrison, allocating entire town reserves to purchase it from Celestino López.

In an alliance with property owners, the Civil Guard steps up rural surveillance. Arrests of village poor and leftists increase 3,000 percent during 1935 over levels of arrests in 1932 and 1933.

Spring: Town Council reconstitutes tax commissions with property holders, revising tax levies.

Winter: In anticipation of forthcoming parliamentary elections, politicians of every persuasion hold public meetings.

Oct. 29: Lerroux resigns over *straperlo* scandal.

Dec. 29: Benjamín Caro Sánchez of Partido Agrario takes office as governor of Huelva, serves one week.

1936

Jan. 5: Fernando Olaguer Feliú takes office as governor of Huelva.

Jan. 15: Popular Front pact unites parties of the Left.

Jan. 28: Vicente Marín Casanova becomes governor of Huelva.

Events in Los Olivos	Events in Spain
Feb. 18: Fifteen Socialists, including the Socialist leaders, arrested in wake of Feb. 16 elections.	Feb. 16: Popular Front electoral victory.
Feb. 20: Governor's delegate removes council of Tomás Nogales and restores Socialists to office.	Feb. 19: Azaña forms government. Political prisoners freed.
Socialists replace most town functionaries with political allies.	Feb. 23: Azaña reinstates lease law.
Mar. 28: Council reestablishes Junta de Policía Rural to regulate employment.	Feb. 29: Miguel Luelmo Asencio becomes governor of Huelva.
Apr. 6: Council fires Francisco Javier Núñez from post of secretary, appointing Celestino Munís.	Mar. 16: Land reform resumed.
Apr. 11: The Council suspends tax assessments and forms new tax commission.	Apr. 4: Azaña government vows to fulfill Popular Front platform for land reform, school construction, re-employment of laborers fired for political reasons. Municipalities promised more autonomy.
Spring: Socialists allot laborers to property owners, forcing them to pay wages whether they utilize the labor or not.	
Villagers butcher livestock taken from private estates and distribute meat in the town. The belief spreads that there will no longer be private property.	June: Construction and electrical workers of UGT and CNT strike.

Events in Los Olivos	Events in Spain

June: Council cancels pa-
tron saint's festival and
schedules a secular school
festival for July 18–20.

July 18: In the midst of the
school festival, villagers
learn of the Levantamiento
by radio.

July 17: Insurgents begin
revolt in Morocco and on
mainland.

July 27: Insurgents take
Sevilla. Atrocities begin,
attributed to Moroccan
troops.

Early August: Militants,
outsiders, and Juventud Socialista burn the church
after the saint's images have
been removed. A few days
later, the images are burned.

Aug. 14: Insurgents take
Badajoz and massacre hun-
dreds of prisoners in the
bullring.

Aug. 22: As Socialists
watch from a promontory,
insurgent troops occupy
the town, installing property owners in a puppet
town government.

Former Socialist coun-
cillors and other prominent
local leftists go into hiding
or flee. Other villagers return and are questioned.

Late August: Falangists
shave heads of Socialists'
wives and daughters, feed
them castor oil, and parade
them through the streets.
Beatings of Socialists'
brothers and sons begin.
Falangists organize *batidas*

Events in Los Olivos	Events in Spain
to hunt down leftists hiding in the countryside.	Sept. 3: Talavera falls to insurgents.
Sept. 9: Falangists round up and kill 10 men, all brothers or sons of leading Socialists.	
Late September: Falangists kill a second batch of men.	Sept. 28: Insurgents take Toledo.
	Nov. 8: Siege of Madrid begins.

1937

Events in Los Olivos	Events in Spain
Aug. 24: Falangists round up a third batch of men and kill them in a nearby town.	

1939

Events in Los Olivos	Events in Spain
Some Socialists, promised amnesty, surrender and are jailed.	End of Civil War.

1940–42

Events in Los Olivos	Events in Spain
Famine years.	Famine years.

late 1940's

Events in Los Olivos	Events in Spain
Local agriculture flourishes around export of fruit.	

1950's

Events in Los Olivos	Events in Spain
Exodus of labor begins, reaching massive proportions after 1966.	End of economic autarky. Spain and United States sign bases treaty. Labor migration to Europe encouraged. Industrialization of Catalonia begun. Rural exodus begins.

Events in Los Olivos	Events in Spain

1960's

Rural exodus afflicts Los Olivos as villagers seek jobs in Catalonia.

1970's

Franco dies, Nov. 20, 1975. Juan Carlos crowned king, Nov. 22.

Cortes approves Law of Political Reform, Nov. 16, 1976, reestablishing democracy.

Socialist party holds 27th Congress, Dec. 5, 1976, the first in 40 years.

1980's

Socialists, led by Felipe González, win massive electoral victory, form government, Nov. 1982.

References Cited

References Cited

Aceves, Joseph B. 1976. Forgotten in Madrid: Notes on Rural Development Planning in Spain. In *The Changing Faces of Rural Spain*, ed. Joseph B. Aceves and William A. Douglas. Cambridge, Mass.

Aceves, Joseph B., and William A. Douglas. 1976. *The Changing Faces of Rural Spain*. Cambridge, Mass.

Aparicio Albiñana, José. 1936. *Para qué sirve un gobernador . . . : Impresiones ingenuas de un ciudadano que lo ha sido dos años de las provincias de Jaén y Albacete*. Valencia: Imp. La Semana Gráfica.

Barrett, Richard A. 1974. *Benabarre: The Modernization of a Spanish Village*. New York.

Ben-Ami, Shlomo. 1978. *The Origins of the Second Republic in Spain*. Oxford.

———. 1983. *Fascism from Above: The Dictatorship of Primo de Rivera in Spain, 1923–1930*. Oxford.

Bernal, Antonio-Miguel. 1974. *La propiedad de la tierra y las luchas agrarias andaluzas*. Esplugues de Llobregat: Editorial Ariel.

Bolloten, Burnett. 1979. *The Spanish Revolution: The Left and the Struggle for Power During the Civil War*. Chapel Hill, N.C.

Bourdieu, Pierre. 1977. *Outline of a Theory of Practice*. Cambridge, England.

Bowles, Samuel, and Herbert Gintis. 1986. *Democracy and Capitalism: Property, Community, and the Contradictions of Modern Social Thought*. New York.

Brandes, Stanley H. 1975. *Migration, Kinship, and Community: Tradition and Transition in a Spanish Village*. New York.

———. 1980. *Metaphors of Masculinity: Sex and Status in Andalusian Folklore*. Philadelphia.

Brenan, Gerald. 1943. *The Spanish Labyrinth: An Account of the Social and Political Background of the Spanish Civil War*. London.

Bright, Charles, and Susan Harding. 1984. *Statemaking and Social Movements: Essays in History and Theory*. Ann Arbor.

Buechler, Hans C., and Judith-Marie Buechler. 1981. *Carmen: The Autobiography of a Spanish Galician Woman*. Cambridge, Mass.

Butterfield, Herbert. 1965 [1931]. *The Whig Interpretation of History*. New York.

Calero, Antonio M. 1976. *Movimientos sociales en Andalucía (1820–1936)*. Madrid: Siglo XXI de España Editores, S.A.

Campbell, J. K. 1964. *Honour, Family, and Patronage*. New York.

Caro Baroja, Julio. 1957. El Sociocentrismo de los pueblos españoles. In *Razas, pueblos, y linajes*, by Julio Caro Baroja. Madrid: Revista de Occidente.

Carr, Raymond. 1966. *Spain, 1808–1939*. Oxford.

Carr, Raymond, and Juan Pablo Fusi. 1981 [1979]. *Spain: Dictatorship to Democracy*. 2d ed. London.

Carrión, Pascual. 1932. *Los latifundios en España: Su importancia, origen, consequencias y solución*. Esplugues de Llobregat, Barcelona: Ediciones Ariel.

Castillo, Juan José. 1979. *Propietarios muy pobres: Sobre la subordinación política del pequeño campesino, La Confederación Nacional Católica Agraria, 1917–1942*. Madrid: Servicio de Publicaciones Agrarias.

Checkland, S. G. 1967. *The Mines of Tharsis: Roman, French and British Enterprise in Spain*. London.

Collier, George A. 1975. *The Fields of the Tzotzil: The Ecological Bases of Tradition in Highland Chiapas*. Austin.

———. 1978. The Determinants of Highland Maya Kinship. *Journal of Family History* 3: 439–53.

———. 1982. In the Shadow of Empire: New Directions in Mesoamerican and Andean Ethnohistory. Introduction to *The Inca and Aztec States, 1400–1800*, ed. G. Collier, R. Rosaldo, and J. Wirth. New York.

Collier, Jane F. 1973. *Law and Social Change in Zinacantan*. Stanford.

———. 1975. Legal Processes. *Annual Review of Anthropology* 4: 131–63.

———. 1979. Stratification and Dispute Handling in Two Highland Chiapas Communities. *American Ethnologist* 6: 305–27.

——— (with Michelle Z. Rosaldo). 1981. Politics and Gender in Simple Societies. In *Sexual Meanings*, ed. S. Ortner and H. Whitehead. New York.

Creighton, Colin. 1980. Family, Property, and Relations of Production in Western Europe. *Economy and Society* 9(2): 129–67.

Davis, John. 1977. *People of the Mediterranean: An Essay in Comparative Social Anthropology*. London.

Díaz del Moral, Juan. 1967. *Historia de las agitaciones campesinas anda-luzas.* Madrid: Alianza.

Douglas, William A. 1975. *Echelar and Murelaga: Opportunity and Rural Exodus in Two Spanish Basque Towns.* London.

Driessen, Henk. 1981. Anthropologists in Andalusia: The Use of Comparison and History. *Man* (N.S.) 16: 451–62.

———. 1983. Male Sociability and Rituals of Masculinity in Rural Andalusia. *Anthropological Quarterly* 56(3): 125–33.

Durán Alonso, Antonio. 1985. *Estructura socio-económico de una comarca deprimida: La Sierra de Aracena, Huelva.* Huelva: Excma. Diputación Provincial de Huelva.

Federación Nacional de Trabajadores de la Tierra. 1932. *Memoria que presenta el Comité Nacional al Congreso Ordinario que ha de celebrarse en Madrid durante los días 17 y siguientes del mes de septiembre de 1932.* Madrid: Gráfica Socialista.

Fourneau, Francis. 1980. *Huelva hacia el desarrollo: Evolución de la Provincia de Huelva durante los veinte ultimos años.* Huelva: Excma. Diputación Provincial de Huelva, Instituto de Estudios Onubenses "Padre Marchena."

Fraser, Ronald. 1972. *In Hiding: The Life of Manuel Cortes.* London.

———. 1973. *Tajos: The Story of a Village on the Costa del Sol.* New York.

———. 1979. *Blood of Spain: The Experience of Civil War, 1936–1939.* London.

Gilmore, David D. 1980. *The People of the Plain: Class and Community in Lower Andalusia.* New York.

———. 1983. Sexual Ideology in Andalusian Oral Literature: A Comparative View of a Mediterranean Complex. *Ethnology* 22(3): 241–52.

———. 1985. The Role of the Bar in Andalusian Rural Society: Observations on Political Culture Under Franco. *Journal of Anthropological Research* 41(3): 263–77.

Gironella, José María. 1953. *Los cipreses creen en Dios.* Barcelona.

Gregory, David Dreutzer. 1972. Intra-European Migration and Sociocultural Change in an Andalusian Agro-town. Ph.D. Diss., University of Pittsburgh.

———. 1978. *La odisea andaluza: Una emigración hacia Europa.* Madrid: Editorial Tecnos.

Hajnal, John. 1965. European Marriage Patterns in Perspective. In *Population and History,* ed. D. V. Glass and D. E. C. Eversley. London.

Harding, Susan Friend. 1984. *Remaking Ibieca: Rural Life in Aragon Under Franco.* Chapel Hill, N.C.

Harvey, Charles E. 1981. *The Rio Tinto Company: An Economic History of a Leading International Mining Concern, 1873–1954.* Penzance, Cornwall.

Herr, Richard. 1971. *An Historical Essay on Modern Spain*. Berkeley, Calif.

Hijos de Santiago Rodríquez, eds. 1957. *Nueva enciclopedia escolar: Grado segundo*. Burgos: Hijos de Santiago Rodríguez.

Instituto de Reformas Sociales. 1913. *Memoria redactada por la comisión nombrada por el Instituto para estudiar las condiciones del trabajo en las Minas de Riotinto*. Madrid: Imp. de la Sucesora de M. Minuesa de los Ríos.

Instituto Nacional de Estadística. 1964. *Primer censo agrario de España, octubre de 1962*, Vol. 22, *Huelva*. Madrid: Instituto Nacional de Estadística en colaboración con el ministerio de agricultura y la organización sindical.

———. 1973. *Censo agrario de España, 1972. Serie A—Primeros resultados, Huelva*. Madrid: Instituto Nacional de Estadística en colaboración con el ministerio de agricultura y la organización sindical.

Jackson, Gabriel. 1965. *The Spanish Republic and the Civil War, 1931–1939*. Princeton.

Kaplan, Temma. 1977. *Anarchists of Andalusia, 1868–1903*. Princeton.

———. 1981. Class Consciousness and Community in Nineteenth-Century Andalusia. *Political Power and Social Theory* 2: 21–57.

Lisón Tolosana, Carmelo. 1983 [1966]. *Belmonte de los Caballeros: Anthropology and History in an Aragonese Community*. Princeton.

Maddox, Richard. 1986. Religion, Honor, and Patronage: Culture and Power in an Andalusian Town. Ph.D. Diss., Stanford University.

Malefakis, Edward E. 1970. *Agrarian Reform and Peasant Revolution in Spain: Origins of the Civil War*. New Haven.

Marcus, George E., and Michael M. J. Fischer. 1986. *Anthropology as Cultural Critique: An Experimental Moment in the Human Sciences*. Chicago.

Martínez Alier, Juan. 1971. *Labourers and Landowners in Southern Spain*. Totowa, N.J.

Meaker, Gerald H. 1974. *The Revolutionary Left in Spain, 1914–1923*. Stanford.

Mintz, Jerome R. 1982. *The Anarchists of Casas Viejas*. Chicago.

Moore, Barrington, Jr. 1966. *Social Origins of Dictatorship and Democracy*. Boston.

Moreno Alonso, Manuel. 1979. *La vida rural en la Sierra de Huelva: Alajar*. Huelva: Instituto de Estudios Onubenses "Padre Marchena."

Ordóñez Márquez, Juan. 1968. *La apostasía de las masas y la persecución religiosa en la Provincia de Huelva*. Madrid: Consejo Superior de Investigaciones Científicas, Instituto Enrique Florez.

Organización Sindical de Huelva. 1975. *Los 79 municipios de Huelva, 1975*. Huelva: Servicio de Información y Publicaciones Sindicales.

Pascual Cevallos, Fernando. 1983. *Luchas agrarias en Sevilla durante la segunda república*. Sevilla: Excma. Diputación Provincial de Sevilla.

Payne, Stanley G. 1984. *Spanish Catholicism: An Historical Overview*. Madison, Wisc.

Pérez Díaz, Víctor. 1966. *La estructura social del campo y éxodo rural: Estudio de un pueblo de Castilla*. Madrid: Editorial Tecnos.

———. 1976. Process of Change in Rural Castillian Communities. In *The Changing Faces of Rural Spain*, ed. Joseph B. Aceves and William A. Douglas. Cambridge, Mass.

Peristiany, J. G., ed. 1966. *Honour and Shame: The Values of Mediterranean Society*. Chicago.

Pitt-Rivers, Julian. 1954. *People of the Sierra*. Chicago.

———. 1966. Honor and Social Status. In *Honour and Shame: The Values of Mediterranean Society*, ed. J. G. Peristiany. Chicago.

Plath, David W. 1980. *Long Engagements: Maturity in Modern Japan*. Stanford.

Preston, Paul. 1978. *The Coming of the Spanish Civil War: Reform, Reaction and Revolution in the Second Republic, 1931–1936*. London.

———. 1984*a*. War of Words: The Spanish Civil War and the Historians. In *Revolution and War in Spain, 1931–1939*, ed. Paul Preston. London.

———. 1984*b*. The Agrarian War in the South. In *Revolution and War in Spain, 1931–1939*, ed. Paul Preston. London.

Price, Richard, and Sally Price. 1966*a*. Noviazgo in an Andalusian Pueblo. *Southwestern Journal of Anthropology* 22: 302–22.

———. 1966*b*. Stratification and Courtship in an Andalusian Pueblo. *Man* 1: 526–33.

Rosado, Antonio. 1979. *Tierra y libertad: Memorias de un campesino anarco-sindicalista andaluz*. Barcelona: Editorial Crítica.

Roux, Bernard. 1975. *Crisis agraria en la sierra andaluza: Un estudio económico de las empresas ganaderas de la Provincia de Huelva*. Ediciones del Instituto de Desarrollo Regional, No. 3. Sevilla: La Universidad de Sevilla.

Schneider, Peter. 1969. Honor and Conflict in a Sicilian Town. *Anthropological Quarterly* 42(3): 130–54.

Sevilla Guzmán, Eduardo. 1979. *La evolución del campesinado en España*. Barcelona: Ediciones Península.

Shubert, Adrian. 1984. *Hacia la revolución: Orígenes sociales del movimiento obrero en Asturias, 1860–1934*. Barcelona: Editorial Crítica.

Skocpol, Theda. 1982. What Makes Peasants Revolutionary? *Comparative Politics* 14(3): 351–75.

Stein, Louis. 1979. *Beyond Death and Exile: The Spanish Republicans in France, 1939–1955*. Cambridge, Mass.

Suero Sánchez, Luciano. 1982. *Memorias de un campesino andaluz en la revolución española.* Madrid: Queimada Ediciones.

Tuñón de Lara, Manuel. 1978. *Luchas obreras y campesinas en la Andalucía del siglo XX: Jaén (1917–1920), Sevilla (1930–1932).* Madrid: Siglo XXI de España Editores, S.A.

Tusell [Gómez], Javier. 1976. *Oligarquía y caciquismo en Andalucía (1890–1923).* Barcelona: Editorial Planeta.

———. 1977. *La crisis del caciquismo andaluz (1923–1931).* Madrid: Cupsa Editorial.

Yanagisako, Sylvia J. 1985. *Transforming the Past: Tradition and Kinship Among Japanese Americans.* Stanford.

Index

In this index an "f" after a number indicates a separate reference on the next page, and an "ff" indicates separate references on the next two pages. A continuous discussion over two or more pages is indicated by a span of page numbers, e.g., "pp. 57–58." *Passim* is used for a cluster of references in close but not consecutive sequence.

nance, 25, 82; petitioned from
Los Olivos, 81, 83, 86, 105, 109,
126; intervention in Los Olivos,
81, 83, 87, 225–26, 229; in labor
conflicts, 114
————of Huelva: Dionicio Caro
López, 81; Francisco A. Rubio
Callejón, 83; Braulio Solsano
Ronda, 86–87, 90, 105, 114;
Enrique Malboyssón Ponce,
106–17 *passim*, 127; Jeró-
nimo Fernaud Martín, 117–18,
120, 126; Fernando Olaguer
Feliú, 133; Benjamín Caro
Sánchez, 133; Vicente Marín
Casanova, 133–34; Miguel
Luelmo Asencio, 141–42
Grains, 24, 29
Gregory, David, 188
Gutiérrez Prieto, Juan, 133–34

Hajnal, John, 181
Harding, Susan Friend, 14, 173f,
179, 188, 217–18
Harvest conflict, *see Rebusca;*
Strikes
Herr, Richard, 162
Historical analysis, 166, 201,
203–4; Spanish history, 12–18,
207–10, 216, 218–19
Historical consciousness, *see*
Negative dialogue
Historical memory, vii, 1, 17f, 21,
32, 148, 164, 201, 219
Homage to Catalonia, 148
Honor, 16, 96, 174, 181, 183; and
autonomy, 5, 90, 206; and poli-
tics, 12, 90, 183; and stratifica-
tion, 174
Household registers, 8f, 189
Households, 173–74, 188. *See
also* Autonomy; Conjugal fam-
ily system
Huelva, in nineteenth century,
24–31

Ideology: postwar, 2, 6, 14, 16–
17, 21, 168, 178, 209, 216–17;
of working-class rank and file,
46–48, 135–36, 182, 208; of
FNTT, 62; sources of commit-
ment, 135–40. *See also* Catho-
lic mutualism; Corporatism;
Cumplir; Education; Literacy;
Negative dialogue; News-
papers; Propaganda; Schools;
Unión
Iglesias, Pablo, 107
Iglesias family, 51, 68, 126, 223
Igualatorio Médico, 172–76
Imprisonment, 35, 72, 155f. *See
also* Arrests
Industry, *see* Agrarian industry
Inheritance, 22–23, 33, 173, 181,
212, 215
Insurgents, 145, 152, 232
Interpretive analysis, 2–4, 205–9
Interviews, 8–9, 31–32, 146, 148
Irrigation, 27, 29

Jaén, *see* Aparicio Albiñana
Judicial reforms, annulled in
1934, 128
Jurados mixtos, see Mixed juries
Justice of the Peace, 36, 109, 128–
29, 140
Juventud Socialista, 77, 120, 138,
149, 151, 154

Killings: methods for identifying
victims, 8, 12, 32, 146; of Los
Olivos Socialists, 20, 51, 146–
61 *passim,* 178, 233; in Civil
War, 32, 35, 41; of wife of *cacique* Fermín Moreno, 50; at
Badajoz, 145–46, 232; as Nationalist reprisals, 151; attribu-
tion of blame, 162–64
Kinship: and factionalism, 11, 77,
121–22, 124, 212; and property
relations, 23, 214–15; threat-

.

Library of Congress Cataloging-in-Publication Data

Collier, George A.
  Socialists of rural Andalusia.

  Bibliography: p.
  Includes index.
    1. Socialists—Spain—Andalusia—History—20th
century—Case studies. 2. Socialism—Spain—Andalusia—
History—20th century—Case studies.   3. Spain—History
—1931–1939.   I. Title.
HX345.A53C65   1987   335'.00946'8   87-9929
ISBN 0-8047-1411-8 (alk. paper)